IT'S TIME... FOR NETWORK MARKETING

**THE MOST
REMARKABLE
FORM OF
FREE ENTERPRISE
EVER CREATED**

EDITED BY JOHN MILTON FOGG

IT'S TIME... FOR NETWORK MARKETING

THE MOST REMARKABLE FORM OF FREE ENTERPRISE EVER CREATED

EDITED BY JOHN MILTON FOGG

Lou Abbott, Margie Aliprandi, **Robert Allen,** Scott Allen, **Jim Bartlett,** Richard Brooke, **Bob Burg, Art Burleigh,** Corey Citron, **Leonard Clements,** Anthony Diaz, **Michael Dlouhy,** Steve Dom, **John Milton Fogg,** Monique Gallagher, **Jim Gillhouse,** Lim Eng Hai, **Art Jonak,** Nicki Keohohou, **Robert Kiyosaki,** Kim Klaver, **Brian Klemmer,** Terri Levine, **Mike Lewis,** Linda Locke, **John David Mann,** Jillian Middleton, **Kathi Minsky,** Warren Nelson, **Rod Nichols,** Shelley Penney, **Paul Zane Pilzer,** Mike Potillo, **Paula Pritchard,** Bob Proctor, **Lorna Rasmussen,** Kimberly Rhodes, **Kathy Robbins,** Teresa Romain, **Tony Rush,** Tim Sales, Tom Schreiter, **Bo Short,** Roberto Torres, **Ty Tribble, Jackie Ulmer,** Dr. Denis Waitley, **Diane Walker,** Wendy Weiss, **Lisa Wilber,** Dennis Williams, **and Mark Yarnell**

EMBASSY BOOKS
www.embassybooks.in

It's Time... for Network Marketing
The most remarkable form of free enterprise ever created

© Copyrights 2007 All rights reserved by the authors: Lou Abbott, Margie Aliprandi, Robert Allen, Scott Allen, Jim Bartlett, Richard Brooke, Bob Burg, Art Burleigh, Corey Citron, Len Clements, Anthony Diaz, Michael Dlouhy, Steve Dom, John Milton Fogg, Monique Gallagher, Jim Gillhouse, Lim Eng Hai, Art Jonak, Nicki Keohohou, Robert Kiyosaki, Kim Klaver, Brian Klemmer, Terri Levine, Mike Lewis, Linda Locke, John David Mann, Jillian Middleton, Kathi Minsky, Warren Nelson, Rod Nichols, Shelley Penney, Paul Zane Pilzer, Mike Pottillo, Paula Pritchard, Bob Proctor, Lorna Rasmussen, Kimberly Rhodes, Kathy Robbins, Teresa Romain, Tony Rush, Tim Sales, Tom Schreiter, Sue Seward, Bo Short, Roberto Torres, Ty Tribble, Jackie Ulmer, Dr. Denis Waitley, Diane Walker, Wendy Weiss, Lisa Wilber, Dennis Williams, and Mark Yarnell

Edited by **John Milton Fogg**
Copyedited and Proofed by **Claudia Volkman**
Book Design and Layout by **Tom Bellucci**

First published in India 2009

All rights reserved. No part of this book may be used or reproduced in any manner whatsoever without written permission except in the case of brief quotations embodied In articles and reviews.

Published in India by :
EMBASSY BOOK DISTRIBUTORS
120, Great Western Building,
Maharashtra Chamber of Commerce Lane,
Fort, Mumbai - 400 023.
Tel : (+91-22) 22819546 / 32967415
Email : embassy@vsnl.com
Website: www.embassybooks.in

ISBN: 978-93-80227-84-9

Printed in India by Repro India Pvt Ltd., Navi Mumbai.

CONTENTS

Foreword

1	**Lou Abbott**	
	To Live, to Love, to Learn... to Leave a Legacy	
5	**Margie Aliprandi**	
	It's Not Just the Money	
11	**Robert Allen**	
	An Open Letter from New York Times Best-Selling Author, Robert Allen	
23	**Scott Allen**	
	What's So Special About Network Marketing?	
27	**Jim Bartlett**	
	Put a Price Tag on That... If You Can	
31	**Richard Brooke**	
	Network Marketing: The Four-Year Career™	
35	**Bob Burg**	
	The Blessing of Free Enterprise Is that Everyone Benefits!	
41	**Art Burleigh**	
	Travel Isn't a Luxury— It's Homework for a Meaningful Life	
51	**Corey Citron**	
	What's So Great About Network Marketing?	
55	**Leonard Clements**	
	The Four Greatest Fears of Starting Your Own Business	
63	**Anthony Diaz**	
	Abide & Abound	
67	**Michael Dlouhy**	
	The #1 Most Motivating Benefit of MLM	
73	**Steve Dom**	
	Full-Time Income Working Part-Time	
77	**John Milton Fogg**	
	The People's Franchise	
89	**Monique Gallagher**	
	Network Marketing: A Divorced Woman's Hope	
97	**Jim Gillhouse**	
	Why I Think Network Marketing Is a Perfect Opportunity For Anyone In The Military	
103	**Lim Eng Hai**	
	Celebrating Network Marketing—The Business of Uplifting People	

It's Time... for Network Marketing

- **111 Art Jonak**
  The Freedom To...
- **121 Nicki Keohohou**
  You CAN Have It All in This Amazing Profession
- **125 Robert Kiyosaki**
  Rich Networker Poor Networker
- **135 Kim Klaver**
  A Chance to Make Money Doing Something I Love
- **143 Brian Klemmer**
  The Greatest Thing About Network Marketing
- **149 Terri Levine**
  Talk About a Win-Win-Win!
- **157 Mike Lewis**
  It Must Be a Cold Day in Hell... Right?
- **161 Linda Locke**
  Women Plus Network Marketing: A Perfect Match
- **167 John David Mann**
  Cutting a New Path
- **177 Jillian Middleton**
  Myths and Legends
- **187 Kathi Minsky**
  Leaders Made Here
- **195 Warren Nelson**
  What if...
- **201 Rod Nichols**
  The Most Remarkable Business
- **205 Shelley Penney**
  It s Not the Marketing...It s the Network
- **211 Paul Zane Pilzer**
  The Next Millionaires
- **227 Mike Potillo**
  The Key to Success
- **231 Paula Pritchard**
  Stay the Course Long Enough to Discover the Magic for Yourself
- **237 Bob Proctor**
  The Network Marketing Success Puzzle

245 **Lorna Rasmussen**
What if...
251 **Kimberly Rhodes**
A Level Playing Field and a Great Game to Play
259 **Kathy Robbins**
My Best Decision
265 **Teresa Romain**
It's Not the 'Big' Money. It's the 'Little' Money...
271 **Tony Rush**
Passive, Recurring Income and Leverage
277 **Tim Sales**
Network Marketing Is an Organic Business
281 **Tom Schreiter**
So, How Ugly Can Your Relatives Be?
285 **Bo Short**
Network Marketing Can Provide a Venue for You to Become a Great Leader
293 **Roberto Torres**
Lifestyles of the (Virtual) Rich and (Not So) Famous
299 **Ty Tribble**
MLM Goes Mainstream
303 **Jackie Ulmer**
The Business of Hope
309 **Dr. Denis Waitley**
The Biggest Business Trend in Business History
317 **Diane Walker**
Never, Ever Quit
327 **Wendy Weiss**
Is Network Marketing Selling?
333 **Lisa Wilber**
The Power To Amaze Yourself
339 **Dennis Williams**
Network Marketing. It Almost Sounds Like a 'Fairy Tale'...
343 **Mark Yarnell**
My Passion for Network Marketing

348 **Acknowledgements**

vii

FOREWORD
BY JOHN MILTON FOGG

It's Time... for Network Marketing

... the most remarkable form of free enterprise to get the respect and recognition it deserves. It's Time... network marketing went beyond being accepted. It's Time... network marketing became truly admired.

There's a whole new way of doing business happening all around the world. Literally, a transformation is taking place in the way people buy and sell everything. At the same time, there's a radical transition in what people are willing and able to do to earn a living today. You see it everywhere. You can feel it... everywhere. Everything's changing fast.

Blame the Internet most of all.
Thank the Internet most of all.

Network marketing is leading this transformation.
The "others" will have to follow or get out of our way.

Network marketing is all about doing things differently. "Business as unusual" is what we're all about.

We are "business for the rest of us" and the number of "us" is growing by more than 70,000 new people around the world every day!

ix

It's Time... will once-and-for-all set the record straight about what makes this business of ours so different... and so remarkable.

It's Time... will show why more and more people are noticing what a brilliant business model this is (and this book will have even more people than ever sit up and take notice).

It's Time... will silence the critics who call our industry a farce and give voice to the real people who know the truth: network marketing is a *force*. It's life-changing, and it's unstoppable.

It's Time... network marketing went beyond accepted.

It's Time... network marketing became truly admired.

Network marketing is the leading edge of free enterprise.... (Not just "on" the leading edge." It IS the leading edge.)

And the world doesn't know it—yet.

Network marketing is the most powerful and persuasive way to introduce consumers to new products and services they don't know exist.

And the world doesn't know it—yet.

Network marketing turbocharges person-to-person (P2P), word-of-mouth recommendations by brilliantly adding an incentive/reward compensation program.

And the world doesn't know it—yet.

Network marketing is the business model where relationships rule.

Foreword

- the only real, level, commercial playing field open to anybody regardless of age, sex, race, education, or past success...
- the best way for ordinary people to achieve extraordinary income...
- the only business structure designed to build successful organizations through cooperation, not company politics and competition...
- the proven, affordable "People's Franchise"...
- the only business system that encourages you to creatively "do it the best way for you" and succeed...
- the best choice today for the growing number of "terminally unemployable" entrepreneurs and intrapreneurs...
- the authentic, intelligent, credible, moral business design that pays you what you are truly worth...
- the business model that provides both time and financial freedom...
- the business that lets everyone in on the "secret" of leveraged, residual income...
- the business that lets everyone in on the "secret" of loverage, of contribution, of making a difference for a living...
- the business that has changed millions of people's lives for the better forever...

Successful network marketers know all of that. And now...

It's Time... everybody knew it!

Enjoy the book.

I appreciate you.

John Milton Fogg
Crozet, Virginia

LOU ABBOTT

To Live, to Love, to Learn... to Leave a Legacy

The good news is that the network marketing industry keeps getting better and better. Professionals in the industry are demanding more from themselves and from the companies they work with.

To live, to love, to learn, to leave a legacy.... Those life activities, according to Stephen Covey, are the four basic needs and motivations of every human being... of every one of us. When we live a life that addresses all four, we are empowered. We have boundless energy. We are fulfilled. We live a great life.

More often than not, however, our lives end up differently. We get caught up in "the thick of small things." Yes, we are alive, but only barely it seems, as we go to work, pay the bills, care for our families, and eke out an existence.

Hardly a great life, yet almost all of us have been there.

I remember worrying about that when I was about seventeen years old. I was thinking about college and what I would do with my life, where I might like to go with it, when a very sobering thought occurred to me. I'll never forget that moment. I looked forward in time to that day I would be lying in bed with only hours remaining of my life.

It's Time... for Network Marketing

"What if," I thought, "in that final hour, I looked back over my entire life and, with no time left to change anything, realized that I had missed the point of it all?"

I have never forgotten that frightening possibility.

By contrast, it seemed like my father had it all figured out. At age ten, he knew he wanted to be an attorney. He studied hard, put himself through college, and graduated well from the USC law school.

For his whole life, he loved his profession. It held great meaning for him. It allowed him to live comfortably, to work with love and passion, to constantly be learning, and I think when it was all over, he felt he had made a difference, that he had left a legacy. He found a profession and with it, he found the vehicle that would give him his "voice" in the world.

And, to my recollection, he never lost a case.

I was not so fortunate. I did go to a great university—for a couple of years anyway. But I didn't find my direction there. When I went to work, I quickly came to the conclusion that an hourly wage, even a good one, wasn't very fulfilling either. I started several businesses. Each one gave me a chance to learn and do new things. That was fulfilling... at least for a while.

It wasn't until February 1997 that I found the profession that would allow me, in fullest measure, to live, love, learn, and leave a legacy.

It was at the first network marketing convention I ever attended. I particularly remember the personal story of one of the leaders that spoke that day. Rick Petersen recalled how he had reached the end of his financial rope. He and his wife had evidently made some bad decisions. There was no income coming in—I don't remember why—and they were thinking they had to sell their second car in order to buy food. The problem is, they had already sold their first car and were living in the second one.

That's when Rick found this particular network marketing opportunity. Somehow, he dug deep for the courage and conviction. He drew a line in the sand and started a new life.

By the time I heard him tell his story, only a few short years later, he was earning a serious six-figure annual income, had built his dream house, and was living not only a new life, but a great life. His tears of gratitude on stage that day touched many hearts. I began to appreciate how incredibly valuable an opportunity can be, at least for those who willfully and courageously embrace it. His story changed my life.

What I saw, and many others have seen since, was a vehicle where I could earn a great living—the upside potential was, in fact, unlimited. What could I do if money were no object? I saw a profession where I would learn and grow constantly. I found a place where I would be surrounded with positive people, people who don't see problems, only challenges to meet and conquer, people with whom I could form relationships that could last the rest of my life.

And, most importantly...

> I found a place where I could make a real difference to others, to help people change their lives and find new hope and new direction.

Finally, for the first time, at age forty-two, I knew the profession that I wanted to embrace. It was network marketing.

The good news is that the industry keeps getting better. Professionals in the industry are demanding more from themselves and from the companies they work with.

This has become my mission: To set, teach, and model the highest standards so that the reputation of network marketing will be what it truly deserves to be: a noble profession.

This noble profession of network marketing has:

- Allowed me To Live more abundantly than I ever could have otherwise—to have more options, more choices and more freedom.
- To Love more fully and express that in ever widening circles.
- To Learn about myself and others, about what is really possible to do in life, and how powerful our minds and belief systems are...

And most fulfillingly, through network marketing I have found a way To Leave a Legacy.

Lou Abbott started in network marketing with a brief participation in Amway 30 years ago. A self-employed entrepreneur from age 21, now at age 51, Lou has built many successful businesses including rising to the top 1% or better with his successful network marketing company.

Lou's useful, info-rich website provides services and reference material for the professional network marketer.

To learn more about Lou and his mission, visit his website at: http://MLM-TheWholeTruth.com

MARGIE ALIPRANDI

It's Not Just the Money

I'm convinced no other business model could have given me the lifestyle I enjoy today. And the dear friendships I've developed with people around the world adds a richness and texture to my life that's beyond compare.

There is no question that the lifestyle of a career network marketer is enviable. I love my life, and I love network marketing. I believe, however, that the most important thing that happens to us in network marketing is not necessarily what we achieve or accumulate, but what and who we become.

If we embrace its principles, network marketing forces us to grow our strength of character and professionalism in order to grow a business. This growth evolves naturally from leaving our comfort zone, motivating ourselves to become the best that we can be, and helping others do the same.

Unlike the corporate business model where employees depend on the employer and where people must compete with each other in order to advance, the network marketing model encourages people to take initiative and help each other to reach mutually beneficial goals. The wealth you create is proportional to the number of people you help, how well you do it, and what they do about it.

> So network marketing, more than anything I know, empowers people to contribute and make a difference. And I believe that in the final analysis, the difference you make is what counts.

When we leave here, we leave the money behind. But we take with us who we've become and the positive influence we've had in the lives of others.

This personal growth stuff is really exhilarating. I can tell you, I'm not even remotely the same person who joined this business back in 1989. Living in Utah meant being pitched on every new thing that came along. So I had to overcome a huge resistance to network marketing. My dad was a distributor for the "granddaddy of all networking companies" and repeatedly tried to recruit me. Once, out of exasperation, I told him "I'd rather clean toilets than do that kind of thing!"

That attitude changed when I came across the one and only company I've been with for seventeen years now.

> I joined because I'd fallen passionately in love with a product, and that made me see network marketing for what it's really supposed to be.

I began with no particular qualifications except determination, which is another great thing about network marketing. Desire and drive go a long way. As for me, I had no previous network marketing experience—I was a music teacher. I was newly divorced with three very small kids, a big mortgage on a new home, and no money to start a business. Just those kids alone would be three reasons for some people to say they would NOT do this business. But I knew that my children were the reason why I MUST do it. Somehow I could see the big picture of where I could go with it, and for starters I needed to save our home.

The product I fell in love with was the type of thing that needed to be demonstrated, so I decided to hold home meetings. I invited a ton of people to my first meeting. Only four came, but two of them joined. I thought to myself, "This is all right! I can see there's a ratio here! If I invite enough people and half of them join, this is going to be good! I can already see the light at the end of the tunnel!"

> So I doubled my efforts. The following week I invited twice as many people, and nobody came.

But I persisted. Within a matter of months there were 100-150 people hanging over the banisters and standing in the doorways of my home waiting for a demonstration in our Tuesday night meetings. I was doing home meetings almost every night, and sometimes two or even three in a single night.

Within one year, I was making as much money in a single month as I would have in an entire year teaching school. When I began with my company, they were doing $28,000 a month worldwide. Within fourteen months, we were doing $2 million a month in my group alone, and I made my first million dollars by the time I was thirty-five. Now, you tell me how I could have done that in any other business.

If you have a willingness to do whatever it takes, you can achieve financial freedom in network marketing. And what is required of one person for success may not be the same for another.

Building a network marketing business is similar to planting a garden. You've got to sow a lot of seeds and you've got to plant them all the time. You can't just plant one and think it's going to feed you for a lifetime. Nor can you expect your seeds to produce an instant harvest. There's a sowing season and a reaping season. It takes time for seeds to mature and you have to have the right elements to cultivate and grow them. Of course, this timeless principle goes hand-in-hand with the idea of tenacity and persistence and hanging in there.

Once I drove from Utah for thirty hours to plant some seeds in Louisville, Kentucky. Nobody at that meeting is still with me, but they signed up some people, who signed up some people, who signed up some people who did stay. Seventeen years later those people are adding $20,000 per month to my residual income.

A single seed I unwittingly planted in New York City is quite another story. This meeting seemed destined to be a disaster.

The cab driver got lost, so I was thirty minutes late and really sweating it. The hosts had barely managed to hold things together and the atmosphere was heavy with the audience's irritation. When I finally got up to the front I could see there was no way I could retrieve this crowd. So I gave a very short presentation and said I'd stay for any questions. A few people came up to me. One was a Russian gentleman. He shook my hand, and through a very thick accent told me he was going to take the business to Russia!

At that point in my network marketing career, I had learned not to take grand promises like that seriously. So I just kind of shook his hand and patted him on the back and said, "That's great! Yeah, why don't you do it? Why don't you take this to Russia!"

A few months later I noticed these names I couldn't pronounce on my commission report. Soon there were pages and pages of them. At one point, I had over 500,000 Russian distributors on my team. Half a million people!

You just never know, do you? You do one

> meeting and no one comes, you do another and you sponsor a nation.

Network marketing creates more stories like mine than any other business.

Today my company is well on its way to $1 billion in annual revenues. I have networking teams in twenty-three countries, and among them are more friends for life than I can count.

Because of network marketing, despite my humble beginnings, I've been able to give my children everything they need and more, including private school and travel around the world.

Each of my children has been able to travel with me throughout Europe, Australia, Japan, and Southeast Asia. We've been diving together in the Red Sea, hugged dolphins in crystal blue Caribbean water, ridden elephants in Thailand, and camels in Egypt. How can you put a price on these kinds of experiences?

But most importantly, I've been able to give them my time in an environment where we're not worried about how the bills will be paid and we can focus on something besides basic survival.

> I've been able to live my life my way. I can do what I want, when I want to do it!

And it's not just the money. The part I value the most is my own personal growth and the tremendous satisfaction that comes from being able to help others grow too.

You might be thinking, "Sure, easy for you to say—it's not the money—because you have the money."

Nope. I hold that growing part most precious.

It s Time... for Network Marketing

> It's the mental muscle and the emotional maturity that I value most of all. It's not what you accumulate. It's what you become, and what you help others to become.

To me, network marketing is as much about personal growth as it is financial growth. It's also about seeing the big picture, and holding a vision of what's possible even when your team members can't see it for themselves—yet.

I'm convinced no other business model could have given me the lifestyle I enjoy today. And the dear friendships I've developed with people around the world adds a richness and texture to my life that's beyond compare.

Margie Aliprandi, with one and only one company, Neways, for seventeen years, has a networking organization of "a few hundred thousand" around the world. She's achieved walk-away income and has no intention of walking away. She's too in love with her products and people for that. Margie has become one of the most respected and successful leaders not only in Neways—she became the first Crown Diamond Ambassador in North America—but also the MLM industry.

Margie has served on the Cancer Prevention Coalition Board of Directors since 1999 and also serves as the Coordinator of International Offices for the CPC. She has produced and recorded several motivational and training audio tapes, and is a sought after speaker.

Margie is also the leading force behind My Mind Makeover, an easy-to-use fully customizable software program that enables you to create empowering affirmations in your own voice with your own choice of music, to change your life for the better forever. (Check it out at http://MyMindMakeover.com)

You can learn more about Margie, and take advantage of her resource-rich website here: http://CrownDiamond.net

ROBERT ALLEN

An Open Letter from New York Times Best-Selling Author, Robert Allen

It's time that a few leaders stepped up and brought network marketing out of its dark cocoon into a new butterfly reality. Wanna play? Wanna be one of them? It won't be easy. But it'll be worth it. Let's earn a huge stream of excellent, enlightened income together and transform our own lives and the image of network marketing forever.

Got a few minutes?

I think it will be worth your time.

Let's chat about financial freedom—as in your financial freedom.

I believe that each of us needs multiple streams of income—real estate, mutual funds, internet marketing, to name a few. But high on the multiple streams short-list is the opportunity of network marketing. It really is the "Ultimate Money Machine."

> Network marketing is probably the least understood, most maligned business opportunity in the world.

And the fault for this misunderstanding lies directly in the lap of many of the people in the network marketing industry itself. That's right. Network marketing is great. But amateur network marketers are fouling the nest and costing you and me a fortune.

Before I continue, I'm assuming that you know what network marketing is. If you're like me when I first was approached about network marketing (and who hasn't been?) I had some preconceived notions that were, at best, inaccurate. For twenty years I kept saying "no" to network marketing based upon what I thought network marketing was.

And what did I think? I thought it was a low class way for small-minded people to make a few extra bucks by harassing their friends and family into buying garage loads of expensive products.

Frankly, that's the way old style multilevel marketing used to be thirty or forty years ago. You know what they say about "first impressions?" Hard to overcome. So when anyone approached me about network marketing, that old MLM image was stuck in my head.

But thank heaven for a family friend. And I mean that literally—Thank Heaven! Collette Larsen was a godsend. She was a close friend that acted like a true friend. She would not let that old MLM image stay stuck in my mind.

> She knew I was stubborn, maybe a bit arrogant, certainly skeptical, and probably a bit fearful. I saw myself as a classy, professional guy that wouldn't be caught dead getting involved in some fly-by-night business opportunity.

She patiently loved me and my wife into the "real" vision of network marketing…gently deflecting my MLM diatribes until I finally agreed to take a more serious look.

An Open Letter from New York Times Best-Selling Author, Robert Allen

And what I saw quite literally stunned me. It wasn't ANYTHING like I had thought. When I researched the major players—the companies that had been around for five, ten, fifteen, twenty years—I could see why they had staying power. These were classy, successful companies with incredible products at reasonable prices. What's more, as a bonus, their ordinary consumers were offered a way to create extraordinary streams of income... residual income (i.e., money while you sleep) for sharing these products with interested others.

Then my wife and I launched our own networking business and, as they say, the rest is history. We worked our way straight to the top and have been in the top ten income earners for almost ten years. The money was (and still is) great. The experience was (and still is) magnificent. Our company was (and still is) peopled by some of the smartest, nicest, classiest people I've ever met anywhere.

> Network marketing is certainly not my only stream of income, but it certainly is my most favorite. I prefer to call myself an author (it has a nice ring to it), but professional networker is a close second.

I'm a big believer in entrepreneurship and the virtues of freedom. In network marketing, I found an industry that leveled the entrepreneurial playing field. Rather than starting a business from scratch (with the high cost of entry and exit), entrepreneurs could let someone else manage the hard parts of the business—product creation, warehousing, distribution, employee benefits, equipment leasing, property acquisition, etc.—so they could concentrate on marketing the products and earn substantial streams of income for doing it.

When done right, network marketing is an enlightened, inexpensive way of getting more people involved in entrepreneurship and ultimately, in controlling their own financial destinies.

That's the good part.

Here's the ugly part.

By leveling the playing field—removing the barriers, lowering the bar—network marketing has attracted an amateur class of people—a get-rich quick crowd of hustlers and fast-talkers trying to make a killing from their downlines and ultimately killing the reputation of our wonderful industry.

And that really frosts me. I'm upset.

I think it's time we took back our industry from these amateurs. Or at least trained them better.

Every profession has its code of ethics and standards of practice and certification. Doctors earn their diplomas. Lawyers have to pass the bar. Pro athletes have to make the team. That's what makes them professional.

It's time that networkers adhered to their own standards of excellence and professionalism.

If I could wave a magic wand and transform this industry, it would be to adopt a new professional designation of entrepreneurial excellence: "The PEN." The Professional Enlightened Networker.

To earn the PEN, a beginning networker would agree to adhere to a Code of Commitments. At the very least, here are five areas of commitment.

I commit to tell the truth.
I hate it when I hear someone talk about how easy it is to build a fortune in network marketing. Easy money! That's a lie. A flat-out lie. There is no easy money in this or in any other business. It's going to be hard yards from day one. Don't come in if you think the money will be easy. Stay away. It'll be cheaper—for

An Open Letter from New York Times Best-Selling Author, Robert Allen

all of us. Come in only after you understand the costs. My wife and I worked hard to build our downlines. It took several years. But now that the residual streams of income are pouring in, it's been the most lucrative thing we've ever done.

This is the truth:

> It will be harder than you think. It will take longer than you hope. It will cost more that you want. But when you succeed, it will be worth more than you can possibly imagine.

Can you handle the truth?

I commit to plant realistic expectations.
There is so much disappointment with amateur networkers because their expectations are out of whack. After all, this IS marketing. And any professional marketer will tell you that it's a numbers game, and the numbers are extremely low. In other words, a direct mail letter will rarely find more than one in two hundred people willing to pull out a credit card and buy something. One in a hundred is an excellent response. Two or three in a hundred is incredible.

But beginning network marketers are encouraged to make a list of their hundred top friends with the expectation of signing up a bunch of them! Unrealistic! One sharp new associate out a hundred close friends would be an excellent response—even if you have the most exciting product on the planet. Two would be excellent. But if a person is not taught the true numbers, they run off to sponsor a few friends and find ninety-nine rejections staring them in the face. After twenty solid rejections, they quit and blame the industry of network marketing. "It just doesn't work!" "It's a scam!"

I'll tell you what's a scam—an amateur who plants the

unrealistic expectation that talking to a few close friends is all that it takes.

> Finding good, solid business associates is HARD. I would rather people expect that it will be hard. Maybe the hardest thing they've ever done.

Then, if they discover that it's a bit easier than that, they're encouraged. They want to forge ahead, through the tough stuff, until they succeed. And success is SO SWEET!

I commit to appreciate the real value of residual income.
If it's slow and hard, just how much income can you earn at this?

> That depends on you: An extra $1,000 a month. $1,000 a week. Maybe even $1,000 a day!

Now let's compare this to incomes from the "non-networking" world. It takes a doctor at least ten years of study and training to become a physician. The average doctor graduates with over $100,000 in tuition debt. It takes several more years for them to be earning up to $365,000 a year, or $1,000 a day. That's a marathon with a big payoff!

Realize the powerful difference between linear income and residual income. Doctors earn linear income. They only get paid when they show up. If they stop working, their income stops.

> The income from network marketing can be residual... which means that it can continue to flow to you EVEN AFTER YOU

An Open Letter from New York Times Best-Selling Author, Robert Allen

STOP WORKING.

Not even your high-paid doctor can say that. That's why doctors are joining excellent network marketing organizations in droves.

A thousand dollars a day in "doctor-type" income isn't nearly as powerful as $1,000 a day in "networker-type" income. A doctor-type check is just that—one check. But a networker-type check represents a stream of future checks as far as you can see into the future.

Did you get that?

This powerful lesson came to me three years ago as I was driving home after delivering a speech to 1,000 people in Anaheim, California. The weather was horrible—a pounding rainstorm. My car spun off the road at high speed and smashed directly into a stationery tree. I was moments from death. I ended up in intensive care in a coma.

The doctors and nurses rushed to save my life. Orthopedic and plastic surgeons performed their magic at hundreds of dollars an hour. I was oblivious to their heroic efforts.

When I awoke to see my family at my bedside, I was so thankful to be alive. And then I had the strangest thought:

While I had been laying there in a coma, I had been earning more money than all the doctors and nurses taking care of me.

It felt good to know that even if I had died that night, my family would have continued to receive income from my efforts. Residual income transcends even the bands of death.

That's why you work hard to build your residual streams... just in case there comes a time when you CAN'T work. You want the streams to continue to flow.

Don't you?

I commit to refuse to be offended. This one isn't easy. Most of us are pretty soft and mushy inside. We hate rejection. We hate to look like fools. We hate to fail. And now I'm telling you to prepare for a 98% failure rate?

Actually, there is a simple way not to be offended. The answer lies in this sentence from network marketing guru, Tom "Big Al" Schreiter:

> Amateurs convince; professionals sort.

Amateur network marketers are always selling—trying to convince someone to join their team or to buy their products. No wonder they're so despised. Nobody likes to be sold.

Professionals never sell. They select. They have an image in their mind of the ideal member of their team. They are looking for applicants—someone who is already sold, already convinced. It's a subtle but profound difference—the difference between selling and selecting.

> People who select can't be rejected because they are the ones deciding who's in and who's out. If YOU don't qualify, the professional won't select you.

Did you get that? This is how professionals behave. Do you want to be a professional?

I'll never forget the first time I finally "got it." I was doing a three-way call with one of my team members. They'd run a newspaper ad and had attracted a few interested people. We

An Open Letter from New York Times Best-Selling Author, Robert Allen

were doing one-on-one telephone follow up calls.

A guy comes on the line. He's a bit surly. I don't like the tone of this conversation. I tell him we're looking for a certain type of person to play on our team. He asks me what kind of business opportunity this is. I tell him it has to do with a certain reputable network marketing company, and he goes off on me.

"You people," he snarls. "Selling expensive stuff to your friends and family." He's livid. I don't get offended—after all, this is exactly the way I used to feel. I don't try to convince him, or overcome his objections. I've made my decision. This is not my kind of person. I'm rejecting HIM before he has a chance to reject me. But just before I hang up I have a brainstorm. The words start flowing out of my mouth:

"Come with me on a quick trip into the future... let's say five years from now. You're driving up to your new house in your new car, and you stop at the mailbox. You open the mailbox and find an envelope containing a very large check there. This isn't your monthly check; it's your weekly check. And you smile to yourself and realize that although you worked very hard for five years to earn those checks, you haven't actually done any work for the past six months. And the checks still keep showing up. Amazing, you think to yourself.

You stand there in front of your new house and you hardly believe your new lifestyle. The products you've been taking are making you feel more energetic. You're healthier than you've ever been. You feel fantastic physically, financially.

Now, let me ask you a simple question:

" If that was you and that image was real, would you tell your friends and family about it? Or would you hide from

19

> them how you'd achieved this level of success?"

His answer to me was shocking. He said, "If that was real, I'd tell everyone I knew."

"Well, sir," I said. "That is exactly what happened to me. And that is exactly why I'm talking to you right now. I'm looking for a few sharp people who want to make that happen in their own lives. By the reaction you gave me earlier, you're not the kind of candidate we're looking for. If you know of someone who'd like to live that kind of lifestyle, please give them my number. I'm taking applications."

There is silence on the other end of the line. I wait. He says, "What do I need to do to qualify?"

When I hang up, my team member is amazed. There is no rejection, no failure, no embarrassment. I don't allow it. I'm sorting for the kind of person who is looking for... even praying for... a once in a lifetime opportunity like this. They may only be one or two in a hundred. But those one or two in a hundred are worth their weight in gold.

I commit to finish strong.
Let's review the real numbers again. One out of a hundred is good odds. Two out of a hundred is phenomenal. Get prepared for the ninety-eight rejections that might be your experience. But realize that those few acceptances, if followed through, can earn you a fortune.

> Did you notice the secret in that last sentence? Underline the words, if followed through.

Follow-through—that's the secret.

An Open Letter from New York Times Best-Selling Author, Robert Allen

This is a country of quitters. We're great starters, but lousy finishers. Do you want a formula for failure? Start strong, finish lousy.

Here's a better formula: start lousy (if you have to), but finish strong.

Better yet, here's the best success formula:

Start strong, then finish even stronger.

When it comes to network marketing, you need to make a three-year pledge. Stick to it. Figure it out. The money is at the finish line, no matter how long it takes.

Brian Tracy talks about the two most important characteristics of winners: optimism and persistence.

Optimism is the belief that tomorrow will be better than today. Persistence is the willingness to keep moving even if it isn't.

Think positive. And persist.

And as a final note on follow through: Just as you expect your "newbies" to never give up, they also expect that you will never give up on them. There is a certain type of networker who we call a "sponsor monster." They sign 'em up fast and abandon them just as quickly Their motto: If you throw enough spaghetti against a wall, some of it is bound to stick.

This is not enlightened. This is giving our industry a bad name. I want to grab those people by the neck and scream, "Don't even bring them into your business if you're not prepared to train and support them. If you love 'em and leave 'em, they'll

It's Time... for Network Marketing

not only badmouth you, they'll badmouth network marketing."

Here's the lesson: If you're going to start them, then finish with them.

Let's do for the networking industry what Disney did for the amusement park industry. Before Walt, the amusement park business was full of shifty operators and tattooed carnival barkers—a low class experience. Disneyland became the standard to emulate. A clean-cut, polished, high quality experience—the way it ought to be.

Wanna play? Wanna be a Disney? It won't be easy. But it'll be worth it. Instead of becoming filthy rich, let's earn a huge stream of excellent, enlightened income together and transform our own lives and the image of network marketing forever.

Robert G. Allen is a highly successful network marketer and author of the national and New York Times best sellers: **Nothing Down: A Proven Program that Shows You How to Buy Real Estate with Little or No Money Down;** Creating Wealth, The Challenge; Multiple Streams of Income: How to Generate a Lifetime of Unlimited Wealth, Multiple Streams of Internet Income: How Ordinary People Earn Extraordinary Money Online; The One Minute Millionaire: The Enlightened Way to Wealth; and Cracking the Millionaire Code: Your Key to Enlightened Wealth.

To learn more about Robert, visit his website at:
http://Work-at-Home-Income-Streams.com

What's So Special About Network Marketing?

All the advantages of business ownership- financial freedom, time freedom, decision-making freedom- plus the advantages of a typical job with a large company- a well-refined product offering, reliable accounting, second-tier customer support, and a proven plan for success.

I could make a long list of all the various things that make network marketing great: financial freedom, time freedom, the focus on relationships, and so on. But what makes network marketing not only great, but unique and special as well?

Any form of entrepreneurship can lead to financial freedom.

Any form of passive and leveraged income can lead to time freedom.

Any sales, marketing, or business development job can focus on relationships.

What makes network marketing so special—more than just the combination of these things?

As I see it, there are two things that make network marketing really stand out from all other types of business.

The Best of Both Worlds

In the typical business, there are basically three roles: creators (the people who make the products or service offerings); deal-makers (those who market and sell the product, or who make deals with others to help sell the product); and supporters (the people who take care of the other two types—everyone from the shipping dock to the front desk to the CEO).

As a typical solopreneur, or founder of a small business, you typically have to wear many of these hats, if not all of them.

Not only do you have to create the product offering, you also must develop the marketing strategy, create the marketing materials, go out and sell the product, deliver it, follow up to collect money owed to you, and make sure that your employees and subcontractors get paid.

But in network marketing, you don't have to create the product or service. A group of researchers and developers have already worked to create and test a great product for you.

Professional product managers and marketers have developed the packaging, pricing and positioning, plus most of the marketing collateral you'll need—certainly enough to get you started.

Your upline sponsors will have already developed success strategies that may not guarantee your success, but will at least significantly improve your odds if you follow them.

And a good company also provides most of the support you'll need. Commissions are automatically calculated from orders, and you get your check reliably. A customer service department handles issues that you can't address yourself. In many cases, the company handles ongoing order fulfillment. With the right company and the right upline, you get the best of both worlds.

All the advantages of business ownership—financial freedom, time freedom, decision-making freedom—plus the advantages of a typical job with a large company—a well-refined product offering, reliable accounting, second-tier customer support, and a proven plan for success.

> You're the pilot, but you're never flying solo.

The Ability to Be Small

I know we all have great dreams of growing our business huge one day, but relish in your ability to do things on a small scale, especially when you're first starting out. It is one of the things that make network marketing rare, if not unique.

Some types of business can be started on the side while you hold down another job—Internet businesses, a product you're creating to take to market, etc. But many others can't. You can't do consulting during the day while you're working full-time somewhere else. You can't open a retail store or a restaurant just evenings and weekends.

> An MLM opportunity, though, can be started part-time while you're still working a full-time job. Or it can easily be added in gradually to your mix of other businesses.

It's not just when you're starting out, though. When the company creates a new product or service offering, they assume that development risk, and it's your choice as to how little or much you want to promote it.

It's Time... for Network Marketing

> You can think big, but you don't have to do big- you can do small, over and over and over again.

You can see what works with one customer and then do it again, and again. When you add your first distributor under you, you share what you've done with them so they can try to repeat it. You watch and learn from them, and you refine it. Then you add another, with even more wisdom to share to help them be successful.

When you add these two traits of network marketing to the other obvious benefits—time freedom, financial freedom and decision-making freedom—it's a unique and compelling combination. And that flexibility means that there's no "one right way" to do it—it can be whatever you define it to be in your life.

Scott Allen is a twenty-year veteran technology entrepreneur, executive, and consultant. He now writes, speaks, and trains individuals and organizations on building better business relationships on the Internet using online communities, social networking sites, blogs, mailing lists, discussion forums, and more. He is coauthor of The Virtual Handshake: Opening Doors and Closing Deals Online and is a contributing author to Blog!: How the Newest Media Revolution Is Changing Politics, Business and Culture. You can learn more about Scott by visiting his weblog: http://TheVirtualHandshake.com

JIM BARTLETT

Put a Price Tag on That... If You Can

I know about the freedom that money can buy. But the freedom of your time being YOUR time? Priceless!

The best thing about network marketing is absolutely, positively, unequivocally... the time freedom!

When my aunt called me from Minnesota in September 2003 to tell me my grandpa was dying and that I needed to get on a plane as fast as possible, you cannot imagine the relief I felt in knowing from Minnesota that I did not have to ask for time off; I did not have to decide if I could afford the trip.

Within fifteen minutes, I had my flight booked and was on my way to the Pittsburgh airport. I got there while my grandpa was still coherent enough to know me. I held his hand and prayed with him before he died. I got to tell him I loved him. I heard his last words... I heard him say he loved me.

I'm not saying I wouldn't have gone if I had had a job. But we both know how difficult it that would be... the price we would have had to pay.

To go without thought of answering to anyone... To go with no anxiety about an unforeseen expense... To go with peace of mind... That is freedom.

> And that's the freedom I'm passionate about sharing with others through network marketing.

... The freedom to go wherever you want to or need to, whenever you want to or need to, with no regard to what an employer says or what it might cost financially.

On a lighter, yet more important note: In the three years I've been full-time in network marketing, I am the ONLY father I know of who has gone to EVERY program my kids have had during the school day.

> The guidance counselor told me I'm the ONLY father he's ever seen come in and have lunch with the kids!

Hey! School pizza is really good, and it's cheap! On top of that... when Dad is there, no kids ever get sent to the "bad" table!

Yep, the time freedom is worth WAY more than the money. (Don't get me wrong... the money spends nicely, too! But the freedom of your time being YOUR time? Priceless!)

And one more benefit: Making great friends and seeing them achieve their dreams—making a living and a life working with people you like and who care about you. Put a price tag on that if you can!

Put a Price Tag on That... If You Can

Jim Bartlett lives in Northwestern Pennsylvania with his wife Tonja and their two children, Tiffany and Bethany, ages 18, and 15. Jim was raised on a farm and grew up learning what it meant to work hard and play hard. He went to the 9th grade and then enrolled in technical school to become a machinist. Jim started working full time as a machinist at age 17 and started in sales part time in 1985. He was introduced to network marketing in 1987.

For the next 13 years he struggled in network marketing with little success. In 2000 he read The Greatest Networker in the World and began learning the sound principles that lead to success in network marketing. In just 36 short months with his company, Xango, Jim has built a group volume of nearly $1.5 million dollars a month!

RICHARD BROOKE

Network Marketing: The Four-Year Career™

An income-producing occupation that allows you to not only earn income for now, but more importantly stacks up income for the future. Build something while you earn that keeps on earning. It is called Residual Income or Royalty Income, and the wealthiest people in the world have been focusing on it for hundreds of years.

The traditional forty-year career does not exist anymore. The average person today will change jobs more than seven times in their working career, many of them changing whole careers several times.

The idea of working for forty years to retire on one-third of what was not even enough for the forty years just does not make sense.

Yet it is still the ruling paradigm.

Challenging this forty-year career model is The Four-Year Career™. This trademarked concept is simple: Choose an income-producing occupation that allows you to not only earn income for now, but more importantly stacks up income for the future. Build something while you earn that keeps on earning. It is called Residual Income or Royalty Income, and the wealthiest people in the world have been focusing on it for

31

hundreds of years. Inventors do it. Songwriters do it. Movie producers do it. Actors now do it. Authors do it. Commercial real estate developers do it. And network marketers do it.

Build something that will keep on churning out the income, whether you are there managing it or not. This creates financial freedom, a concept that is not well known, explored, or enjoyed by most people. What does it take to do it in the movies, or publishing, or real estate? For the most part, I don't know. There are experts to guide you if that is your inclination. I do know what it takes in network marketing.

- Is it easy? No.
- Do you need lots of money or education? No.
- Do you need some time, lots of self-motivation, and a great company to stand behind you? Yes.
- Can you do it? Yes.

Financial freedom means different things to different people. It depends on one's appetite. Some people can be free on $1,000 a month, while others need $2,000 or $3,000 per month. Still others desire ten times that much. Regardless of what the amount is for you, think about what your life could be like (or if you prefer, what it could have been like) had you not had to work most of it.

Think of the interests you could have explored.

Think of the places you could have gone.

Think of the time you could have invested in your relationship with your children in their street-smart education.

Think of the fun you could have had.

Think of the things you could have created: writings, paintings, buildings, and gardens.

It's not too late to think in the present tense.

I think about the quality of life that most of us live now. We have good lives. We get to experience, for the most part, a fair amount of what life has to offer.

But what could we do? What could we build? What could we create and contribute if "earning a living" were not the mandatory daily grind?

What if we had our basic finances handled by age thirty or forty or fifty? What quality of life could we enjoy?

I am not suggesting that money is the most important thing in life. It is just that we spend most of our time earning a living, so we must place a pretty high value on what it provides. Just think of the time you could free up and what you could do with it that is more important than money.

It seems that maybe, when it comes to quality of life, we could turn our own society upside down and inside out by pioneering the paradigm of The Four Year Career™. Dive into a royalty income opportunity you enjoy and do it passionately and powerfully enough to get yourself set up for the rest of your life. You can continue that career for as long as it suits you, or you can launch another without sacrificing income.

With financial freedom your dreams can come true—even if you live to be 120. Imagine living twice as long as your forefathers/mothers, with ten times the quality of life. I think that adds up to twenty lifetimes. Financial Freedom. The Fountain of Youth. Network Marketing.

It's Time... for Network Marketing

Richard Bliss Brooke became a full-time network marketing distributor in 1977. He has been a successful sales leader, corporate executive and/or MLM company owner since that time. He has served on the Direct Selling Association's Board of Ethics, and as a board member for the MLMIA. Brooke is the author of The Four-Year Career: Wealth Building Through Network Marketing; Mailbox Money: The Promise of Network Marketing; and the highly acclaimed Mach II with Your Hair on Fire: The Art of Personal Vision and Self-Motivation. Brooke was featured on the cover of the March 1993 issue of SUCCESS magazine, the first time in the history of the industry that a mainstream magazine promoted the virtues of network marketing. RichardBrooke.com features dozens of free articles, audio recordings, and information on Brooke's passion for leadership and character development, as well as building wealth through network marketing. Richard and his wife Chris live in Coeur d'Alene, Idaho and the Yosemite area of California.

To visit Richard's website and subscribe to his free monthly newsletter, go here: http://RichardBrooke.com.

The Blessing of Free Enterprise Is that Everyone Benefits!

The beauty of building a successful network marketing business is that it can **only** be accomplished by serving others.

In a free enterprise-based economy, the amount of money one makes is directly proportional to the number of people they serve.

The Reverend Dr. Martin Luther King, Jr. said, "Anyone can be great, because anyone can serve."

Imagine that; anyone from any background, should he or she decide to serve others, can become successful. And a deserved part of success is wealth—the ability to live life more and live more life.

Financial success via network marketing—based on the above premise of free enterprise—can allow you to be more, have more, and do more. Building a vibrant and successful network marketing organization, you can work with whom you desire, travel or not travel as much as you want, send your children to the schools you see fit, donate more to the charities in which you believe, and overall... simply have more choices in life.

Wow!

And all this, because you got behind a particular product or service aligned with a company you believe in, a group of people you've gotten to know, like, and trust, and decided to serve growing number of people by bringing to them the benefits of the products, services and/or opportunity you represent.

> Free enterprise rewards that which is good about human nature and discourages that which is bad.

How so? Perhaps an explanation is called for due to today's general misconception of what the term "free enterprise" actually means... as well as what it doesn't mean.

Free enterprise, the economic and political doctrine holding that a capitalist economy can regulate itself in a freely competitive market through the relationship of supply and demand with a minimum of governmental intervention and regulation, should not be confused with "making the sale by illegal or unethical means." That is not free enterprise; that is not capitalism. It is theft. (Example: Enron was not an example of capitalism/free enterprise. Mrs. Fields' Cookies is an example of capitalism/free enterprise.)

The natural tendency of human beings (both buyers and sellers) to want what is best for themselves is the very best regulator of business that has ever been discovered. Because of this, the good in businesspeople is rewarded, and the bad is discouraged.

> Those who build their business with honesty and integrity develop great

The Blessing of Free Enterprise Is that Everyone Benefits!

> reputations; people begin to "know them, like them and trust them." People desire to do business with them... and they do.

A sale can be made via dishonest means, maybe several—and let's face it, at times and in certain circumstances and situations, even many. An organization can begin to form through false promises and can even be momentarily profitable. However, all too soon a person attempting to build a business that way will see their lack of ethics catch up to them. Their negative reputation spreads, and their sales and business structure will crumble faster than a stale cookie that falls on the floor and gets stepped on.

On the other hand, those who've proven to be long-term, mega-successful leaders have consistently learned how to do the business, they've worked at it consistently, and they've led their organization by way of example.

> Their example says, "Keep your eye on the ball and take your eyes off yourself. Keep serving others. Provide the best value to your customers and the best leadership to your organization."

More network marketing superstars have achieved great success in this manner because it coincides with a basic human principle: "All things being equal, people will do business with and refer business to those people they know, like, and trust."

There's nothing "namby-pamby" about this. It's based on what is called "enlightened self-interest."

> In a free enterprise economy, we benefit ourselves only by benefiting- and to the

degree to which we benefit- others.

As Adam Smith explained in his classic, The Wealth of Nations, 'It is not from the benevolence of the butcher, the brewer, or the baker that we can expect our dinner, but from their regard to their own interest."

In other words, they must serve us to make money. Not only that, they must do so better than their competitors. Well, it's just the same for a network marketer.

You are challenged to share your products, services, and/or opportunity with others and to educate and persuade them that, as a result of doing business with you, their life will be better.

Depending upon your product or service, it will provide them with more convenience, health, beauty, safety, peace of mind, protection, or whatever advantage it provides. If you're sharing your opportunity with them, then it is the lifestyle of time and financial freedom you are selling.

Either way, it's in your best interest to be of benefit to them and to serve their best interest.

Can you think of any other business model that, by the very nature and structure of its design, encourages one person to benefit so many others? I mean, unlike the corporate structure of defensively feeling the need to keep those who joined after you and are lower on the "totem pole" down and struggling, in network marketing, you actually advance the more you help those who joined after you to advance!

There are many fine businesses out there. A very good living can be made in numerous fields. And, owning a traditional business is typically a good idea, so long as you're prepared to work

The Blessing of Free Enterprise Is that Everyone Benefits!

hard, learn your craft and, in most instances, work with employees and teach others in your company how to do your job.

One disadvantage is that, often, the very people you've invested time, energy, and money in training will go off on their own and (Heaven forbid) compete for your customers! How many times has that happened? Far too many for those it's happened to even once.

In other words, if you're in a traditional business and you grow a successful "employee," you have more than likely just home-grown your future competition!

Conversely, in network marketing, because the person in your organization will always be in your organization, the best thing you can do for yourself is to help this person grow their business. Why? Because, since they'll always be in your organization, you have a "vested self-interest" in helping them to become successful (which, by the way, is the same vested self-interest the person who recruited you into the business had for himself or herself... and ain't that great!).

It seems as though, if you keep your focus on serving and leading (what the Reverend Dr. King referred to as "Servant Leadership") then you have an opportunity to live a life and lifestyle only imagined—if even that—by most people. Even better, you will be in a position to help others do the same.

The beauty of building a network marketing business—perhaps the most remarkable example of free enterprise ever created—is that a person who truly seeks an opportunity to better himself/herself, their family, and their general lot in life can take themselves from wherever they are now to a much better economic place in the world by serving others—and only by serving others. Remember...

It's Time... for Network Marketing

> " In a free enterprise-based economy, the amount of money one makes is directly proportional to the number of people they SERVE."

And it follows, of course, if you want to make a lot more money, then simply find a lot more people to serve... and serve them very well.

Bob Burg is an internationally known speaker and the author of the underground best seller ENDLESS REFERRALS: Network Your Everyday Contacts into Sales. This business classic (over 150,000 sold!) has just been totally revised and expanded. You can purchase the book and/or sign up for Bob's weekly "Endless Referrals Video Briefs" by going to Bob's website at: http://Burg.com.

ART BURLEIGH

Travel Isn't a Luxury- It's Homework for a Meaningful Life

It's a lot of fun when all the key elements come together- and the commissions constantly flow to you and to a slew of other deserving leaders on your team!

Chuka-Chuka-Chuka-Chuka-Chuka-Chuka-Chuka-Chuka-Chuka-Chuka-Chuka-Chuka. **"Wow, look at that, Dad!"** Chuka-Chuka-Chuka-Chuka-Chuka-Chuka. Chuka . . .

The motor drive on our long-lensed Canon SLR camera had just responded to my 16-year-old son's anxious finger as he'd quickly squeezed off twenty-three shots in rapid-fire succession of the pride of lions trotting through the tall, sunset-washed savannah grasses just thirty feet from our big safari van in Kenya's Masai Amboseli National Park.

Seth's upper body extended up through the photographers "pop-top" on our van, his elbows rested on the roof, and he continued photographing these lions as they came to rest atop a huge, rounded termite mound, settled down, and gazed off toward the antelopes and zebras grazing on the plains—with massive Mt. Kilimanjaro looming above it all, yet fully seventeen miles away!

The sunset cast its orange glow over everything, and even the

It s Time... for Network Marketing

white snow and ice atop Hemingway's mountain looked like it was on fire before the sun finally set rapidly—as it does near the equator—plunging us into early nightfall as we headed back to our luxury lodge for some drinks at the bar before settling in for our first night "on safari" in East Africa.

Eighteen years prior to that, my fabulous wife, Marlyn, had stood on the 19,340 foot summit of Kilimanjaro with several other friends from our first safari to East Africa, and now, we were back here together, with new friends, and with our son. It was pretty special, and we were just at the beginning of what would be yet another month-long, fantastic family vacation.

All this was possible because we now enjoyed both the time-freedom and a large, steady flow of passive income... the result of several years of serious, focused, part-time work building an active team with a great network marketing company.

That is what Marlyn and I most appreciate about this business—the opportunity we've had to significantly improve the quality of our future by building an enduring and lucrative income-producing asset (our organization) with our network marketing company.

Money isn't everything, but it's right up there with oxygen.

> The many benefits of an extra stream of strong, recurring income allows us to enjoy more options and get to where we really want to go in life- much sooner, and in style!

And because "success is a journey, not a destination," we're still on that journey, and we're actively building and supporting our networking team.

How was our trip to Africa inspired?

Ten months prior to it, I'd received a call from a leader on our team with the network marketing company we'd been building with for four years (and are still with today). She said, "Hey Art, my brother, who has been to Africa sixty-three times and runs a safari company, is going to Kenya with our family and a few others. We are taking a small group, and we want to know if you guys want to go too."

So I said, "Sure!"

That was a $24,000 decision, and I could make it right there and then on the spot, because of the time and money freedom this business provides.

So we got to take this great, luxury safari to Kenya with an expert guide, and it was really rewarding for me and Marlyn to be able to provide that exceptional and unique experience for our son, who was then only halfway through high school.

On that same trip, we got to meet some Samburu natives and toured their village. At the end, after the tour, the chief's son brought us around a corner onto the pathway back to our vehicle, and all the women of the village were lined up along it.

They had spread out their wares, and they wanted us to buy everything that they had! Jewelry, trinkets, bows, arrows, spears, bowls, carvings... all this stuff. It was both breathtaking and heartbreaking, because with their poverty and their hardships with drought, we wanted to be able to buy from everyone.

Realistically, of course, we couldn't do that, as there were only about ten of us and over sixty of them. Also, because we had a limited amount of time and not enough of the smaller Kenyan shilling notes with us, we couldn't buy as much as we wanted to.

What's really great is that our son learned the value of hot and cold running water on that trip. He experienced the contrast between how we were traveling and how these African natives really lived.

It was an eye-opener, and I think it's very valuable to get that kind of firsthand experience, especially when you're young—it really expands your perspective.

On the way back from Africa, we stopped over for a week in London and a week in Paris. And those were fabulous experiences, too. We were away for a month together, and we got paid our networking commissions the whole time we were gone.

Who else can do that with their teenaged son when they're in their early 50s?

VERY few besides successful network marketers, successful investors, or independently wealthy people! Wealthy retirees can travel, but often not until they're much older, and if they have to work for a boss at a day job until they're sixty or sixty-five or older, they can't benefit their kids with the essential experience of extensive travels. Their kids aren't kids anymore by that time!

Personal development is another big benefit of being around smart people in network marketing, and the educational escape that travel provides from one's routine allows for more reading and introspective personal development.

We know that your business will only grow as fast as you do. So, unless you engage personal development, your chances of really expanding your business are limited, because you're probably not growing much yourself—expanding your abilities, your insights and your skills.

One experience that helped me a lot occurred about two years into our association with the company we're now with. We were making enough money that we could take our

Travel Isn't a Luxury- It's Homework for a Meaningful Life

first long family vacation.

We'd just finished up a week's vacation at the UCLA Family Camp in the Southern California mountains at Lake Arrowhead, where we go every year, and six days later, we returned home, packed our brand-new luxury car, and we were off again—for a five-week driving vacation from Los Angeles to Cape Cod, Massachusetts and back.

It was terrific. It was just the three of us—Marlyn, Seth and me—and we drove at whatever pace we wanted for 8,200 miles. We saw five major league baseball games along the way. We stopped to visit family and friends, stayed in motels or hotels when we needed or wanted to, ate at restaurants all along the way. We visited national parks, the Baseball Hall of Fame in Cooperstown, New York, big city sites, and cool museums.

We were able to show our son this great country of ours from the ground up, instead of just down through the clouds. Our neighbor took in our mail and deposited our network marketing checks at our bank for us, so we could simply go to any ATM machine and take out the cash we needed.

We got paid by our company every week we were gone on our trip- and THAT is such a HUGE benefit of this business!

Before we left, I invested $300 in a bunch of training albums from Upline®—John Fogg's excellent Conversation with the Greatest Networkers in the World tape series and The Women's Tapes. And that's how I was first introduced and came to appreciate industry leaders like Richard Brooke, Tom "Big Al" Schreiter, Randy Gage, Steve Spaulding, Russ DeVan, Jan Ruhe, Mark & Rene Yarnell, Peggy Long, Rita Davenport, and Sandy Elsberg. And as we listened to those tapes in our car as we drove all across the country, I learned a lot. And so did Marlyn and Seth!

It's Time... for Network Marketing

On this trip across America, we got to spend quality time with many special friends and relatives. We had lunch with the parents of our company's president in Cape Cod, and then we drove twenty minutes up the road and had dinner with cousins of mine I'd known since my childhood.

We spent time with my dad both in Boston, where he was visiting his girlfriend, and then in Baltimore, where he was still living. And, for the first time, I visited our "family plot" where my grandparents and my brother are buried. All together, we visited twenty-two states, plus Canada.

> Chances are, you don't know any thirteen-year-olds who have done that, and very few, if any, adults!

When our son was fourteen, he had the opportunity to go to Europe with an organization called People to People Student Ambassadors. It was a soccer tour—some thirty kids from all around the US met at the Los Angeles airport. They flew to London and toured southern England, Holland, Germany, and France, and they played soccer games with other students their age in all these different countries.

They had the chance to go sightseeing everywhere, and they happened to be in Paris the day the French won the World Cup. At fourteen, it was great for Seth to be able to go to Europe on his own, and it was nice for us to be able to easily afford that experience for him.

A few years later, Marlyn had the chance to take her mom to New York City. She was trying to figure out what to give her for her 80th birthday. Marlyn's mom had grown up in New York City, but she hadn't been back there in sixty years. She had come out to California as a young bride, so Marlyn took her back home.

It was wonderful that just the two of them could do that together.

> Two years later, her mom passed on. Without the income from our network marketing business, Marlyn and her mom wouldn't have been able to share that very special experience together.

Because of our successful home-based networking business, Marlyn was also able to retire early. She taught elementary school for thirty years; she did a great job and loved teaching and the kids and classroom, but she got tired of all the state-required testing, the politics involved, plus the time required outside the classroom spent grading papers, attending meetings, and bargaining for the teachers' contract renewals.

That same year, our son started his first year of college at the University of California at Berkeley, and two months later, Marlyn and I celebrated her early retirement by taking a six-week vacation to Australia and New Zealand.

> Once again, our residual income flowed into our mailbox every week while we were away!

We have never missed getting a weekly check in over ten years, and our networking income has also paid for our son's college education.

Another great trip was our ten-day visit to Guernsey, the beautiful British channel island off the coast of France, where we stayed with fabulous new friends we'd met on our New Zealand tour a couple years prior.

They live in a 500-year-old granite farmhouse built in 1493.

It's Time... for Network Marketing

And that twenty-five-square-mile island is the most charming area of lushly bordered country lanes, gorgeous farms, flower gardens, and quaint village areas that we've every seen. Their main town, St. Peter Port, was celebrating their 800th anniversary when we were there!

In the fall of 2005, as our son was in his senior year at college, Marlyn and I flew to Melbourne to attend the wedding of another wonderful friend we'd met three years prior on our trip to Australia. We spent the weekend in Sorrento and Port Sea—two beautiful little villages on the peninsula south of Melbourne.

While strolling through the shops in Sorrento, Marlyn and I saw a beautiful, seven-foot-long, dark red, antique Chinese sideboard. It was just exquisite, 150 years old with beautiful black distressed markings. My wife said she didn't even want to see the price tag, figuring it would cost just as much to ship it home all the way from Australia.

Well, the clever storeowner overheard us and said, "Well, you'd be surprised." It was going to cost us only about $750 to ship it home, so we bought this unusual, eye-catching sideboard with a credit card, and it now graces our dining room! The kind of freedom to be able to snap up spectacular "souvenirs" like that is so nice!

Even though our Aussie friend's wedding was beautiful and fun, you know it's virtually impossible to spend any time with a friend at their wedding, so the arrangement we made with her was that we'd come if we could spend some time with her and her new husband after their honeymoon.

So, after their wedding, while they were off honeymooning, Marlyn and I spent another week sightseeing in Melbourne, then over a week touring beautiful, remote Tasmania. Then we flew up to Sydney and met our friends as they returned from their honeymoon on the South Sea island of Vanuatu. With a slew of our extra Marriott points, we treated them to some nights at the Sydney Marriott as part of our wedding gift to them, and we had a blast together sightseeing all over Sydney for five days!

Of course, we were paid our weekly commission checks the whole time we were on that vacation, too!

> Time freedom. Financial freedom. Thanks to network marketing! What magnificent benefits these are for parents and their kids!

Marlyn and I sleep until we wake up. We're no longer jarred awake by alarm clocks every morning. We decide when and where we're going to travel—anywhere. There's no more commute that consumes hours every day, or hundreds of gallons of costly gasoline every month! So there's much less wear and tear on our cars, and on US!

Having those freedoms relieves stress, because we have enough income to provide options and flexibility. We can travel almost whenever we want to—including during the "off season" when the crowds are gone and the weather's cooler. We work seriously at our business, so we're certainly not traveling all the time, but I believe...

> ...travel is not a luxury- it's homework for a meaningful life.

When you can expose yourself and your children to travel, I think it has a very positive and important impact on them and on the quality of your family relationships. It provides a very important perspective, and it nurtures fun, rewarding relationships.

Plus, if you're doing any prospecting or "research" for the future growth of your networking business, then some of your travel expenses could be tax-deductible—check with your tax advisor.

Being able to live your life in a comfortable, flexible way is a huge benefit of network marketing! Freedom!

It's not easy growing a network marketing organization. You have to be blessed with finding the right company—one that's got excellent management, great leadership, and a strong, appealing, consumable product line which creates a positive impact on the quality of people's lives—and you need a good marketing plan and strong support from the company.

Then you have to work smart with consistency and focus, usually for several years, to get your group large enough to develop its own growth momentum and for leaders to emerge and develop.

You want a flagship product with uniqueness, exclusivity, and appeal with some sizzle that can create impact and duplication. Some buzz in the marketing arena helps too, empowering a lot of other people so that they can create success for themselves and grow their organizations.

It's a lot of fun when all those key elements come together, and the commissions constantly flow to you and to a slew of other deserving leaders on your team! These are some of the very best benefits of growing a network marketing organization in the right way

---

Art Burleigh is Double Diamond Executive distributor and also the Chairman of the Executive Advisory Council for Essentially Yours Industries (EYI). His team of over 150,000 distributors now spans the North American continent and has also grown throughout Asia.

To learn more about Art and to subscribe to his free training newsletter, Accelerate Your MLM Success!, visit http://ArtBurleigh.com.

What's So Great About Network Marketing?

I truly believe that we have entered the Renaissance of network marketing- the lightbulbs are going on and attracting freethinking, abundant people at an accelerating pace that cannot be stopped.

I'm sitting here in the Frankfurt airport waiting to catch a flight back home after a whirlwind tour through Germany, with a couple of stops along the way to Gotenberg, Sweden and London, England, and it just hit me.

I was honored to be asked by John Milton Fogg to write this chapter on what's so great about network marketing—but ever since he asked, I must admit, I've been stumped.

Not because I couldn't think of anything that's great about network marketing, but rather because I could think of too many things! How to narrow it down to just one thing I am most passionate about is a difficult task.

I have seen and experienced such great camaraderie, been able to travel distant lands, helped my mom buy the house of her dreams, and purchase a ski condo for myself. I have helped countless people get out of debt and go on to build a lifestyle that makes most CEOs green with envy, I've been able to donate money to my favorite charities, and the list goes on and on.

> But all of these wonderful blessings really come down to one thing and one thing alone: People.

Great, wonderful, open-minded, positive people are what I am most passionate about.

Most people mistakenly think that their main product is whatever it is they're selling, and of course, it is in one way. But your real product, whether you're marketing cosmetics, skin cream, juice, nutritional care, jewelry, or cookware, is PEOPLE.

But not just any kind of people: more specifically, people who are seeking change.

> But not just people seeking change: people seeking change who are ALSO willing to do something about it.

Network marketing gives these types of individuals a track to run on that comes complete with a system and a support team to facilitate the process. Our business model creates a culture that embraces the concept of abundance, and the belief that more for you is more for me, not the corporate-think of more for you is less for me.

An extraordinary thing happens when all of these elements are present—the result is positively combustible. When this happens, we get to witness the most magical of all human processes: transformation.

> People transforming their lives by helping others succeed is the network marketing paradigm.

Watching the lightbulbs turn on as people realize that not only are they in control of their lives, but also that anything is possible, is one of the most magical things I can imagine—the field of infinite possibilities... the domain of GOD.

No matter what your religious leaning, I think that we can all agree that there is a whole lot of God in each one of us. And when people are in trouble and need help in the form of more money, time, love, or caring—it's the God within another person that comes to the rescue.

To me, network marketing is a lifeline available to those special individuals who are willing to rock the boat, face some adversity, yet (not but) want to climb onboard despite all that—or even because of all that—and paddle like mad to safety and success together.

> People who transform their own lives and then help others to do the same are the people who build the largest empires.

And it is the ability to interact and learn from these kinds of people that excites me most. I get enthusiastic about people with the courage and the determination to follow their dreams, especially in trying circumstances.

These are people who focus on the solution rather than the problem... people who understand that it's not the obstacles we face, but the overcoming of those challenges that really matters. The struggle gives us the opportunity to develop character, become true leaders, and as a result, attract other leaders into our enterprise.

For, after all, we are in the business of building and attracting people and leaders. And there's nothing I'm more passionate about than spending quality time with leaders around the world.

I truly believe that we have entered the Renaissance of

network marketing.

The lightbulbs are going on- attracting freethinking, abundant people at an accelerating pace that cannot and will not be slowed or stopped.

The reasons for this Renaissance are obvious: the Internet and other hi-tech tools have leveled the playing field and have empowered ordinary people to duplicate success far faster and more efficiently—and more globally—than ever before. Marketing plans have evolved, making the business more accessible and equitable to all.

Finally, any network marketing company that understands that PEOPLE are the lifeblood of the business should have at its core a charitable partner or a charitable culture.

It's often said that you are only as strong as your weakest link, so improving the quality of lives around the world fits into my humble yet unshakable belief that PEOPLE are what makes this industry of network marketing so great.

And once that lightbulb is turned on, it will never, ever go off!

Corey Citron is a network marketing superstar who has built an international Xango organization of more than 40,000 networkers in only twenty-four months. He's an Internetwork Marketing pioneer as well. He created the first online marketing system to enroll 100,000 members, and he did that in only eighteen months.

An entrepreneur since the age of nine—when he sold pita bread pizza to his classmates to finance the purchase of his first computer—after graduating from Stanford University, he opened a nightclub on South Beach at the age of twenty-two. After being introduced by a nurse in his father's office to direct selling, he realized that he had found his calling and has never looked back. You can learn more about Corey on his website, http://CoreyCitron.com

The Four Greatest Fears of Starting Your Own Business

... and how network marketing blows them all away with the force of a 20-megaton thermal nuclear explosion! I dare you to honestly and openly look at network marketing and not be impressed and intrigued!

Way back in the last century (1991), a survey was conducted by my research firm, MarketWave, Inc., of almost 7,000 people who were not, nor had ever been, business owners of any kind. The question was a simple one:

If all obstacles were removed, would you like to own your own business?

In other words, if whatever was stopping you from starting a business didn't exist, would you at least attempt it? Would you prefer to be an entrepreneur, or an employee?

Eighty five percent said Yes, they'd prefer to work for themselves. Which means that 15 percent misunderstood the question on the survey. After all, if whatever concerned you enough to not attempt a business venture didn't exist, then you'd have no fear of doing so.

I mean, who wouldn't want to be in control of their own life? To have the freedom to make their own decisions, work their own hours, and write their own paycheck?

Even using the conservative 85 percent figure, that meant about 200 million Americans wanted to start their own business but have never even attempted it! We thought there must be some pretty compelling reasons why, so we set out to find out what they were.

> To no one's surprise, it was never about preferring to work for someone else's business, but rather the incapacitating fear of starting your own.

And it was the same four fears, every single time.

It takes too much money.
People didn't have tens of thousands, or hundreds of thousands of dollars to invest in a business (and they didn't know anyone else who did).

It takes too much time.
People didn't want to work eighty hours a week for the first year or two to get their business going.

There's too much risk.
Over 56 percent of all businesses fail in the first two years, and they'd have to quit their job, so there was no safety net.

They didn't know how.
Most people had never taken any business courses. They had no business experience. They didn't know anything about taxes, accounting, marketing, and the myriad of other skills a good entrepreneur must possess.

Not all responded with all four objections, although most responded with more than one. Surprisingly, "I don't know how" was the single most common response. A lot of folks said

The Four Greatest Fears of Starting Your Own Business

they wished they had taken the plunge earlier in their lives, but they just weren't the mavericks they once were. They had a mortgage to pay and a family to feed. They felt it was "too late."

Now comes the fun part.

Would you ever consider going into business for yourself if:

The total start up costs were under $500... the total time investment could be as little as 5-15 hours a week... you could continue to work in your present job until the income from your business was sufficient to earn you at least an equal income, so there would be little risk... and best of all, there were numerous consultants available to you who are experts at running this business, who would train and advise you personally for an unlimited number of hours, for the entire life of your business, absolutely free!

Not only that, but there is another company that will take care of all your research and development, labeling, inventory, shipping, payroll, various taxes, most legal questions, and so on. And this company will do this for you every month, for the life of your business, for around, oh, $35.00 a year.

Right now, you're probably remembering the old adage, "If it sounds too good to be true... " Fine.

But, just hypothetically, would you consider going into business for yourself IF all this were true?

"Well, sure..." you're probably thinking, "... but there's got to be a catch."

Not only is there no catch, I didn't even hype the pitch by one iota. These are exactly the conditions in which tens of

> thousands of successful network marketing ventures have begun.

Sure, some overly zealous networkers may tell you how rich you're going to get, how easy it is, and how fast it will happen. Please note, I didn't say any of that!

> Network marketing is a serious business, no less so than any other way you might consider earning your living for the rest of your life.

The reality is that network marketing is hard work, it takes time, and you'll probably lose some money in the beginning.

The difference is that most of the hardest work is done by someone else, your work is done when you choose to do it, it typically takes a few months to turn a profit (some accomplish this in the first month) rather than a few years, and whatever amount you might lose at first has one, two, or maybe even three fewer digits compared to the start-up losses of most conventional businesses.

Yet you can still reap the tax benefits of operating your own business, and you can have just as much, if not more, income potential as most conventional businesses!

Imagine becoming financially independent in one to three years...

> Without having to spend thousands of dollars each month...

> Without having to work long hours seven days a week...

Without even having to quit your job during the development stage and...

Without having to get a business degree or hire someone who has one...

If you are considering starting your own business, and you've got access to, let's say, $50,000 in startup funds (a very modest assumption), imagine how profitable you could be, and how quickly, if you didn't have to hire employees, you didn't have to lease an office... and/or storefront... and/or warehouse, you didn't have to pay sales or payroll taxes, you didn't have to spend one penny on R&D, graphic design, or the development of promotional material, and you didn't have to hire an accountant, lawyer, or business consultant.

And imagine how much more money might go into your pocket if you didn't need business partners to help you finance and run the business. Think about it—and try not to become giddy.

Now for the really fun part...

Imagine buying a McDonald's franchise for the modest sum of one million dollars. The business fails. You call up McDonald's corporate headquarters and ask for a "Return Authorization Number" so you can get your franchise fee back along with a reimbursement check for your unsold supplies and stock.

(While imagining this scene, also imagine the sound of sirens wailing in the background. That would either be the paramedics coming to assist the poor corporate officer who you've just induced into a fit of hysterics, or an ambulance coming to take you to a really nice, soft, baby-blue colored room.)

In network marketing, not only is this not an absurd scenario, it's the law!

One of the aspects of a legitimate, legal network marketing company is the ability of a failed distributor to get a full refund (usually less a 10 percent restocking and processing fee) on all product and marketing material that is in resalable condition.

So, if pursued conservatively and intelligently, there is a monumental reduction in risk relative to conventional business start-ups, yet with a comparable or even greater profit opportunity.

Those of you who are already actively involved in network marketing, be aware that the vast majority of your "outer circle" prospects (those who've never been involved in network marketing) do have at least the desire to own their own business, as opposed to working for someone else. You don't have to talk them into the benefits of something they're already dreaming about.

But they also have some very powerful, legitimate fears about starting their own business.

> You've first got to open their minds to the idea that there is still a realistic way to achieve that dream and then define, or perhaps defend, the concept of network marketing.

Only then should you introduce the benefits of your particular network marketing program.

Think of it like this: Before you can pour fresh, hot coffee into a thermos, you must first open it up and pour the old, stale coffee out, right? So, think of your business-phobic prospect as a sealed mind full of cold, stale ideas. First open it up (to the concept of starting a business), dump the old information out (about MLM, if necessary, and for sure about what's involved in starting a new business), and then pour the new, hot, fresh information in (about your specific opportunity).

The Four Greatest Fears of Starting Your Own Business

If you are considering starting your own business, or you want to, but have always been apprehensive, open your own mind to network marketing.

Think it's too good to be true? I challenge you: Find the catch!

If you've never pursued a network marketing venture, it must be for one of two reasons: You just didn't know about it, or you have a prejudice against it.

And that's exactly what it is, a prejudice. You have prejudged this business based on what someone else has told you about it (usually someone who has failed at it or who has also never been involved themselves).

In other words, you've chosen to adopt someone else's opinion of this business. Don't let other people do your thinking for you. Make your own decision based on your own evaluation.

Check this business out. Really, do your due diligence.
And when you are done, I would defy anyone, even the most devout skeptic, to not experience a significant, positive paradigm shift.

I dare you to honestly and openly look at network marketing and not be impressed and intrigued!

Leonard Clements is a speaker, trainer, and author who has concentrated his full-time efforts on researching and analyzing all aspects of network marketing since October of 1990. He conducts "Inside Network Marketing" seminars throughout the world. Len is the author of the controversial book Inside Network Marketing (Random House) and the best-selling audios Case Closed! The Whole Truth About Network Marketing and The Coming Network Marketing Boom. He is also a court certified expert in the field of network marketing and the co-owner of a successful network marketing company.

It's Time... for Network Marketing

To receive additional information about MarketWave and its products, please call 1-800-688-4766, or write to MarketWave, Inc., 2406 Canberra Ave., Henderson, NV 89052, or visit http://MarketWaveInc.com.

Abide & Abound

If we abide by the principles and philosophies of this industry, we will abound. We will succeed. We will become financially independent and enjoy all the freedom that this industry offers, but more importantly, we will become better people in the process.

Every day of the week, millions of network marketers are canvassing the globe—sharing, representing, recruiting, supporting, promoting, and duplicating their particular home-based business opportunity.

There is a sense of urgency, even desperation, as people from all walks of life seek deliverance from financial bondage. The phenomenal growth, success, and resilience of this billion-dollar industry is not a fluke—it's a revolution, the last bastion of free enterprise.

Every attempt to suppress, control, and destroy this industry has and will continue to fail, as it is impossible to extinguish the hopes and dreams of millions of self-motivated distributors who yearn for nothing more than a chance to experience the equivalent of the American Dream—the freedom of financial independence.

To add to its strength, network marketing has become a vast melting pot of cultures, peoples, races, creeds, and sexes of all ages with no barriers or limitations, except for those we place on ourselves.

One might as well try to defy the law of gravity as to defy the underlying laws that drive the human spirit—the spirit of inspiration and determination.

Network marketing ultimately thrives upon these same principles. To tap into this billion-dollar industry, you must tap into the human soul. You must tap into the underlying principles that make this thriving phenomenon possible. You must embrace what network marketing represents:

A new frontier of self-functional individuals all led by one common law: the law of the harvest- you reap what you sow.

The seeds of this industry have always been people, not products or pay plans. When we abide in developing people and inspiring the human spirit to thrive, our harvest abounds.

Unfortunately, people enter this industry with the false notion that the best way to succeed is to promise financial salvation at no cost, with little or no effort, and with little or no skills. This welfare mentality and free-ride approach to network marketing has created a financial windfall for a few and mass havoc and even ruin for the many.

Like any frontier, network marketing can be cruel and unforgiving, particularly in today's cultural environment, where personal responsibility and achievement are all too unfamiliar territory. To succeed long-term in this business, you must build and uplift the human spirit—not tear down and destroy it by encouraging sloth or promising instant gratification.

You must build upon the strengths and abilities of each individual by dedicating yourself to helping them acquire the skills that enable them to rise above their personal fears and weaknesses. What is needed in this industry—now more than ever—is an experienced guiding hand, not corporate excuses or individual failings.

In many respects, network marketing has taken the brunt for our own personal individual imperfections and failings. What other industry is so authentic that it reveals our weaknesses and shortcomings?

Think about it...

- If we're lazy and lack ambition, we'll fail.
- If we don't put forth the effort and acquire the skills required by this industry, we'll fail.
- If we continue to blame others for our problems, we'll fail.

On the other hand...

- If we're ambitious, dedicated, and self-motivated, we'll succeed.
- If we take personal responsibility as a business owner, we'll succeed.

It's an unwritten law in this business without shortcuts, and there's no getting around it by taking the easy way out:

Network marketing exposes who we really are by mirroring our character- our weaknesses as well as our strengths.

Often we become disgruntled with this business, when we should be disgruntled with ourselves. That's why I love and respect this industry so much. It is unforgiving. It demands competence. It forces us to improve, which makes us grow.

Abide and abound is the governing and underlying law of network marketing. If we abide by the principles and philosophies of this industry, we will abound. We will succeed. We will become financially independent and enjoy all the freedom that this industry offers, but more importantly, we will become better people in the process.

In the end, we discover that, within this industry, we can be our own best friend or our worst enemy. Network marketing gives us the power and freedom to choose.

Anthony Diaz has over two decades of experience in the direct sales industry as a successful distributor, marketer, business consultant, motivational speaker, professional trainer, and company owner. He is know in Asia as "The Messenger" and "The Innovator" and has a reputation as a marketing maverick who has developed countless innovations and trends that have created paradigm shifts in network marketing internationally, including personal import, the binary and hybrid compensation plans, matching bonuses, relationship-based training systems, advanced marketing techniques, interactive CD ROMs, product packaging, and presentations that are widely used throughout the world today.

Anthony is the CEO of Life Quest Network of Japan and has recently brought his company to America as Zenza Life Sciences in the first step of his commitment to global expansion.

You can learn more about Anthony Diaz on his website at: http://Zenza.us.

The #1 Most Motivating Benefit of MLM

Network marketing is about relationships. When you build relationships and then sponsor those people into your business, you have a business that grows, built by people you love to spend your time with... and you have ongoing income for life.

When you work for someone else, your and your family's future is in their hands. The only way to ever reach your dreams is to work for yourself.

You've seen companies get eaten up by bigger corporations... lifetime employees turned out on the street. What if that happened to you? You don't know what the future will bring.

Listen—it wasn't raining when Noah built the ark. But when that flood came, he was ready. Being ready is a GOOD idea. Having an income from your own home business might be YOUR ark. It could save your family.

There are a LOT of home business models to choose from. But there is one characteristic that elevates network marketing above all the other business models... and this is crucial for you to understand. Otherwise, you may make a big mistake... huge!

My wife Linda and I have been doing network marketing for twenty-eight years. We have a life today that most people only dream about. The number one feature that caused us to fall in love with network marketing is the recurring income that this business model creates.

With non-MLM business models, you start over every month from zero. But in MLM, you get paid like an author, or a rock star. Stephen King still earns a bit on books sold today that he wrote twenty or thirty years ago. Lisa Marie Presley gets about $25,000,000 a year of ongoing income from people buying CDs of "Don't Be Cruel" and other songs her dad recorded. Elvis has been dead thirty years! THAT is recurring income.

Twenty-eight years ago, I had my own construction business. An insurance agent knocked on my door. He said,

"Listen, Michael. What if I could show you a way to work for a little less money, building these homes... but then the houses would pay you on ongoing income for the rest of your life? Even if you quit, never built another house, the checks would keep coming in."

I thought that idea was incredible.

Then the guy said to me,

> " Well, there's an opportunity that creates recurring income like that. You work hard for a couple years, then you get a check in the mail every week, even if you quit working!"

I had spent seven years busting my back, working, slaving, building my carpentry business. The thought of getting paid in the future for work I'd already done really lit my fire. And THAT is how MLM works.

So today, twenty-eight years later, we still get a check the first week of January every year, from the same company, on the business that I did twenty-eight years ago!

Is your job COSTING you money?

By 1994, a good friend of mine had spent sixteen years driving a bus in Miami. When you drive a bus, you get paid for working. If you don't work, you don't get paid.

But in April of 1994, my friend ran his first full-page national ad. The response to that ad built him a recurring income. **In fact, that ad my friend wrote in 1994 still pays income today!** Is that amazing? He'll tell you, it takes his breath away, just thinking about it.

And after he ran his second national ad, he decided he couldn't afford to drive a bus anymore. That job was costing him too much money... too much time. He quit. That bus-driver income ended. But here we are thirteen years later, and that ad he wrote is still paying income!

THAT is what makes the network marketing business model so superior to any other. But it's not the ONLY way to get recurring income.

You could write a #1 best-selling novel.... You could sing and record a CD that goes Platinum.... You could invent the next Post-It® Note... uh-oh!

Come to think of it, maybe network marketing IS the only way regular people will ever get recurring income!

MLM is the only way that normal people like you and I can get paid like rock stars. If you open a shop in a mall, you may make good money, but you start over from zero every month. And, of course, your expenses are astronomical, so there's big pressure on you to produce immediately... constantly... from then on.

The key to creating a high level of ongoing income is to build strong relationships with the people who join you in your network marketing business. When you sponsor a person, plan on being in business with them the rest of your lives. That's the only way you can create a dependable ongoing income. Your income is built on those relationships.

MLM is the most unique business model ever created. It is relationship marketing. It's all about partnering up for life.

My mentor, Tom "Big Al" Schreiter, gave me a gold nugget about fifteen years ago. He told me, "Never sponsor anybody into your business that you wouldn't want to be on a one-month cruise with." Before that, I thought that if they could fog a mirror, you'd sign them up. But that doesn't work. Network marketing is about relationships. When you build relationships and then sponsor those people into your business, you have a business that grows, built by people you love to spend your time with.

What more could you possibly want?

Most people mess up and choose the wrong system.
Listen. This is crucial. To have real recurring income, you need a GREAT value-priced product that's consumable—that people get automatically, every month, like a book club subscription.

If you just sell books, you start over every month, from ZERO. But if you sell subscriptions, all the people who ordered in the past order again this month. You'll get new customers, too. So your income actually increases every month. THAT is a beautiful thing. Believe me. It's amazing.

The #1 Most Motivating Benefit of MLM

If you have to start from zero every month, you'll NEVER retire.

I've talked to plenty of people who did it the wrong way. They'd love to go back and start over. Crucial point: You need a hot, consumable product to create a recurring income.

"Big Al" once described to me how he got started in network marketing. He went to a meeting. Afterwards, the person who invited him walked up to him and said,

"Listen, Big Al. When you join our business, here's what happens. Six months from now you walk into your boss' office, lean back in the chair, put your feet up on his desk, dig in some little scuff marks with your heels, and calmly tell your boss you can't fit him in your schedule any longer. You're resigning, effective today.

"If they need any help after you leave, they can call you any Tuesday at your normal consulting rate. Then you leave his office, go out to your desk, pick up your personal stuff, wave good-bye to all your fellow employees who told you it couldn't be done, then hop into your brand-new bonus car. You burn rubber out of the parking lot, zip on down to the bank, pull up to the drive-in teller and say, 'Deposit this commission check. I don't know... put it in savings or checking... I don't know. I get these things all the time.' Then drive home and have a nice glass of your favorite beverage."

"Big Al" heard this and he said, "How do I join?"

Michael Dlouhy started in network marketing in 1979 and began his full-time career in 1991. Michael joined over 100 MLM companies in 1992-94, to find out everything he could about how the business really worked. Today, Michael does fifteen hours a week of network marketing training by phone for anyone in any company via his Mentoring for Free program.

71

It's Time... for Network Marketing

Michael has written 2 e-books: Success in 10 Steps and Powerful Networking Secrets!

Michael transcended his 8th grade education and difficult early family background to become a multimillion dollar network marketing leader and top producer in his company. (He says, "It turned out to be a good thing. I had to make it on my own in life from an early age. I learned to be an entrepreneur from the start.") He's been married to wife Linda since 1970, and they have two children: Matthew, 23 and Amanda, 20. Michael lives in Brooksville, Florida.

To visit Michael's website and get your free e-book, read his informative weblog, learn about his free teleconference calls, and more, go to: http://AskMichaelDlouhy.com.

Full-Time Income Working Part-Time

Treat your network marketing business as a business and eventually it will pay you as a business... and best of all, it can pay you a full-time income while you are working part-time from home.

What I like most about network marketing is the ability to earn full-time income while working part-time from home, but as much as that remarkable possibility excites me... it seems network marketing is not for everyone.

In March, I was chatting with a neighbor about how my network marketing business allows me to work at home and spend time with my family. He commutes two hours every day (which he hates). When I asked him if he was interested in starting a part-time business from home, he said,

> " I can't do that marketing stuff right now; the basketball finals are just starting."

In April, I was leaving the restaurant that I own, and just as I unlocked the door to my new Jaguar I heard someone say, "Boy, that's a great looking car." I turned around and said, "Thanks—do you like Jags?" He replied, "Sure, but who can afford one?"

It's Time... for Network Marketing

I told him that my part-time network marketing business more than paid for the Jag. We chatted for a few minutes and then I asked if he was interested in a second income from home. He said no, because he was "so busy all the time." He climbed into his clunker and drove off. I guessed he was probably feeling sorry for himself.

While it is true that we are all busy, it is also true that everyone has the same twenty-four hours in a day.

> Most people feel they do not have time, because by habit they are constantly working on the wrong things.

In other words, they're busy, but they are wasting their time and nothing important is being accomplished.

Network marketing represents the last—and perhaps the only—chance for financial freedom for most people. Where else can you start a business for a few hundred dollars, with almost zero risk, and have the possible outcome of a lifetime of financial abundance—and at the same time get to help others achieve success as well? Nowhere else that I know of.

As a former "normal" business owner, I've had millions of dollars on the line, secured by all my personal resources, including my house. If that business failed, I could lose all I had built...all I had saved...and I would have to restart my life with zero assets.

> I really appreciate the low entry cost of starting a network marketing business and the low downside risk.

As I said at the beginning, what I like most about network marketing is the ability to earn full-time income while working

Full-Time Income Working Part-Time

part-time from home. That's what makes this business the most remarkable form of free enterprise ever created.

Steve Domitrecz, a.k.a. Steve Dom, is a national director with Innerlight, Inc. He earns a six-figure income every year while working his networking business part time. Steve is an entrepreneur who recognized the ability of a good network marketing opportunity to generate lifetime residual income. Visit Steve's website at: http://PhMiracle4u.com

The People's Franchise

> Network marketing is the most remarkable business model developed so far for ordinary people to achieve extraordinary success. Now is the time of best investment for greatest returns in network marketing. It's like having the chance to buy gold again at $49 an ounce!

" I would rather have one percent of a hundred people's efforts than 100 percent of my own."

— Andrew Carnegie

I'm going to be telling you about The People's Franchise— how ordinary people can achieve extraordinary success.

Now, it's probably bad form to begin with a quiz—but just for fun, let's do it anyway. Don't worry. This is really easy—and it's multiple-choice, too.

Read the following statements, then choose the correct answer from the list of choices at the end:

> 'In most Americans' minds, it's a scam and a scheme - questionable or unethical at best, immoral and illegal at worst.

It's Time... for Network Marketing

> "Many own-your-own entrepreneurial hopefuls have been hyped into turning over their life savings, only to see the company go out of business, taking their dreams down with them.
>
> "Politicians, regulators, and the media (especially the media) cry 'foul' whenever its name comes up. Newspapers, magazines, and television news and talk shows regularly expose it for the 'flimflam rip-off it really is.' Major corporations who get involved go out of their way to avoid any appearance of doing so. There is even a move in Congress to outlaw it altogether!"

Now, guess: which one is the right answer?

a) TV ministry scams
b) Offshore investment schemes
c) Multilevel/network marketing
d) None of the above

Did you pick a), b) or c)? Well, there's probably some truth to all those choices—but none of them is the right answer.

The truth is, it's a trick question. The right answer, "d) None of the above," WAS correct—more than forty years ago! Back then, that's exactly what people were thinking and saying about a radical, revolutionary new business concept called franchising.

In the 1960s—before Ray Kroc and McDonald's, before Dunkin' Donuts, Midas Mufflers, Molly Maid, Pizza Hut... and all the other successful franchise companies established franchising as a legitimate industry—all of those negative things were being said and done about franchising. And yes, there was even a move in Congress to outlaw franchising.

And today...?

Today, experts say the franchising industry is responsible for more forty percent of all the retail goods and services we buy and sell in the United States alone—over one trillion dollars!

Not bad for what just a few years ago was labeled " a scam and a scheme."

Let's take a closer look at franchising.

Franchising truly was a revolutionary business concept—and it still is.

Take a look at your alternative: approximately eighty percent of all small business fail in their first year. Eighty percent of those that make it don't survive to see year five—and of those that do, even fewer will last another five.

Think about it: how many companies do you do business with that have been around for ten years or more?

Not very many....

Franchising is a way for the small business entrepreneur to boost the odds of success. A franchise takes the guesswork out of building a business from scratch. The franchise company creates a "turnkey opportunity"—a ready-made, off-the-rack business, complete with products or services, logos, uniforms, training, vendors, policies, and procedures. Virtually anyone with the desire and start-up capital can climb into this vehicle, turn the key, and drive off down the highway of entrepreneurial success.

It's truly brilliant.

You don't need to know all there is to know about building a franchise to own one. The franchise company has done all that work for you. You simply pay your franchise fee, build or rent your location and furnish it with the equipment the company has already designed and successfully tested for you, hire your people, and then pay the company a percentage of your sales and profits.

A question: How well do franchisees do?

According to its critics, the truth is about one third of all franchises fail. Another third breaks even, and one third makes a profit. In fact, some franchise veterans say you can't make money in franchising today unless you own at least five or more individual franchised units! Still, that's a much better average than the 80/20 failure/success rate of conventional small businesses.

Question: How much does it cost to own a franchise today?

Ahh, there's the rub.

Franchise fees range between a low/low/low of $1,000 to $500,000 and more. The average fee today comes in at around about $50 grand.

You can get a Molly Maid or a Thrifty Car Rental franchise for a fee of $17,500. Sir Speedy is $25,000. And the big guys, like McDonald's... well even if you could find one—forget it! It's in the millions....

The really bad news is that's only the fee. You've still got to pay for the building, equipment, initial inventory, etc.—all of which can run into the millions or more. The average investment in a proven franchise opportunity is $250,000! Not quite what the average person can afford. PLUS, most franchise companies take a percentage of your sales—not just profits, SALES—as their royalty commission!

The People's Franchise

It's tough to start a franchise today. It's not like it was back when the industry was young and unknown. Just as in real estate, the stock market, or most other opportunities, the real money is made by those who get in early.

> There's a higher risk and a higher reward. Once anything is a sure thing, it seems everybody's doing it.

Today franchises are proven profit centers. That's one reason why they're so expensive. You pay for having less risk than a conventional business start-up—and you pay for being a johnny-come-lately, as well.

But there is a way to have the low-to-no-risk benefits of a proven, duplicatable business system like franchising and still enjoy the rich rewards of a ground floor opportunity.

Frankly, most Americans don't have the extra $25,000 to $250,000 or more that it usually takes to own their own franchise business. But almost every one of us can afford to have the next best thing. And that's exactly what I'm telling you about here: The NEXT... BEST... THING.... The People's Franchise...

... Network Marketing.

> **Network marketing has taken the concept of franchising- providing independent entrepreneurs with a ready-made, low-risk, proven, turnkey, small-business opportunity- and made some genuinely remarkable improvements on it.**

Low Capital Investment—Little or No Risk
How much money do you need to become an independent network marketer? There is usually no fee required to start your networking business. You'll typically commit between a few hundred dollars to a few thousand dollars for your sales kit, your training and sales and marketing materials, and your initial product inventory (if you need it).

The Benefits and Tax Advantages of a Home-Based Business
For most participants, network marketing is a home-based business, so you don't have the high overhead of a retail or office location. The equipment you need to begin your networking operation can be as simple as a telephone, desk and file cabinet. And the potential tax advantages of owning and operating a legitimate home-based business represent one of the last forms of tax relief available to the average American today.

No Employees—You Are in Control
As a network marketer, you are an independent contractor—the CEO of your own businesses. Think of it as "Me, Inc." You have no "employees." The men and women with whom you'll work are also CEOs, running their own independent networking businesses. In network marketing, you don't simply "own your own job"—you own your own business.

And unlike most entrepreneurs, your business does not own you! You are truly in control of your work- and your life.

More Choices—Part-Time, Full-Time, Travel, National, and Global Businesses
Every network marketer is a volunteer: You don't "have to" do anything. You're free to work the days and hours you want, where you want, doing what you want—and perhaps most important of all, you're free to choose the people with whom you work.

Although the majority of networkers work their businesses part-time—currently about 85 percent of the industry are part-timers—more and more men and women are pursuing network marketing as a full-time career. Some work exclusively from their homes; some choose to set up formal offices; others enjoy traveling to other cities and even to other countries, building their businesses on a global scale.

Personal and Professional Support
In network marketing, you're in business for yourself—but not by yourself. Your network marketing corporation's success depends on your success—they're your business partners, so they give you the most support possible, each step of the way.

As a good franchise company would do, a good network marketing company provides you with the product or service to market, plus an R & D department, new product development, field training, sales and marketing literature and promotional materials, a distributor service department, and more. And today every network marketing company is Internet-friendly. You and your company are truly partners in a win-win opportunity.

Sound incredible? It is—but there's more. There's another very special reason network marketing is the next step beyond franchising. Which is why it's sometimes called...

Franchising2

When you buy a franchise, you acquire the right to market the product or service provided by your company. It's much the same in network marketing, except that you don't have to pay a franchise fee nor the huge start-up and overhead costs, have a retail location and/or elaborate equipment, hire and manage employees, and there are no geographic restrictions on your marketing territory. You also don't have to pay a percentage of your sales back to the network marketing company, as you do in franchising. What's more, you are an independent contractor—you work for you—not for "the company."

And as if all of that were not remarkable enough, a network marketing company does one more truly revolutionary thing for you.

> It gives you the ability to offer the opportunity to build a successful business to others in partnership with you, too!

In network marketing, you not only get to earn income from marketing your company's products or services (like a franchisee), you can also earn income from the sales generated by people you enroll into your own network organization (like a franchise company). They're your "Business Partners," men and women who, just like you, own their own independent network marketing businesses.

That's why we call it Franchising2.

And that's what creates one of network marketing's most powerful and profitable features: it allows you to leverage your time, talent, and energy to earn commissions from the sales made by all the other people you bring into the business.

> Remember, Andrew Carnegie said, " I would rather have one percent of a hundred people's efforts than 100 percent of my own." That's just what network marketing enables you to do.

This explains why so many "ordinary" people can achieve extraordinary success in the network marketing industry. Conventional sales and distribution methods depend on a few, select high-performance sales superstars, who each do a huge amount of sales volume. Network marketing is just the opposite: it's based on a lot of people—doing a little bit each.

The People's Franchise

That's why we call this concept "The People's Franchise."

Network marketing powerfully combines all the income-building benefits of being both a "franchisee" and a "franchise company" at the same time- while cutting out the major stumbling blocks of both.

- There's no fee, because you're an independent network marketer.

- You don't pay royalties from your sales back to the company.

- There's no hiring, firing, or managing employees.

- There are none of the all-consuming demands of a seven-day-workweek and a 15-hour-a-day retail operation.

- There's the powerful marketing advantage of offering superior quality, one-of-a-kind specialty products and unique services that meet high consumer demand with exceptional value through relationship marketing.

- There's the independence of choice: choosing with whom you work, when, where, and how you work.

- There's the freedom of owning your own home-based business—and the tax-saving advantages that come with it.

- There's the flexibility of part-time or full-time involvement, as your unique situation allows... as you choose.

- There's the opportunity to leverage your time and energy and earn income from the efforts of others: in time, tens, hundreds, even thousands of others.

- There's the limited risk of a start-up that requires only a few hundred dollars.

- There's the proven potential reward of both earned income and residual income—which can range from an extra $300, $500 or $1,000 per month up to $10,000, $25,000 and more.

- It's a great business for the Internet, too. When you combine the high-touch of network marketing with the high-tech of e-mail and the World Wide Web, it just might be the most perfect business of all....

- And finally, there is still the opportunity for you to be one of the first to enter an industry—an industry that has just begun its dramatic growth curve... an industry that is creating a revolution in the way the world buys and sells everything!

There has never been a better time than now to take a serious look at network marketing. "The People's Franchise" is an extraordinary concept whose time has come- today!

Now is the time of best investment for greatest returns in network marketing. It's like having the chance to buy gold again at $49 an ounce!

Make the time today to check out the benefits of building your own network marketing business. It's a straightforward and simple, low-risk investment—and it promises to return the most remarkable rewards you can imagine.

The People's Franchise.

John Milton Fogg is an author, editor, and speaker. His books and audios have sold over three million copies worldwide.

He is the founder and former editor-in-chief of the highly regarded publication Upline®, was a contributing editor to SUCCESS magazine, the founder and former editor-in-chief of Network Marketing Lifestyles magazine, founding editor of Networking Times... the founder of GreatestNetworker.com... cofounder of TheNetworkMarketingMagazine.com and is the creative force behind TransformingMLM.com, Speaking and Listening.com, Belief Busters.com and The MasterMind Sessions.com and his latest, The Magazine for Network Marketers, Upline2.

John is the author of the best-selling industry classic, The Greatest Networker in the World, which has been read by more than two-and-a-half million people around the world, and he has edited and contributed to far too many books to be mentioned here. His latest book is, It's Time... for Network Marketing. In December of 2006, after twenty years of self-imposed "retirement," John became a network marketer again and is actively building an organization.

He has spoken around the globe, throughout Canada and the United States, in Australia, China, Costa Rica, Crete, Iceland, India, Indonesia, Korea, Malaysia, New Zealand, Russia, Singapore, Trinidad, and Ukraine.

John is 59 years old, is married to Jekaterina (Katyusha), has a daughter Rachel (25), a son Johnny (20), a daughter Eleonora Milena (Ele) who's 5, and Anais Polina (his "last child") was born in March, 2006.

Network Marketing: A Divorced Woman's Hope

> Once I replaced my old negative blueprint about networking marketing, the difference was like night and day. I no longer had any trepidation talking with someone about the products I offered. I didn't have to beg them to purchase again. And people were sticking in my organization.

It was late fall. The weather was turning cooler. I was standing, looking out the kitchen window of our family home, talking on the phone with my upline.

I felt curiously alive, noticing everything around me. Like when someone is in shock, I suppose. Everything around me was crystal clear and sharp, like I was looking down at myself, seeing myself as an actor in a play. I knew intuitively that it would be a day I would remember forever.

I had called my upline to ask her a question. I explained that my husband had just told me he had filed for divorce. I was not asking her for marital advice—or more rightly said, divorce advice. I was asking a fundamental question.

"Theresa, do you think it is possible for me to make a living networking? I need to bring in enough money now to pay for the mortgage and all our expenses. I really want to do this. My heart is in networking, but I am afraid I might have to get a job and give it up."

She took a deep breath and said, "Yes, I do, but I think for right now, you had better get a job."

I was devastated. I thought she would tell me what I wanted to hear, but she told me the truth.

> Network marketing is not a quick fix. It is a long-term solution and one, for most people, best done on a part-time basis.

Yes, I know everyone says that, but I found that it's really true.

After I got off the phone with Theresa, my mind started to race on all the things that I had to make decisions about. But I wasn't ready to make those decisions. I felt pushed, forced into a corner, and I wanted to fight, to yell.

I did not want to be divorced, let alone, a single mother! Yes, there were problems in our marriage, but I thought everybody had them and we would work them out. We had a young child together. I had been a stay-at-home mother for ten years, caring for both of his children from a prior marriage and our new child.

When the shock settled in, I became determined that my son was not going to lose both parents. My intention was to do whatever I could to bring in an income and still stay at home. It was important to me to maintain some semblance of normality in our world that had just been turned upside down.

As my mind raced, I was reminded about my prior work experience and skill set, and I struggled to understand why I had not had success in networking. Only twelve years before, I was living in my favorite place on earth, Windsor, England (yes, right next to Windsor Castle). I was a successful project manager that Sun Microsystems had hired as a consultant to implement a new accounting system throughout Europe. I was being paid a six-figure income, had a company car, and an expense account. People paid over $200 an hour to listen to what I had to say. I was good at what I did—but, alas, that was over twelve years ago.

Over the last six months of my marriage, I had dabbled in network marketing, but I never truly thought it would ever need to be my primary source of income... until now.

My checks did not even cover the required monthly product purchase. What was I to do?

Given my newfound determination to make a living from home doing network marketing, I sought out everything I could on how to build a successful business. That's what I did to become a project manager.

I went to university for accounting, companies sent me on very expensive residential training programs to learn how to become a project manager, and I had extensive on the job training. I brought to it all my people skills, pipeline of trust, integrity, high worth ethic, and it paid off. I was making very good money and was in a satisfying position. And I just could not understand why I was not able to apply all those same skills, confidence, and ability to become a success at network marketing.

Are you sitting down? Are you ready for the answer I came to? Before you read the next line, I want you to open your mind and not just read this and file it away. Truly see if my reason might resonate with you.

I was ashamed of being a network marketer.

There—I said it. I felt that networking was a last-ditch option for people, similar to car sales and real estate. People with education and options did not do network marketing. They got "real" jobs.

When I got in touch with this mindset that was running in the background, I was reeling from the truth of it. I asked myself, "If I feel like this about it, why would anyone want to join me and become part of this disrespected profession?" It was no wonder I had no success attracting people to my business.

Well, that realization was fine and dandy, but what do I do with it? It felt almost like I had this blueprint that kept making my days the same way they were the day before, like the movie Ground Hog Day. I wanted to rewrite that blueprint, because that belief was not what I wanted my experience of network marketing to be.

The people I encountered in networking were some of the most intelligent, kindest, and most helpful people I had ever met. They didn't keep their secrets of success to themselves. They shared them openly with me, and they introduced me to people whom I needed to meet.

> The support network was incredible and very different from what I experienced when I was in the corporate world.

People there did not want to see me promoted, because it meant they would possibly become stuck where they were.

I remember one woman in particular who was in the accounting department of the first company I worked with in England. She was in her forties and had some measure of success in the company, but she was stagnating. She was an accountant and would likely always be an accountant. Here I was, twenty-eight years old, being offered the coveted position of European Accounting Implementation Project Manager.

Although she was my friend, I always felt she held something back with me. Her advice and guidance only went so far. It stopped when she saw that I was going to get the job of her dreams. I would be traveling throughout Europe, implementing the new accounting systems. Why me and not her?

I thought it might have been that I was not perceived as only an accountant. Yes, I was a trained accountant, but I also had experience in customer service and extensive computer experience. That made me a compelling person to hire for the job.

When I compared my current experience of the supportive ecology of network marketing to my previous experience of competition in the corporate world, I became inspired. It was not my nature to hold something back that could help someone. My philosophies and nature fit networking perfectly.

> I always wanted to see people fly to their highest heights and create greater joy and ease in their work and life.

I guess that's why I enjoyed systems analysis and project management. I could improve the quality of people's work lives; I could shorten processes and improve information flow so they could get back to their real life at home.

Even though I read many books, listened to tapes, and took courses—in addition to asking anyone I could how to change that negative mindset—I didn't find the answer until many years later.

When I did replace my old blueprint about networking marketing, the difference was like night and day. I no longer had any trepidation talking with someone about the products I offered. Previously, I would be excited with an order of $50, but now I was getting orders of $200 and more. I didn't have to beg customers to purchase again. And people were sticking in my organization.

Did the products change? Did I change companies? Did the comp plan change? Did my upline change?

The simple truth was...

> I changed my mind about how I viewed network marketing.

My belief is unshakable. When I sell someone products now and they ask if it is possible for them to do what I do, I no longer cringe at that question. I look them in the eye with confidence and pride and say, "Yes, you just need to become an associate, and this is what you need to purchase to get started."

Do I accept everyone as a business partner? No way—I have customers and I have partners. There are criteria for someone who wants to be in my organization. Gone are the days of the desperate network marketer, grateful for a pitiful one-time order.

Now in its place is a proud network marketer who is able to assist others in their journey of healing—physically and emotionally (and financially, too).

The healing not only comes from the products, but from the journey of becoming a networker itself.

The truth is, it's an inside job. You not only become what you think about... you become what you believe.

So how is my network marketing career going now?

Well, I would say, well. No, I would say more than that... swimmingly well.

Network Marketing: A Divorced Woman's Hope

For this single mother, network marketing was not only her hope, it was her healing and the renaissance of her life.

I am proud to be a networker and I would stand on rooftops now and scream it. I can't even begin to think how much longer my transition back to the working world and becoming a successful single mother would have taken, if it were not for network marketing. It kept me out there talking with people, sharing what I had to offer, and growing into the person I am today.

Monique Gallagher is an author and coach. She developed an interest in human growth and development during her teenage years in California. In 1982 she began her studies at SUNY Binghamton. Upon graduating in 1986 Monique moved to England and accepted a lucrative position in Project Management working throughout Europe.

By 1991, she had moved to Venezuela, and enrolled in an international master's program for teachers in Caracas while working as a substitute teacher at an international school. She returned to the United States in 1993. Her curiosity became her passion as she probed the human mind and cognitive behaviors, completing her degree at Rutgers University.

As a Health and Success Coach, Monique is a dynamic speaker and trainer producing profound results in assisting others in overcoming what they previously thought were impossible roadblocks. She has recently expanded her professional repertoire to include assisting parents in raising strong-willed children to be respectful, caring, and accountable.

Monique resides in San Diego, California, with her remarkable 10-year-old son, WG, and their adored cat.

To learn more about Monique and her life, business, and health coaching, visit her website at: http://LifeDirectionCoaching.com

JIM GILLHOUSE

Why I Think Network Marketing Is a Perfect Opportunity for Anyone in the Military

I believe that this business is a gift- perhaps the best gift that someone in the military could possibly receive. Service men and women make excellent network marketers. Plus they get to leverage their unique circumstances and experiences, giving them a running start towards success in this industry.

Being a member of our armed forces is a noble and honorable profession in pursuit of duty, honor, and country. Unfortunately, the members of our armed forces do not enjoy a wage that corresponds with the amount of time that is sacrificed by being away from their loved ones—nor the obvious "hazard pay" given in other occupations.

So, why do I think that network marketing is such a powerful opportunity for someone in the military?

The answer is simple, but multifaceted, so I'll start by making a list of points and then come back and go into more detail about each one.

- Relationships
- Leadership
- Circle of Influence
- Geography
- Spousal Work Opportunities

- **Finances**

As I drill down into each of these topics, you'll notice they are all pretty much interrelated with each other.

Relationships
Network marketing is a business that is built one hundred percent on relationships. So too are the friendships formed in the military.

One of the strongest bonds that can ever exist between two people comes as the result of having had to depend on each other in a combat or life-threatening environment. The military spouse also develops strong relationships with friends they make in their unit support groups while the service members are deployed.

Military people move around a lot. They're thrown together with men and women of all races, religions, educational experiences, personality types, interests, values, strengths, weaknesses....

> They're either very good at relationships, or they get good. Their lives depend on it.

Leadership
Network marketing is also built one hundred percent on leadership. Every network marketer is the leader of his or her organization, and success or failure in this business is based on one's skills and ability to lead.

Military service is all about learning how to lead and learning how to follow.

> I don't think anybody knows more about leading and leadership than someone who has served in the military.

Why I Think Network Marketing Is a Perfect Opportunity for Anyone In The Military

In every organization, civilian or military, there are two separate chains of command—the formal and informal.

In the formal chain of command, the authority figure is empowered by the business or the military itself. However, in the informal chain of command the leader is empowered by the people that willingly follow them and look to them for direction or advice. That's the way it is in network marketing.

As a military service member, you know leaders that you would follow into the fires of hell and back. Unfortunately, you've also been exposed to so-called leaders that use their people as stepping-stones only to serve their own purpose. That doesn't work in network marketing.

The beauty of network marketing is that we get to pick whom we choose to partner with and invite to join our business. And we get to choose our leaders for who and how they are.

Indulge me for a moment, while I address the subject of being choosy about whom you invite to be a member of your business team.

I believe that this business is a gift. Therefore, when I interview a prospect as a perspective member of my business I don't know yet, I start by having a conversation with them to determine if I really want them on my team.

Keep in mind that this is a business, and you don't want just anybody working with you as your partner. It's okay to be persnickety—not everyone gets a waiver (an exception to policies and/or procedures), not everyone gets promoted below the zone (ahead of their year group), and not everyone gets to be on my team.

Circle of Influence: The People You Know
The military family member knows many more people than the average person, because they are forced to relocate much more often than most people do. The average American never moves more than one hundred miles away from where they graduate from high school. Yet the military family member quite often has friends that are stationed all around the world, and they are constantly meeting new people.

In network marketing we speak about your "circle of influence"—all the people you know—and being a "center of influence"—that means that those people know, like, and trust you.

> Military people all have large circles of influence and many are commanding centers of influence, as well.

Geography
The fact that military people travel so much gives them a fantastic advantage to develop a large and wide-reaching business—even reaching worldwide.

Most people in the "home-based business world" would love to have this opportunity—yet most military people take it for granted, or even consider it a form of punishment by not being able to be close to home.

I say, take advantage of the situation as the blessing that it is and use it to build a great, big network marketing business.

Spousal Work Opportunities
This is a topic that's a sore subject with me. Over the years, I've seen so many military spouses have to give up a good paying job at one duty station and take a significant cut in pay at the next location they were assigned. Worse yet is the spouse

that can't find a job in their career field at the new duty station.

Every military person I know, or have known over the years, has either experienced this personally, or knows someone that has.

With a home-based network marketing business, you have the ability to take your business with you everywhere you go, and when you work for yourself, you never have to look for a job again (or a better boss).

Finances

Most people in the military are living paycheck to paycheck and don't have a lot of cash to start a business of their own. Unlike a franchise that has a minimum startup cost of tens of thousands of dollars (along with restrictions like territories and regions), a person can often own their own home-based network marketing business for five hundred dollars or even less (and no territorial restrictions apply).

There are many benefits to owning your own home-based network marketing business, such as:

- Setting your own work schedule
- Taking your business with you wherever you move
- Choosing the people you partner with
- Being your own boss
- The tax advantages only available to a business owner
- The ability to make some fantastic friends all over the country and around the world

Every person- military and nonmilitary- that is associated with our armed forces should take a long, hard, serious look at the network marketing industry and the opportunity it provides.

It's Time... for Network Marketing

In all my time on active duty, I never found a business that I and/or my spouse could be involved with—at every location where I was stationed—with the exception of this remarkable industry.

My only regret is that I wasn't smart enough to have gotten involved sooner than I did. I've spent the majority of my adult life as a leader, instructor, trainer, mentor, and coach in some capacity or another. I have yet to find something that I can do that benefits the lives of more people than network marketing.

Jim Gillhouse has been involved in the network marketing profession since 1997. He is a founding distributor with XELR8 and a charter member of the XELR8 X Factor Plus Leadership Development Team. When Jim's not network marketing, he's a colonel in the army, instructing military pilots how to fly helicopters. Tellingly, Jim and his wife Annette hail from Enterprise, Alabama.

"One of the things that moves me is a desire to save others from the frustration, anxiety, pain and 'brain damage' that I, and some other people experienced while getting started in this industry... the vision of providing the highest quality of life for my family that I possibly can... I am motivated by helping others to overcome their fears, go for their dreams, and reach their goals."

You can hear "Jim's 4 Minutes" every week at the conclusion of Tom Chenault's Home-Based Business Radio Show and learn more about Jim on his weblog. "Jim's Final Four Minutes," here: http://Jims4Minutes.blogspot.com

Celebrating Network Marketing- The Business of Uplifting People

One of the most fulfilling or heartwarming aspects of the business, if done right, is how it uplifts people, helps them to feel better about themselves and eventually become more and better than they were.

In a world where people struggle every day in a rat race just to make ends meet, network marketing professionals offer a way out of the drudgery.

In a world where people are too busy to listen to each other and yet yearn to be listened to, network marketing professionals provide just what people need—listening ears and understanding hearts.

In a world where people can't help but complain of having no time, no money, no fun, and no health, network marketing professionals offer a happier balance in life between work and play, financial wellness and physical wellness, and present-day needs and future provisions.

In a world where people walk with low self-esteem and frail or badly dented egos, long conditioned to think and feel they are never good enough for the critical tasks at hand, network marketing professionals offer a guiding hand, a caring heart, and a reliable companion in a happier walk to a better life.

It's Time... for Network Marketing

In a world where people are routinely told to "get real" and forget their childhood dreams, network marketing professionals can help people rediscover their core desires and show them a way to fulfill them.

And yes, I do mean network marketing professionals, as opposed to the hordes of others who are just trying their luck, usually for a short period only, who won't do whatever it takes to get good at the game.

For all the good that we can contribute to people's lives, of all professions, we should not have to keep justifying and defending ourselves—what we do, what we stand for, and why we deserve the financial riches and other rewards that come our way. But we do.

I remember a conversation with a business partner, where I advised her to simply stop feeling embarrassed, defensive, or apologetic about her network marketing business and encouraged her to be proud, very proud.

She has been building her network marketing business alongside a five-year-old conventional business where she acts as an agent for a European supplier of certain industrial goods. In the conventional business, she works largely alone, trading her time for money, scouring the region for business.

The reason she became involved with network marketing is that she saw a source of leveraged, residual income in the future— an income stream that would keep flowing long after she stopped working, something she does not expect from her conventional business.

Yet when she encounters someone who scoffs at the MLM way of doing business, she gets tongue-tied, feels awkward, and quickly changes the subject.

As our conversation progressed, we established that the root cause of the awkwardness was not having sorted out her own feelings about the business yet. She conceded that she continues to feel embarrassed about building a network marketing business alongside her conventional business. She fears that it will invite speculation about how she is faring in her conventional business.

All that was needed, I suggested, was a realignment of her mindset to one which she is all too familiar with. To illustrate what I meant, I asked her these questions:

1. Do conventional businesspeople go around justifying to prospective customers why their business model works?

2. Do conventional businesspeople, on the slightest prodding, open up and bare all about how they make their money and why they deserve the huge markups (if any) that they enjoy?

3. What would conventional businesspeople do or say, if anything, when prospective customers ask how much money they really make from their business? Will they wave their equivalent of the latest bonus check to prove a point?

4. Do conventional businesspeople try to convert every good customer into a business partner or stakeholder in their business, or do they wait for the right customers to show an interest in the business before they let them in on selected nuggets of information?

5. What would you think of a businessman who tries too hard to sell you a stake in his business, even when you have expressed a lack of interest in his way of making extra money?

The general point of these questions is simply this:

> **Network marketers tend to explain, defend, justify, and expose themselves too much, too readily.**

It is time we change tactics, get professional, and learn to walk and talk with an unshakeable belief and a quiet confidence that draws the right people out and makes them want to find out more.

We need to begin to carry ourselves with at least the same self-respect, dignity, or verbal restraint that conventional business people do.

And why not?

We have many reasons to hold our heads up high and be proud of what we do to make a good living.

My favorite reason is that...

> **Network marketing is simply a good business, one that pays us fairly and according to the good that we do in other people's lives, directly and indirectly.**

The good that we do includes how the products or services we sell make life better for people, but it is by no means restricted to that.

One of the most fulfilling or heartwarming aspects of the business, if done right, is how it uplifts people, helps them to feel better about themselves, and eventually become more and better than they were.

Here is how that happens:

Empathize with listening ears and understanding hearts

We uplift people first by offering listening ears and understanding hearts. Only by listening well can we determine if there is a good fit between what people are looking for and what we can offer. In the process, even if we do not find a customer or a new recruit for the business, we satisfy people's yearning to be listened to with care and sincerity and to be understood.

> Where a good fit does not (yet) exist, good listeners will know how to let go. Where a possible fit is identified, good listeners will know how best to take the conversation forward.

Engage them to uncover core desires

Not everyone who signs up to venture into a network marketing business hits the ground running or flies from the word "go." As the enterprise attracts all and sundry, including many not yet equipped with the required business mindset, few are resourceful or hardy enough to figure it all out quickly and do well on their own. Often people stumble over their doubts and fears, dragged down by the lack and limitations they have long been conditioned to believe in and have allowed to govern their lives.

To succeed in this business, we have to first help people uncover their heart's core desires—the dreams and ambitions that once moved them, but which they had long abandoned as they strove to meet urgent present-day needs—and the one or two biggest reasons why they would never, ever give up.

Encourage them to believe in themselves

We will also need to make time to help people uncover their underappreciated strengths and talents and overcome or side-step overaccentuated weaknesses and limitations.

Having done that, we can then show them a way to pursue their dreams, desires, and ambitions that is customized and personalized to suit their unique abilities and strengths and accommodate their frailties.

> In the process, we simply encourage people to believe in themselves once again and help them realize that they can do much more than they thought possible.

The whole process is liable to be time-consuming, and it certainly does not fit the misconception of network marketing as a get-rich-quick, mass-recruiting scheme.

However, this time-consuming process, which honors people and what matters most to them, is one that is necessary and worthwhile—as necessary and worthwhile as it is for a property developer to take time and resources to ensure a solid and sound foundation before he erects a skyscraper, building upwards floor by floor.

This is the essential, people-oriented ingredient that tends to be missing when network marketing leaders promote and emphasize duplicable systems that are supposed to work for all.

> Taking time to empathize with, engage, empower, encourage, and enrich people is what makes our business special.

To me, it is the one reason why we deserve the exceptional income and lifestyle that comes with the business, and it is also the reason we can walk with quiet confidence and do our business with self-respect, dignity, and verbal restraint.

Lim Eng Hai is a journalist-turned-stockbroker-turned-network marketer, and fiercely proud of his professional transition and personal transformation. Eng Hai sees himself as a coach to his business apprentices and personal nutrition consultant to his customers.

He works from home in Singapore, having more time than the average dad to enjoy time with his two children, and yet able—with the powers of the Internet, budget air travel, and the people-to-people business—to build an international network marketing business, extending to as many countries as he can find "the right people." Without having to travel too much, he is earning income from up to ten countries.

He is in partnership with a US company which offers an extensive range of nutritional and personal care products, embracing the corporate mission of "eradicating heart disease—naturally."

Visit Eng Hai's weblog at: http://EngHai.blogspot.com.

ART JONAK

The Freedom to...

Can you truly be happy suppressing the passion to live life your way? Can you achieve happiness without freedom? I know network marketing is the single best way to for an average person without any skills like me to live a life filled with freedom- real freedom, boundless, unrestricted, ultimate freedom.

The club known as "The Bayou" occupied the aging building at 3135 K Street in Georgetown for forty-five years. It smelled like an outhouse on an asparagus farm, but it occupied a place in rock and roll history—so the smoke, sweat, and stench didn't much matter. The heavy metal band Tesla was putting on a show certain to burn brilliant for a long while in the hearts and minds of the fortunate fans who were in attendance—and particularly bright for one fan.

Fighting my way to the bar to beat the last call, the singer's voice resonated in my ears as clearly as the Vienna Boy's Choir at Christmas in the Sistine Chapel...

> And the sign said 'Long-haired freaky people need not apply"
> So I tucked my hair up under my hat and I went in to ask him why
> He said ' You look like a fine upstanding young man, I think you ll do"
> So I took off my hat, I said 'Imagine that. Huh! Me

workin for you!"
Whoa-oh-oh

Now, hey you, mister, can t you read?
You ve got to have a shirt and tie to get a seat
You can t even watch, no, you can t eat
You ain t supposed to be here
The sign said you got to have a membership card to get inside
Ugh!

Sign, sign, everywhere a sign
Blockin out the scenery, breakin my mind
Do this, don t do that, can t you read the sign?

—Tesla cover of the 1971 hit single
"Signs" by the Five Man Electrical Band.

One heavy-metal cover song experience...

That's all it took for a jarring reminder that society has boxed us into thinking small, into conforming to unwritten laws of what we can and can't do, and has us working jobs we hate so we can buy junk we don't need.

That night in Washington D.C. confirmed that my generation has been raised by television and magazines to believe that one day we'll all be millionaires, movie gods, and rock stars... but we won't.

Suffice it to say, I never did get that drink to warm me up. I didn't need it! I was fired up! I was excited!

The song shows how someone must decide whether individuality of expression or conformity to societal standards is the preferred way to live. If your choice is with the former, then you must put up with the judgment of others as a consequence of that choice.

The lyrics went straight into my heart, into every cell in my body, and have never left me! They spoke to my core. I knew beyond a shadow of a doubt what I really craved in life.

I craved the Freedom to do what I wanted, where I wanted, with whom I wanted.

To NEVER concern myself with what others may think of my lifestyle!

To never have ANYBODY tell what I could or could not do!

The good news was I knew what I wanted in life. The bad news was... finding what I wanted was like climbing a cactus! No matter where I looked, who I asked, what I tried—nothing allowed me to live the life I wanted!

It is a well known fact that 75 percent of our population is happiest with only a "six-pack of beer and a half tank of gas." But that wasn't me. I wanted more, much more!

I could try the Small Business America route. But I would have to go to work and dress and act a certain way.

I could try the Corporate America route. But then again the shareholders, board of directors, CEO, etc. would expect me to "fit the mold." (Richard Branson, one of my heroes, being the rare exception to the rule here!)

Small Business America and Corporate

It's Time... for Network Marketing

America could earn me a ton of money, but in return they would strip away my 'Time Freedom' to do what I wanted, when I wanted, with whom I wanted!

I could start my own business. But I'd be stuck watching over the business, managing employees, putting in extra-long hours for decades, etc. (Chad Hurley and Steve Chen being one of the few rare exceptions- selling YouTube to Google for $1.65 billion after just a few years! Way to go, boys!)

Every profession put a gun in my back and robbed me of my Freedom of Time or shoved conformity in my face. Or worse, the profession couldn't pay me anywhere near the income needed for true financial freedom!

I couldn't hold a job for more than six months without getting fired because of my deep craving for the ultimate freedom of not having anyone tell me what to do! I was unemployable!

I started to despair. Was I doomed to live being an employee and having to behave how society "expects" me to be? A life-sentence of someone telling me what I could or couldn't do?

I was running out of choices! I had to become a ten-times-platinum rock star, an ultra best-selling novelist, or somehow find a few million dollars to invest so I could collect a nice dividend check every month. Those seemed to be the only options that would allow me to be myself, to do what I want, when I want, with whom I want, without anyone dictating what I could or could not do!

Heck—even being a soccer, basketball, or tennis superstar was out of the question! Even they had to conform to what the league expected! And then there was the constant barrage of fans and paparazzi!

Behind every door I opened, there was a solid brick wall with a "NOT POSSIBLE!" sign on it... and finally network marketing found me! It didn't take me long to realize that...

Network marketing is the perfect option for nonconformists and the unemployable!

Network marketing is like toilet paper, Pampers®, and toothpaste. It's definitely proven to be effective. If you don't think it works—don't tell my bank or they won't cash my weekly bonus checks! And today, because of network marketing I am as happy as a 60s psychedelic band, hanging out between Frank Zappa and Jimi Hendrix! Finally, I can do what I want, when I want, with whom I want, without worrying about the money or about what society thinks!

This is not an editor's note for John Milton Fogg. It's not an open letter. It's not even an impassioned plea. It's a primal scream through a bullhorn into a microphone rigged to Metallica's mammoth concert amps:

" NETWORK MARKETING IS THE FREEDOM TO DO WHATEVER THE HECK YOU WANT!"

He wakes up in the morning
Does his teeth, bite to eat and he s rolling
Never changes a thing
The week ends, the week begins

Driving in on this highway
All these cars and upon the sidewalk
People in every direction
No words exchanged
No time to exchange

> And all the little ants are marching
> Red and black antennas waving
> They all do it the same
> They all do it the same way
>
> — "Ants Marching" by Dave Matthews Band

Look around. Sit in rush hour. Watch people in lines. They are all "Ants Marching." This is no way to live! Every day there's someone telling you what to do. This is NOT FREEDOM!

The price of regret is a pain that can't be healed. The game of life is happening. Don't stand on the sidelines, sit in the bleachers. Claim what is rightfully yours. Choose Freedom!

> **Freedom to do..**
> **What you want.**
> **When you want.**
> **With whom you want.**

Without worrying about the money.
Without worrying about what society thinks.
Without anyone dictating his or her beliefs of what you should or shouldn't do.

Life is about "life, liberty, and the pursuit of happiness"—your happiness. Can you truly be happy suppressing your inner desire to be a rebel? Suppressing the daily passion within your soul to live life your way? Can you achieve happiness without boundless, unrestricted, ultimate freedom?

> Look, if you had one shot, one opportunity
> To seize everything you ever wanted- one moment.
> Would you capture it or just let it slip?
>
> —"Lose Yourself" by Eminem

My biggest advantage is "I know it's possible."

I know network marketing is the single best way to for an average person without any skills like me to live a life filled with freedom, real freedom.

The freedom to see a movie during the afternoon on a weekday and have the entire theater to yourself!

The freedom to drive my luxury Lincoln or Viper with a three-day-old beard to the gym at 11 a.m. blaring "Signs" from the 500-watt speakers and have all those "Ants Marching" assume I'm either a gansta' or a rock star!

The freedom to roll over, yank the covers over my head, and wake at the crack of noon—because I wanted to!

The freedom to get on a jet plane and fly anywhere in the world up front and just for fun!

The freedom to order one of everything on the menu at a restaurant, so everyone can enjoy a feast filled with great conversation, fun, and friendship.

The freedom to see my daughter off to school every morning and invite all her friends for a pool party after school, grinning as each parent comes marching home from work hours later to pick up their child.

I love network marketing!

My friend Tim was catching a flight back to Norway from Florida after speaking at one of our events. As he sat on the on the plane, he thought:

> "I have the freedom to walk off this plane and, instead of flying to Norway where it's cold, I could book a flight to Hawaii where it's warm. I won't, but it's nice to know

that because of network marketing I have the freedom to...'

Tim then picked up the in-flight magazine. Inside was a picture of a 75-foot yacht. He thought:

"I have the freedom to buy that yacht if I want to. I won't, but just knowing I could is good enough!"

We're in the business of freedom: freedom from worries—freedom from worries due to the lack of money. Freedom to do whatever our hearts' desire—that's how powerful network marketing truly is!

> We have absolutely no freedom as a child.
> We rebel in our teen years and scream for freedom.
> We die for the right to be free.
> We fight vicious wars to have the seemingly innocent ability to choose.
> We reach adulthood and we relinquish freedom because we think it is too difficult.
>
> —Author Unknown

With network marketing, you can take a group of like-minded people and together achieve this ultimate freedom! Imagine! Now you have a group of people who can go do what they want, when they want, with whom they want, without worrying about anyone telling them what they can or can't do! Now, that is FUN!

Your team must be attractive to attract others.

People succeeding are attractive, but a group of people living life their way, with ultimate freedom, is irresistible!

Hanging in my office is a handwritten brush calligraphy frame with the Chinese symbols for "freedom." I watched a very nervous calligrapher date and stamp his work while I was in Guangzhou.

What's so great about Network Marketing? It's all about FREEDOM.

The Freedom to Do Whatever the Heck You Want!

The ultimate intention and expectation of network marketing is to make someone's life better. How better than to help them achieve true FREEDOM—real freedom, boundless, unrestricted, ultimate freedom.

And now, the end is here
And so I face the final curtain
My friend, I ll say it clear
I ll state my case, of which I m certain

I ve lived a life that s full
I traveled each and ev ry highway
And more, much more than this, I did it my way.

Live LARGE and Expect Success!

Art Jonak has been doing network marketing for a living since 1991 and is one of the early pioneers of InterNetwork Marketing. Art is the founder of Network Professionals, the owner of MLMPlayers.com (where he offers a host of resources including FREE online e-courses) and numerous other top-ranked websites. He is the founder of the Network Marketing Mastermind, the world's largest, most intense and educational generic MLM event. Art cohosts the Annual Network Marketing Cruise with Tom "Big Al" Schreiter. He also writes The One Minute Sponsoring Tip for Network Marketers. Cut and paste the link above to receive Art's FREE Tips newsletter.

You CAN Have It All in This Amazing Profession

When you choose this profession, you are given a gift that can make a significant difference in the lives of your children and every person you touch- your customers, your team members, and your family.

Women are tired of the rat race... trying to do it all and stay sane. Today, they are leaving the corporate world and coming to network marketing and party plan companies in larger numbers than ever before.

Seventy-nine point nine percent of all participants in this business are women, and there's a reason why.

They have found a place where there is no glass ceiling- where they can have a career, raise their families, and make a significant income from the comfort of their homes.

Women are natural networkers and natural nurturers. This profession allows you to meet new people and connect with and support other like-minded and like-hearted individuals.

Women love doing business in the course of simply living their lives—waiting in line at the grocery store, at their clubs and civic activities, or sitting in the stands at their children's sporting events. My sister, who is a very successful direct seller, shared with me that at my nephew's last baseball game of his high school career, the mother of every player on his team was either a customer, one of her consultants, or a hostess. She hadn't wasted a minute in those bleachers.

This form of free enterprise is a great training ground for children to be mentored by their parents.

> A direct selling business can provide women with the opportunity to teach their children money skills, people skills, business management, and most importantly, the life skills of relationships and partnering.

I am proud to say I raised two entrepreneurial children, each with a tremendous work ethic as a result of being brought up in a direct selling home. They saw me work, earn income, lead others, set goals, win, and sometimes they saw me lose (I call those "learning experiences"). It was during the "learning experiences" that my grown children say they gained the most. They saw me "keep on keepin' on."

When you choose this profession, you are given a gift that can make a significant difference in the lives of your children and every person you touch—your customers, your team members and your family. What a wonderful place to lead by example!

The flexibility of direct selling is also a big plus for married or single women with families. This business can be worked around the schedule of others. You may not get to every activity your children have, but you can make the majority.

You can be there after school to hear about their day, and you can enjoy the morning drive taking them to school without the pressure of fighting a commute.

> You can stay home with your kids when they are ill, without questions from your "superiors" or fear of losing your job.

You can be your own boss, and you will undoubtedly be a great boss to yourself.

Many women start their direct selling careers on a part-time basis, either in conjunction with a full-time job or while raising small children. You have the opportunity to become full-time when it is right for you and your family. There are no timelines or bosses pushing you to make career choices that are not in your best interest.

Women love winning prizes—and with this career, there are wonderful awards and incentives. From diamond rings and spa retreats to cruises and all expense paid family vacations, if you are willing to meet the challenges, the awards and recognition are waiting to be earned.

The direct selling community offers great opportunities for personal growth and education. Training and support is readily available from the companies, from books, from audio programs and from a wide variety of personal and professional development organizations.

> Everyone has the same opportunity to be successful in this profession. Whether you are a college graduate or didn't finish

high school, everyone here has the same chance to succeed.

It is not education, job titles, or past experience that are the deciding factors in how successful people will be. It has more to do with your coachability, desire, persistence, and willingness to take action. Every person in this business determines their own destiny and their own paycheck.

This is not a get rich quick business. It takes dedication and work to build a solid residual income. And no one is forced to choose between family and career.

You CAN have it all in this amazing profession.

Nicki Keohohou, began her career as a direct seller more than thirty years ago. Today she teaches and motivates direct sellers around the world through her workshops, seminars, and tapes.

Nicki has been a successful distributor, corporate executive and consultant for hundreds of corporations including many of the industry's leading companies.

Through conference trainings and keynote addresses, Nicki is known for inspiring attendees to greater achievement with her enthusiasm, passion and industry insights. Her innovative workshops are filled with content and exercises that teach direct sellers how to perfect the skills that yield lasting success.

As a result of years of experience in direct sales, and now serving as CEO of the Direct Selling Women's Alliance, Nicki has acquired a broad base of knowledge that can make a significant difference for distributors, leaders and corporate executives.

To learn more about Nicki and the DSWA, visit the website at: http://dswa.org or contact us at info@mydswa.org.

a conversation with ROBERT KIYOSAKI

Rich Networker Poor Networker

Is network marketing the best system for the average person? Kiyosaki says, 'Yes,' and explains, 'In the corporate world, if you don't sell, you're fired. In network marketing, they'll work with you to achieve. What a deal that is! That's revolutionary.' And much more...

Robert, this quote has been attributed to you:

'If I had it to do all over again, rather than build an old style type of business I would have started building a network marketing business.'

Did you really say that?
I said something like that, yeah!

Is it true?
Yes, when I looked at the problems I had to go through, but it's how I started. I still like building companies, but it was harder.

When you and I first spoke, many years ago, you were not all that "high" on network marketing. What caused you to change your mind?
Let me explain. When I started as an entrepreneur, I had to learn how to sell. I started with Xerox in 1974.

125

It's Time... for Network Marketing

Today, when people ask me, "How would you start a business?" I always tell them to start with a network marketing company. Not because of the network marketing company per se, but for the training you get from the network marketing company.

> The reason I say that is because what makes people rich is not money. What makes people rich are skills. And the number one skill of an entrepreneur is the ability to sell.

That's why I recommend network marketing. It's not that I've ever been high or low or anything on it. When I first started out, I just didn't realize how good the training was with that business model, because my training came from the corporate world of Xerox. Not too many guys are going to get hired by Xerox today, and they don't do as extensive a training anymore because people quit too early.

So my whole point on recommending network marketing is you go there and you gain priceless business skills. That explains further what I'm saying about if I had to do it all over again— I would probably go and get training through a network marketing company.

Robert, can you break down what some of those skills are and why they are important?
SELL! Sell, sell, sell, sell, four-letter word, you've got to sell. And that's the word everybody's afraid of! But... sales = income.

So when someone has low income, 99% of the time it's because they can't sell something; they have nothing to sell or they can't sell. You've got to learn how to sell.

If I'm going to be an entrepreneur then that is THE number one skill. That's the theme to everything I tell you. You read Rich Dad Poor Dad, and it says, "I'm not a best-writing author, I'm a best-selling author."

Here's where most people make a mistake. They go into things looking at how much money they can make versus what skills they need to make the money.

> I keep saying, ' Just get the skills, and the money will show up!'

Robert, can you talk to me about the components that go into 'sell, sell, sell'?
It's a training. You have to know you're going to make mistakes. Look at the way the corporate world trains you.

When I was working at Xerox, every month they would post my record and if I was in the bottom twenty, one of us got fired. They fired two guys and they hired two new guys. So, the only reason I learned how to sell was because I was afraid of getting fired.

At least in the network marketing world, they'll train you. It's a whole different way of being taught. If you're not making it, someone will be there to encourage you. It's a lot more humane way of being taught that vital, vital life skill called sales.

Jesus Christ was probably the best salesman in the whole world, and Buddha and Mohammed, they were all great at sales. Look at the presidential candidates—the one that wins is the one that does the best job of selling his point of view.

There are two subjects that nobody wants to talk about; one is money and one is sales. Everyone seems to think of "cash" as a four-letter word and "sale" as a four-letter word, yet I'm a teacher and I make more money than most teachers in the academic world simply because I can sell better than they can.

When I recommend network marketing to people, it is for one simple reason: you gain a life skill. It's called 'overcoming your fear of rejection' - overcoming the client's fear of being sold and breaking through that.

Robert, what makes you say that network marketing is a revolutionary way to achieve wealth?
Because they don't fire you! They'll work with you! They'll help you build a business and once you have a business, you really do have an asset.

Assets are something that put money in your pocket whether you work or not. If you have a job... well, look at some of the big financial houses. One of them is firing something like 15,000 people in the U.S. and hiring 15,000 people in India. The day of the safe, secure job is gone.

At least with a network marketing business, you work really hard to build something that you can pass on to your kids and, if you've done a good job, if you stop working, it will continue to support you. You're not working for the rich, you're not working just for money, you are actually working to build an asset.

Is that what you mean in your book, The Hidden Values, when you speak about the value of a network?
The richest people in the world build networks. That's why they're called television networks or gasoline service station networks. The poor and the middle class and the educated work for networks. I'd rather own the network.

For example, I have a network of bookstores throughout the world that we control. That's worth a lot of money to me. I don't want to work for them; I just want to control them. I think in the form of networks, while the average person thinks about working for money. I'd rather work to build a network. That's why I'm rich.

And that's what we get to do in network marketing. Build a network which we can take anywhere with us?

It's a completely different point of view; it's a different way of looking at the world.

If somebody said to me, "I'll pay you $5 million dollars a year to go work at Harvard University," I wouldn't take it. That's not enough money. Why would I work for somebody else? That doesn't compute for me. They could take it away from me, and that just doesn't make sense. I know it computes to most people, like 401(K)s and mutual funds, which also make no sense to me, but I've been trained differently. I can make more building my own business. I pay more than that in taxes each year.

So what I'm saying is that people have to give up their old ideas of what they were told to do:. go to school, get a job, work hard, save money, get out of debt, invest in the long-term, diversify, buy mutual funds.

That's really stupid from my point of view, but it is good advice for the average person. It's simply a completely different point of view. I am an entrepreneur.

> I don't want to work for someone else. I don't want somebody telling me how much money I can make; I don't want somebody to tell me where I can go in the world, or when I have to come to work.

I'd hate it! Nobody tells me that. That's why I support network marketing!

Talk to me a little bit about the role of leadership in network marketing. How is it different from leadership in other forms of business?
Well, leadership in network marketing means that you are offering no guarantees. All you're offering this person is the possibility that they can be a leader themselves.

But since most people are basically afraid and would rather have a steady paycheck and are more concerned with having a steady job and what other people think of them, network marketers have to understand that these are not leadership skills.

> If you're more concerned with your own self-preservation, what people think of you, and steady paychecks, then you don't have core leadership skills.

To be a leader, you have to be willing and able to take the heat, to stand there and say, "Look, you can do it!"

Leadership in corporate America is called management. Corporate executives aren't true leaders; they're just dangling a paycheck in order to get people to do what management wants them to do.

What are the qualities of leaders you admire most?
I admire someone who will stand there and put their ass on the line themselves. They talk the walk and walk the talk. When I was in Vietnam, there were many 2nd Lieutenants that were shot in the back because they had no leadership skills. Just because you went to college, that doesn't make you a leader. The men in your troop had to believe in you. That's a quality that you don't find very much today.

Unfortunately, we haven't had too many leaders appear in the last few years. The last leader that I really respected was Kennedy, because he really stood up.

You've witnessed a number of leaders in network marketing. What do you see them doing right?
They inspire people to be leaders. A leader doesn't lead, a leader creates leaders. That's why network marketing is so powerful, because if you can get somebody who is not a little paycheck grubbing, security-minded, butt-kissing manager to actually come and lead people, their lives will change.

That's not easy to do because of the mindset of the majority. That's the hardest part.

> So many people are so afraid to say, " I want to do network marketing," not because it's not a good idea, but because of what their friends and coworkers might think of them!

I love the movie, Braveheart, where Mel Gibson says, "They can take our lives but they can't take our freedom!" Most people will sell their freedom so they can have their stupid little lives.

Now, I know somebody has to be willing to do the jobs, be a waiter or waitress, or a schoolteacher, and I appreciate that, but most people who do it are willing to sell their freedom, and what I'm talking to you about is freedom.

> The reason you learn how to sell is so you can become free. The reason you want to be in network marketing is for your freedom.

It's Time... for Network Marketing

Do you realize most people can't go to Mexico and do work because you need a green card? But if I'm a business owner, well, I can go to Mexico or China or wherever I want and do business. That's freedom! But if you're an employee, you need a green card—that's not freedom.

I can make as much money as I like. That's freedom. But if I have to work for someone else and they're going to tell me how much I can make, that's not freedom.

That's really what it comes down to. Do I recommend network marketing? Actually, I recommend freedom!

That's what I stand for. And I don't care what that means to you—just go do it.

For me, freedom means I don't have to answer to anybody, I can leave the country if I want to leave it, I can travel around the world and make as much as I want, legally, ethically, morally and I don't cheat on my wife. I tell you exactly where I'm at; you don't have to guess where I'm at. That's freedom; I don't worry about what somebody else thinks of me. That's what I stand for, not network marketing. Network marketing is one of the ways you get there.

Do you think it's one of the best ways for average people?
I think it's the best system for the average person, yes. In network marketing they'll work with you to achieve. What a deal that is! They will work with you to become free. That's revolutionary.

Robert Kiyosaki is the author of the Rich Dad Poor Dad series. He is an investor, entrepreneur, and educator whose perspectives on money and investing challenge conventional wisdom.

Rich Dad Poor Dad is the longest-running bestseller on all four of the lists that report to Publisher's Weekly magazine: The New York Times, The Wall Street Journal, USA Today, and BusinessWeek. It has held a top spot on The New York Times best-seller list for nearly six years and was USA Today's #1 money book for 2004.

Translated into 46 languages and available in 97 countries, the Rich Dad series has sold over 26 million copies worldwide. In 2005, Robert was inducted into the Amazon.com Hall of Fame as one of the bookseller's Top 25 Authors. There are currently 12 books in the series.

Prior to writing Rich Dad Poor Dad, Robert created the educational board game CASHFLOW 101 to teach individuals the financial and investment strategies that his rich dad spent years teaching him.

Born and raised in Hawaii, Robert Kiyosaki is a fourth-generation Japanese-American. After graduating from college in New York, he joined the Marine Corps and served in Vietnam as an officer and helicopter gunship pilot. Following the war he went to work in sales for the Xerox Corporation and, in 1977, started a company that brought the first nylon and Velcro "surfer wallets" to market. He founded an international education company in 1985 that taught business and investing to tens of thousands of students throughout the world. He sold his business in 1994 and, through his investments, was able to retire at the age of 47.

To learn more, visit Robert Kiyosaki's website: http://RichDad.com

A Chance to Make Money Doing Something I Love

The reason most folks stay in network marketing is they love something about it madly: they love the products, or they love making a difference, or they love having something of their own. These are the very reasons two-thirds of Americans want to start their own business

"If drug dealers make so much money, why are they still living with their mothers?" was a question asked by the authors of Freakonomics, a top-selling economics book. The answer?

'Except for the top cats, they don't make much money. They have no choice but to live with their mothers.'

If they don't make much money, why do they do it?

We could ask the same question about our own industry. Although the potential for big money is real in network marketing, most network marketers, except for the top cats, don't make much money.

Why, then, do so many continue doing it?

The answer lies beyond the money.

First, a few facts about real earnings:

It's Time... for Network Marketing

When Excel Communications, a ten-year old network marketing company, went bankrupt in November of 2004, the corporation reported that as of October 2004, it had 106,426 U.S. representatives that were eligible to earn commissions that month. Of those, 64,967 actually earned commissions. Not bad.

"Not bad" until we learn that 63,733 (98%) of those reps earned $100 or less that month. Only a small fraction of 1 percent—99 out of 63,700 reps—earned more than $1,000 for the month.

According to the DSA (Direct Selling Association), there are some 13 million people in network marketing today. Of those, 85 percent are part-time, 80 percent are women, and like the Excel reps, most are making little money.

So, why do people stay with it?

I've asked that question of many veteran networkers who weren't making much money. Here are some answers that represent many of the responses I've received:

"Oh," said Mary Z, "I love, love, love my products."

"I just love knowing I am making a difference... "

"I've done work in corporate America, but I really always wanted to be my own boss and now I am... "

"It's improving me; I'm learning a lot about me."

"I like helping people, and when someone uses my product and tells me what a difference it made in their lives, that feels really good."

Without folks like these, there would be no big bananas. A lot of people doing a little make the top cats good money—usually after many years of sticking to it themselves, as well as risking

136

A Chance to Make Money Doing Something I Love

their money, their relationships, and their self-esteem.

These few big bananas are showcased on stage or in three-way conversations with prospects, along with the evidence of their financial success—mansions, hot tubs, hotter cars, and a life of tropical vacations—much like the lottery winners on TV with their jackpot winnings.

Most prospects who are tantalized with big money and residual income will drop out when they don't see it happening. They're not losers; they're just not getting what they were promised.

A few stay, however. Why do these faithful keep going even though they're not making much money?

The reasons turn out to be the same ones that another very large group of Americans has given for wanting to start their own business.

A Yahoo survey done in May of 2005 found that two-thirds of Americans had entrepreneurial ambitions. However, only 3 percent said "getting rich" was the main reason they wanted to start a business.

According to the survey:

1. **Doing work that they really love** was the main reason for launching a business.

2. The second most popular reason: ' To be my own boss.'

Perhaps many of the survey respondents were speaking after experiencing twenty-plus years of working at regular jobs "to pay the mortgage, pay for the kids' dentist, etc." or after observing their parents giving their best years to pay the bills.

It's Time... for Network Marketing

Given the specter of a bill-driven life, many Americans are reversing their priorities.

First is something they can love madly... something they care about. Money takes second place.

We all need money, but don't we often take less if it means doing something we love?

Loving the doing of something, pursuing a challenge, and throwing oneself into a cause is what has motivated countless super successful people when they started. At first, they had no expectations of making big money. They were inspired to do their thing, and because they loved it, they stuck with it.

The stories are everywhere: Steve Jobs, Julia Child, the three Google founders, Richard Branson, and many more. A favorite network marketing story of mine is how Sue Burdick went from making a few hundred dollars to $15 million.

> You know, Kim, when I was first approached about this business, I had been looking for something of my own for a few years already. Back then, my husband was a carpenter, and I wanted to do something, too. I had started an aerobics studio, a hair salon, and then a dog-grooming kennel. They all went down the tubes, and we spent most of our savings.
>
> One day, an acquaintance stopped by to show us a little water filter gizmo you could put on your sink- she said we could earn $30 for each one we sold. Since my husband sometimes remodeled kitchens, and since we didn't especially like our drinking water that much, this seemed like a pretty good thing to try. We figured I could set up appointments, and if we sold one per week, we'd add $150 to our monthly income. That sounded good to us.
> Well, you just cannot imagine our excitement when we

A Chance to Make Money Doing Something I Love

brought in an extra $150 that first month. Five sales!

A few months later, it got to almost $500 a month and we thought, 'This is it! We've died and gone to heaven.' I started setting up appointments for myself to show the units too. We were so giddy that our friends asked us what was going on. My husband told a couple of the guys- a plumber he worked with and another contractor- and they decided to do it too. We were just so tickled to see a little income from some of THEIR sales, as well....

It's been nineteen years now, and so much has happened with our business. We've earned $15 million over these past years, and we still find it hard to believe....

Oh, and let me tell you something, Kim. If the guy who came to our house that first time had told us we'd be earning $10K a month, we would NEVER have signed up. We'd have thrown him out for taking us for fools. We've never been much for telling big stories- we believed a couple of hundred dollars was reasonable to expect, and so we did it. It just grew from there. Some days, we still can't believe it.

Love first seems to be the key to long-term success- because it ensures that you stick with it.

According to a 900-page academic book, The Cambridge Handbook of Expertise and Expert Performance, loving the thing you do is the first predictor of becoming good at it.

The three conclusions from this massive study are:

> 1. The trait we call talent is highly overrated.

Expert performers—whether in music or surgery, ballet or

computer programming—are nearly always made, not born.

2. Practice does make perfect.

Michael Jordan, Ben Hogan, and Mozart practiced more than anyone else.

3. When it comes to choosing a life path, you should do what you love- because if you don't love it, you are unlikely to work hard enough to get very good.

The authors added, "Most people naturally don t like to do things they aren t good at. So they often give up, telling themselves they simply don t possess the talent for math or skiing or the violin.'

But the truth, they wrote, is this: "What they really lack is the desire to be good and to undertake the deliberate practice that would make them better.'

Loving something madly fuels the desire to be good at it, which, in turn motivates practice, which is essential for success.

Joseph Campbell was right when he told us, "Follow your bliss."

So what does all this have to do with network marketers?

The reason most folks stay in network marketing is this: They love something about it madly. Either they love the product, or they love making a difference, or they love having something of their own—the very things that the Yahoo survey found were the reasons that two-thirds of Americans want to start their own business.

So let's change our recruiting mantra. Let's go beyond the

A Chance to Make Money Doing Something I Love

money. Let's appeal to deeper yearnings. Let's be in tune with the two-thirds of Americans who want to be entrepreneurs. Let's look for people who are looking beyond the money—people who are looking first for something to love.

Kim Klaver is an author, speaker, trainer, coach, and the mastermind behind BananaMarketing.com. A Harvard, Stanford, and MIT person, Kim's book, If My Product's So Great, How Come I Can't Sell It? is truly a must read classic. She is also the founder and "dean" of the New School of Network Marketing. Be sure to check in with Kim's top-ranked blog here: http://KimKlaverBlogs.blogspot.com

The Greatest Thing About Network Marketing

You can hide out in many companies and organizations, but not in this business. Network marketing requires you to truly be a giver. It requires you to be a true leader. And the success of your giving and leading are fairly gauged by your results.

Two great things about network marketing are:

1. It requires you to truly be a giver.
2. It requires you to be a true leader.

First, let's look at the necessity of being a giver in network marketing.

> The very structure and design of the business model requires you to be a giver, adding value to people and to the marketplace.

There are many fine businesses out there, but the structure of corporations and even most small businesses doesn't require giving. In many corporate environments, you can make yourself valuable by holding onto your knowledge, so that it is hard to replace you. This is called the "middle management syndrome." It forces you to take from others' careers to enhance your own—at least in the short run.

Not so in network marketing. You must share your knowledge. If you don't give your knowledge away to others, you won't make any money, and there won't be real residual income, because you will not build a team.

> In many business environments, you can be greedy for a short time. Witness the corporate scandals of Enron, Tyco, Arthur Anderson, and (too) many others. With greed, you'll never get off the ground in network marketing. You don't have to tell people you are primarily all about your own paycheck, they can feel it and won't do business with you or join your organization.

In most businesses, you can be self-centered and still create a fair degree of success. In network marketing, if you are self-centered, you will wear yourself out on a roller coaster. You may create short-term sales, but not a growing, lasting team that gives you residual income. You are constantly starting over from scratch.

In most businesses, people give what they want to give (which is not really giving). Real giving is giving what is truly needed and wanted, not just what we want to give.

In network marketing, if all you do is talk about your business opportunity—what you think you have to give—very few people will respond.

Once you get into what it is that other people want, what their challenges are in creating that, AND you provide solutions for them, then you make a fortune and feel good doing it.

In many traditional business organizations, you are forced to carry many people who really don't want to contribute, but are there to just get a paycheck. Network marketing, like the Bible story of "The Ten Talents," only pays those that can contribute by giving value to other people and the marketplace.

Let's talk about leadership.

I define a leader as:

> One who interferes in other people's lives and causes them to do what they otherwise wouldn't do, in terms of what matters to them.

Before you choke on that, let's break it into bite-size pieces.

"In terms of what matters to them" means what matters to the other person, not to you. If you interfere and cause them to do what matters to you, that's manipulation.

To "cause them to do what they otherwise would not do," refers to the fact that almost every human being's decisions and behavior are determined by their subconscious belief systems. "As a man [or woman] thinketh in his [or her] heart, so is he [or she]." It's the secret of the ages.

These subconscious belief systems are like colored sunglasses through which we view life. These beliefs often develop so early on that we can't recall being without them. These sunglasses are our belief systems around commitment, trust, and who we think we are. They end up limiting our goals or even preventing us from having goals at all. They determine how we listen or don't listen. They determine whether we prospect people or not, and they impact how we prospect.

When you breakthrough these sunglasses and have a revelation, it affects not just your network marketing business, but every aspect of your life.

Your network marketing business exposes these belief systems.

As long as your sunglasses are making most of your decisions, you are not in control of your life. You know you are not in control when you cannot produce the results you say you want.

Now, let's deal with the word "interfere," since many people have an initial negative reaction to this word.

Most people, very deep down in their subconscious, have bought a belief they are separate from other people. Our eyes tell us that our bodies look different and separate in a thousand ways: color, size, sex, location, dress, etc.

But suppose people were like islands instead. Most of a human being, like an island, exists below the surface where you cannot see what's there. Islands—underneath the water where the eye cannot see—are all connected.

Just like islands, people are connected, too. We just can't see under the surface with the human eye. Interfering in another person's life is, in a very real sense, interfering in our own.

If you care about other people and see they are not getting what they want because of their belief systems—and if we are, in fact, connected one to another like islands—then we are obligated to do something about it.

The Greatest Thing About Network Marketing

This does not mean you can be obnoxious or manipulative under the guise of interfering. This is not a license to do whatever you want. In fact, it naturally limits us to taking action only when we know what it is other people truly want.

There is no fairer way to gauge anything than by results—often harsh, always fair. I must have heard that 1,000 times from my mentor. That is the greatest thing about network marketing.

You can hide out in many companies and organizations, but not in this business. Network marketing requires you to truly be a giver. It requires you to be a true leader. And the success of your giving and leading are fairly gauged by your results.

Brian Klemmer is an international consultant and speaker whose seminars have been attended by tens of thousands of participants in Japan, Canada, the Philippines, Europe, and throughout the United States over the last twenty years. He is a West Point graduate, has a master's degree, and is a member of the National Speakers Association.

Brian is founder of Klemmer & Associates, which has produced results in companies such as ITT Sheraton, Hewlett Packard, American Suzuki Motor Corporation, as well as many network marketing companies. He the author of the best-selling book, *If How To's Were Enough We'd All Be Skinny, Rich and Happy*, which discusses many of the key principles and founding concepts he has used to build both his company and his phenomenal, results-producing seminars: Champions Workshop, Personal Mastery, Advanced Leadership, and Heart of the Samurai. To visit his website and sign up for his free newsletter, go to: http://Klemmer.com

Talk About a Win-Win-Win!

I know that there is money to be made in network marketing, because I've made it; I have enjoyed tangible proof. I have enjoyed incredible success from this business. There is the opportunity to enjoy tremendous financial rewards in network marketing if you are willing to do what it takes to succeed.

Why does network marketing provide such an incredible business opportunity? What's so wonderful about it? Why does it attract so much attention? Why do people either love it or loathe it? Why do some people do amazingly well with it and others fail, and yet others are borderline? What gives? Is it luck?

The two main attractions of network marketing for me are the opportunity to earn a lot of money and the ability to work your own hours from home. The costs to set up one of these businesses is negligible, yet remarkably, the risks are negligible, too.

How many businesses do you know of that have the potential to earn lots of money, can be set up for next to nothing, and are also relatively risk free? Can't think of any?

It's Time... for Network Marketing

No, I didn't think so.

Today people are losing their jobs as companies downsize and regroup, and the employment market is flooded. Younger people cannot find work because they're too inexperienced or there is little available for them. Older people cannot find work because of their age and companies do not want to pay the higher salaries they command. There are those who have young children at home and don't want to leave them to go back into the full-time workforce, or single parents who might not be able to afford childcare so they can go back to work.

When you want to make money and you can't find an employer, the only option is to be your own employer. Be your own boss. Make your own money.

Depending upon how much effort you put into your networking business, you can become a millionaire, or you can make just enough to contribute to your family's income. It is entirely up to you. You can work at your own pace.

There are few other income earning opportunities that will reward you for your effort as easily and fairly as network marketing.

> Take a look at today's large and successful corporations. Do you see them paying hefty bonuses to employees who go the extra mile and put in the extra time? No. You don't.

Many people work overtime and long hours, because if they don't, they'll lose their job. They don't earn any more money for doing it. In network marketing, you can make as much money as you want. If you are going to work those hours and put in huge efforts, why not get paid for it?

Talk About a Win-Win-Win!

Traditional businesses are not forgiving when it comes to women and men wanting to work less hours or flexible hours so they can spend more time with their family. Businesses don't care. If you want a freedom lifestyle with flexible hours, you have to strike it lucky with one of those rare businesses that does care, find a secure part-time job, or work for yourself.

Setting up a business for yourself is a challenge for many people. And yes, setting up a traditional business requires knowledge and a certain set of skills—which can be learned, but this all takes time. On the other hand, with a network marketing business, you can start operating instantly.

There are so many amazing network marketing companies today offering excellent business opportunities that you can pick one that most interests you, and you can set yourself up to work from home easily and cheaply and quickly.

Network marketing companies provide YOU with the guidance, training, and materials you need to succeed.

> A network marketing company wants you to succeed and be wealthy, because the more successful and wealthy you become, the more successful and wealthy they become. It's in their best interests to pull out all the stops and help you as much as possible.

Name one other business opportunity where you get that type of free support!

Then there are those people who simply want the extra income a network marketing business can give them. Maybe they are saving for annual holidays, their children's education, a big boat, a fancy house, or just help with the regular monthly bills.

It's Time... for Network Marketing

The flexibility of this type of business means that you can fit it in at the times that suit you, and if you only want to work it enough to earn "pocket money," you can do that and still be successful on your own terms.

Is it any wonder people are attracted to network marketing opportunities?

One of the main differences between mediocre network marketing people and highly successful ones is their appetite for "more and better"—the successes are ALWAYS hungry for something "more and better." They have the right attitude. If you are saying things to yourself like, "I'll never be able to find enough people," or "I'm not qualified," or "I don't think I can do this," then you are sabotaging yourself. You are convincing yourself you are a not a winner before you even start the game!

> Network marketing is not about selling to people.. it's about serving them.

If your business offers a great product or service that you truly believe in and know will help others, you will love talking about it with people. You will love being able to make a positive difference in people's lives by sharing your knowledge of the product or service with them so they can make an informed decision.

> Forget the days of the old-fashioned salesman who would sell the shirt off his granny's back to make a buck and who would say anything to make a sale, even manipulating people and making them feel bad if they didn't buy.

Network marketing doesn't work like that.

Talk About a Win-Win-Win!

True, not everyone will be interested in buying your product or in signing up under you to be part of your organization, but if you don't tell people about the opportunity, you deny yourself the possibility that some will be interested and will sign up! You should no more prejudge what is right for other people than they should prejudge what is right for you!

You are taught how to present your program and its products or services, and you will have people in your upline who will help you do this until you feel comfortable doing it on your own. With network marketing, your job is to invite people rather than do a hard sell to them. This increases your potential, instead of limiting your success.

As with ANY business opportunity, you do have to take risks, but the good news is that the risk you have to take in network marketing is minimal. You are not risking your life savings or your house or your reputation.. you are risking getting a "no" response. That's all.

People are allowed to say no. When you go into a shop, do you always buy, or do you sometimes just browse and walk out empty-handed?

All you can do is put the opportunity out there. It is up to others to accept it. And just because one person says no doesn't mean everyone will. Others are entitled to be offered the opportunity. It is their choice whether they choose to take it.

Perhaps you are not the world's most confident marketer, but maybe you'll sign up people in your downline who are "naturals" and can do better than you, even though they are below you on your team. You share in their success. You earn passive income. You earn money while others do their work, and the more successful they become, the more successful you become. And again, by helping others become successful, you become successful.

The main drawing card to network marketing for myself and other business entrepreneurs I know is the opportunity for earning passive income.

My personal goal in having passive income streams is to have ways of generating income even while I am sleeping—and not through my regular coaching business where I trade my time for money.

Who doesn't love the idea of earning more money and having more free time in which to enjoy it without having to work long hours for it?

I believe working in a business in which you can choose the product or service that excites you... start up for very little cash outlay... earn passive income... have the ability to expand internationally... and all working from home, choosing your own hours, is an opportunity that is just too good to pass up!

In any event, I know that there is money to be made in network marketing, because I have made it. I have enjoyed tangible proof. I have enjoyed incredible success from this business. There is the opportunity to enjoy tremendous financial rewards in this business if you are willing to do what it takes to succeed.

And you don't have to be an outgoing, extrovert type to be successful. I know a number of shy, retiring network marketers who are now making enough to afford to drive around in a new luxury sports car while they contemplate which part of the world they'll spend their holidays next year!

Network marketing isn't brain surgery. If you honestly feel passionate about your products and services, it's no "biggie" sharing this with other people—and reaping rich financial rewards for doing so isn't bad either! Knowing you are in control of your own earnings and aren't limited by a paycheck or the fear of downsizing and being out of a job tomorrow is both reassuring and liberating. Is it any wonder network marketing is a booming industry?

> To be honest, for me, it is not just about the money. I get a huge thrill helping others to succeed, and the structure of network marketing allows me to help my downline become even more successful than me.

This is important to me. My personal mission is to help others achieve business, personal, and financial success. In network marketing, by bringing in a lot of people, I am able to help create passive income value for others as well as for myself. Talk about a win-win-win!

Terri Levine, master coach, best-selling author, and CEO of ComprehensiveCoachingU.com and CoachInstitute.com, is a successful international network marketing expert. She now coaches network marketers and network marketing organizations around the world and has a passion for coaching them to success. To learn more about Terri's coaching and related programs, or to sign up for her free newsletter, visit http://TerriLevine.com.

MIKE LEWIS

It Must Be a Cold Day in Hell... Right?

After sixty years of probably the most pitiful waste of human talent, resource, emotion, and initiative.. finally.. FINALLY, the network marketing business is turning around!

For those enlightened souls who have always loved the concept of network marketing, but who have been consistently traumatized by the stupidity of the egotistical, manipulative "sales training" that has caused this business to consistently score a more than 81 percent failure rate for six whole decades... your patience has been rewarded... your time has COME!

GONE is the need to hold "opportunity meetings" that have failed to work for most of the people, most of the time, in every company, and in every country around the world!

> REPLACED by intelligent discussion among interested parties at any venue that is comfortable for the parties wishing to talk with each other.

GONE is the need to create a list of 100 people and call them repeatedly to tell them about your wonderful product, your wonderful opportunity, your wonderful company, and your wonderful CEO!

REPLACED by open, authentic dialogue with people you meet during your day-to-day routine about topics that interest THEM, with the door always open to introduce your home-based-business venture to the discussion, IF and WHEN it is appropriate.

GONE is the notion that it is not only possible but necessary for you to create a business with a "duplicatable system," where everyone faithfully follows the exact same method, the same script, and the same agenda.

REPLACED by the certainty that it is impossible to make everyone think the same, talk the same, or do the same.

REPLACED with the knowing that network marketing is truly free enterprise, where everyone can create their business in any way they choose, without fear or contradiction of their upline, crossline, or company ideology.

GONE is the falsehood that you have to be "serious about the business" to make any money.

REPLACED by the reality that if you are having fun and enjoying yourself with your business, your opportunity will shine like a beacon through the darkness and attract people to you, without having to hunt them down like they were your next meal!

GONE is the need to suffer any rejection and disappointment while building your business!

REPLACED by the understanding that if you don't try to

It Must Be a Cold Day in Hell... Right?

manipulate or trick people with outdated, outmoded sales techniques, and you dump the notions that "every no is closer to a yes... it's a numbers game..." and "you must close the sale," you can actually talk with people in an open, honest way so that there will be no reason for them to reject you!

GONE is the insane logic that you have to "get out of your comfort zone" to build a business.

REPLACED by the results that prove you don't! You can do everything you want and grow an enormous networking business totally within your so-called "comfort zone." In fact, the more you work "inside" your comfort zone, the stronger it builds and the faster it goes!

GONE is the requirement to say what someone else says and do what someone else does to be successful.

REPLACED by the knowledge that people don't join your venture because of the product, the company, or the compensation plan—they join because of YOU!

You ARE the most important asset of your business. It's ALL about you!

So, after a six-decade "pre-launch," I feel that network marketing has finally arrived at a point where truth and common sense have prevailed!

People all over the world have at last discovered for themselves that there are NO secrets, NO magic methods, NO elusive leadership skills that you have to learn to create your own winning network marketing business.

Here is the key...

He who looks outside dreams..

He who looks inside AWAKENS.
- Carl Jung

The real solution is found within—just by being YOURSELF!

Just talking with people you meet in your OWN way and in your OWN style. Not trying to convince people about your product or opportunity, but by being genuinely interested and caring enough about the people who come into your life, to see if they are looking for answers to some of life's issues.

Maybe you have the answer for them with your product or opportunity. Maybe you don't. Let those who are looking decide.

If you live your life authentically, if you let your OWN common sense and your OWN intuition be your guide, you won't need any "MLM Expert" to teach you, train you, convince you, or persuade you about what works and what doesn't!

You will discover for yourself that authentic, intelligent network marketing is a wonderful adventure of self-discovery, where the level of satisfaction and fulfillment you receive in helping others is reflected in the size of your commission check!

Mike Lewis has been a results oriented innovator in the Sales, Marketing, and Promotions arena, initially in Europe and more recently in the U.S. for close to twenty-five years. Primarily from an advertising background, Mike started his first entrepreneurial venture in the late 1970s as a small but profitable advertising and marketing company. Since then he has created and developed many businesses and built a strong reputation in the network marketing industry, largely through his marketing & management consultancy firm, Top Gun, which he formed in 1989.

To learn more about Mike and his unique offerings, visit his website: http://AdventuresInNetworkMarketing.com.

Women Plus Network Marketing: A Perfect Match

The top 10 reasons why women plus network marketing is such a powerful combination and why there is no limit to what women can achieve in this business when they put their formidable skills and powerful hearts into it:

Fact #1: Women are opening new businesses in unprecedented numbers because they want the flexibility, opportunity, and power of building a business of their own.

Fact #2: Women are leaving the corporate world in record numbers and are actively seeking an alternative to the traditional 9 to 5 workplace.

Fact #3: Women have buying power. Women make almost 82% of consumer purchases.

Fact #4: Women make up the largest percentage of the sales force in network marketing.

Prediction: Women and network marketing are a perfect match of talent and opportunity, and women will continue to lead the growth of the industry in the future.

Here are the Top 10 Reasons why I believe this is true:

It's Time... for Network Marketing

Reason #1
There Is No Glass Ceiling in Network Marketing
Women are getting increasingly frustrated with the lockstep corporate life and the futile climb to the top that results in higher salaries, but demands total devotion to the job at the expense of a personal life. Women (especially younger women) are no longer willing to tolerate these restrictions.

In contrast, network marketing offers them the chance to build their own business, to live their lives how they want, to choose how many hours they work, and when to work them. They alone get to control how much money they make, not their bosses.

> Network marketing is truly a perfect business for women, allowing them the flexibility to fluidly move between a part-time or full-time schedule as their life flows and changes over time.

Women are realizing that having a career, having a partner, having kids, taking care of aging parents, and trying to make it all work is exhausting and impossible without more flexible options. Women see network marketing as a very viable work from home business option where they can set their own hours, set their own salary, and build a business of their own with the flexibility they need for their personal life.

Reason #2
Explosion of Choice
In the last ten years, there has been an explosion of new network marketing companies coming on the scene, as more and more businesses see the value of selling their products and services through the network marketing model. From tools to candles, crafts to cooking products, no matter what type of product or service is available, there is a network marketing company that offers it.

Women Plus Network Marketing: A Perfect Match

> Companies know the value that women bring to their bottom-line success.

Women like the options network marketing offers them to build a business offline, online, at parties, or through direct sales and to earn a good part-time or full-time income.

Reason #3
A Ready-Made Business with Affordable Startup

Women like the fact that network marketing offers a turnkey business with an affordable startup cost. What other type of business offers women such a wide range of choices for a ready-made business with complete training and support for such a low cost of entry? Women know they can start their network marketing business on a shoestring and build it into an empire.

Reason #4
Women Are Natural Networkers

Women have always been consummate networkers. It's a skill they use every day. They constantly share information and referrals at business networking organizations and in social settings. Women are naturals at networking, and if they find a product or service they like, they tell all their friends about it.

Women also prefer to choose a business or a service through "referrals."

> Before women purchase a service or choose a company, they don't go to the yellow pages; they pick up the phone and call a friend for information and a referral.

When they start their network marketing business, women can just connect with their personal network to get the word out about their new business. Women know that people like to do business with people they already know, like, and trust.

Reason #5
Women Like to Build Relationships and Teams
Network marketing takes maximum advantage of a woman's ability to develop long-term relationships with people in both business and social settings. Women use their natural skills to build teams and solid customer bases, and they instinctively know how to build and plug into a network of connections.

> Women thrive at building and nurturing the cooperative teams that are the foundation of a successful network marketing business.

The bottom line is that network marketing is a people and communication business, and women excel in these areas.

Reason #6
Women Know How to Sell to Other Women
Women know how to sell to other women effectively. Women know that women value relationships and trust and make their decisions to buy a product or service accordingly based on the customer service they receive and their relationships with a person or a business. Women sell effectively by listening to their customers and prospects, by asking questions, and gathering and sharing information, and finding out what they really want and need.

They know that the standard sales pitch isn't going to work with women.

> Women know that women value good service, quality products, good prices and value for their money, not sales hype and false promises.

Reason #7
One Size Does Not Fit All
Women embrace their differences and know that there are many roads to business success and that one size definitely does not fit all. They know that they need to work with the strengths of their team, not shoehorn them into a particular sales method that doesn't fit their talents and personal preferences.

> Women offer their teams a variety of ways to approach the business- not just a "system" using traditional hard sales techniques.

They provide a selection of options to their team, so they have many to choose from, not just one.

Reason #8
The Internet and the Global Economy
The Internet has leveled the playing field for everyone in network marketing, and women are using it to leverage their time, talents, and communication skills to their best advantage. No longer are women confined to a small geographical region in their business.

> The Internet opens up the whole world to women in network marketing and allows them to expand and build their business globally.

Reason #9
Innovation and Creativity
Women bring their own personality, creativity, intuition, and sense of style and fun to their network marketing business. Women are constantly creating innovative ways of doing

business, and network marketing is a better and stronger industry because of it.

Reason #10
Strong Code of Ethics and Integrity
Women believe strongly in operating their business with ethics and integrity and building a relationship of trust with both their customers and downlines.

Women do not believe in taking shortcuts and breaking the rules to make a quick buck.

Women know that this is a great industry, and they understand that to keep it great, we need to follow a strong code of ethics and integrity if we want it to continue to grow in the future.

So, there you have it. Ten of the top reasons why I believe that women plus network marketing is such a powerful combination, and why there is just no limit to what women can achieve in networking marketing when they put their formidable skills and powerful hearts into it.

Linda Locke is the editor/publisher of MLMWoman newsletter and the MLMTalk and MLM Marketing blogs. She has been involved in the MLM and network marketing industry for over ten years and enjoys mentoring women in the business through her website, discussion forum, newsletter, and blogs.
http://MLMWoman.com
http://MLMTalk.com
http://RegentPress.typepad.com/mlmmarketing

Cutting a New Path

It goes beyond our impressive statistics and growth figures. Today, most people you'll talk to about network marketing know of someone who's had a positive experience. We're less apologetic and more sensible. We have a proven track record, and we're getting much, much better at what we do.

I shall be telling this with a sigh
Somewhere ages and ages hence:
Two paths diverged in the wood, and I-
I took the one less traveled by,
And that has made all the difference.
        - Robert Frost, Mountain Interval, 1920

When I was seventeen, I began a brief career in "alternative" education. Some friends and I were dissatisfied with the schools where we punched our time clocks, and wanted to see if we could create a better way.

A way where we took the pursuit of our education into our own hands.

We imagined a school where there were absolutely no requirements—no mandates, no externally imposed strictures—and where each student designed his or her own course of study. In other words, where we learned what we wanted, when we wanted, how we wanted.

Does this sound familiar?

We didn't know it back then, but we were thinking like network marketers. We wanted to be a volunteer army, not a lockstep formation of grudging corporate conscripts.

We were educational entrepreneurs.

Among our motley crew, I was the one blessed with unusually forward-thinking parents who believed in me and in us and our vision enough to let me leave my then-current career (public school, an in-training version of the nine-to-five track) so I could spend the rest of the year spearheading the project.

Now, how on earth does a scattershot band of disaffected sophomores and juniors start their own high school? The answer is, they don't. It's impossible. It can't be done.

Happily, we were not aware of this. Much like the bumblebee—you know, the bug that flies because it never got the memo explaining that it can't—we didn't know it was impossible. So we did it.

The next year the school opened, and it operated successfully for a solid decade onward. We had absolutely no accreditation from any private or state body, but we were accredited by our own results. We successfully placed our graduates into places like Yale, Harvard, and a good crop of state colleges, too. The environment we had pictured, of students voluntarily pursuing their own education, worked.

A few years later, I began another career, this time in "alternative" health. We called it macrobiotics, but what it boiled down to was a bunch of people who looked at the then-current model of "health care" (which was really illness care) and wanted to create a better way.

A way where we took the pursuit of our health into our own hands.

We were nutritional and physiological entrepreneurs.

A few years after that, I put my foot on another career path, this time one in "alternative" business. We called it network marketing, but what it boiled down to was a bunch of people who looked at the then-current model of livelihood and wanted to create a better way.

A way where we took the pursuit of our financial future into our own hands.

We were occupational entrepreneurs.

I seem to keep finding myself on these "alternative" paths. Except something is happening now: we're gradually losing the quotation marks around the word alternative. In fact, son of a gun, I think we're even starting to flirt seriously with losing the term altogether.

I put the term "alternative" in quotes because that's how people often mean it: like something that is not quite real, not quite respectable, certainly not proven, and probably not efficacious. We say it in that open-minded yet patronizing way, making air quotes with our fingers.

At least, that's how it used to be. But now look.

Education? Everyone knows the old system is a dinosaur. The federal government tried fixing it with a plan optimistically named No Child Left Behind, and whoops! A whole generation is getting Left Behind. Suddenly (or finally), the alternatives are starting to look pretty good, after all.

Health care? Paul Zane Pilzer is telling us that what we used to called macrobiotics is suddenly a $400 billion industry—and fast on its way to a trillion—called wellness. Ladies and gentlemen, the alternative, all grown up, wearing long pants and everything.

And network marketing?

Just watch.

Born in the sixties; learned how to ride a bike, played stickball and scraped its knees in the seventies; went through that awkward growth spurt as a talented but tantrumy teenager in the eighties (anyone who has teenagers knows what I mean, and so does anyone who watched network marketing during that decade).

> In the nineties we used to walk around saying, "Network marketing has come of age," and it was true, in the sense that any eager young adult barely out of a four-year college can be said to be of age.

In the nineties, we certainly became more professional. And professionals started showing up: doctors, lawyers, engineers, bankers, "serious" people.

And in the aughts (or whatever this decade is called)?

Now we've finally entered into that age when you've made enough mistakes, embarrassed yourself enough times, and mounted enough earnest efforts at responsible commerce to begin to have some perspective. Not perfect, not even wise, but at least approaching something resembling maturity.

Give you an example.

Used to be, we talked mostly about the merry-go-round golden-ring style of success, the fractional percentage of people with both the exceptionally good timing and the right skill set or personality profile to hit an opportunity just right and catapult to the top. "Success" in those days was mostly shown off in terms of those elite few with yachts, personal jet planes, and ridiculous fortunes. Robin ("Lifestyles of the Rich and Famous") Leach was just hitting stride in the late eighties, and the style resonated with gawky young teenaged em-el-em. Success might happen to only a few, but the rest of us could dream, right?

Today we do more than dream. The way we describe success in the network marketing of 2007 has been shaped by The Millionaire Next Door, the Latte Factor® and...

The hundreds of thousands of serious networkers sincerely and sanely pursuing a reasonable goal of replacement income and financial stability.

Goodbye get rich quick, hello get smart now.

Meanwhile, as we've matured, the world around us has changed. The corporate model of financial security has crumbled away. Two generations ago, going to work for a company was "security"; working for yourself from your home was "risky."

Today, it's gone clear the other way around.

In 2004, the Small Business Administration told President Bush that small business accounts for more than half the nation's

It's Time... for Network Marketing

economic output and employs more than half the country's non-governmental employees—and that more than half of those small businesses are home-based businesses.

Warren Buffet, the "oracle of Omaha" and famed billionaire stock market expert, turned heads on Wall Street in 2002 when he bought a network marketing company. Actually, he doesn't own one direct selling company—he owns three. (And has been quoted, speaking about one of them, as saying, "It's the best investment I've ever made.")

Network marketing today is a $100 billion concern worldwide (some $30 billion of it in the U.S.).

Right now, as you read these words, there are about 70,000 people around the world who are not network marketers- and by this same time tomorrow will be.

The DSA's Neil Offen projects that over the next ten years, more than 200 million people worldwide will join our industry.

Paul Pilzer projects that over those same ten years, the US economy will create ten million new millionaires—and that many of them will be created in network marketing.

And it goes beyond statistics and figures.

Ten years ago, most people you'd talk to about network marketing either knew nothing about it, or knew someone who'd had a negative experience. Today, most people you'll talk to about network marketing know of someone who's had a positive experience. We're less apologetic and more sensible. We have a track record, and we're getting much, much better at what we do.

But don't take just my word for it. Here are some comments from a few of the people I've interviewed for stories in Networking Times in just the past few months, when I asked what were their views of where our business stands in the world:

U.S. Senator Orrin Hatch (R-Utah) is one of our leading friends on Capitol Hill and was the prime mover behind the Dietary Supplement Health Education Act (DSHEA) of '93. Here's what Senator Hatch had to say about our profession:

> "The companies that have developed this marketing approach with truly high-quality products are doing a lot of good in the world. ... [Network marketing] is a critically important way of helping people to use high-quality products ... it's also a way to give certain people an opportunity to sell those products and earn a good living from it. I see it playing a very important role in the twenty-first century."

Jim Turner, author of The Chemical Feast, worked with Ralph Nader in the sixties, then cofounded Swankin & Turner, a D.C.-based consumer advocacy law firm, and now also serves as Chairman of the Board of Citizens for Health, a major consumer-advocacy lobbying group. Jim was responsible, for example, for making acupuncture needles legal in the United States. Here's what Jim told me:

> "Network marketing is in the vanguard of a major consumer movement in which consumers and producers are merging and becoming the same thing. In a very interesting way, the multilevel marketing companies are the first generation of what Alvin Toffler calls 'prosumers.' ... I'd say you could have perhaps 150 million households successfully involved in network marketing, at least part-time.... You could easily become a major part of a majority of the households in America."

It's Time... for Network Marketing

Frank Maguire worked with JFK in the White House, with Fred Smith at FedEx and with Colonel Sanders at KFC. His first job fresh out of college was head of programming for ABC, where he gave Ted Koppel and Charles Osgood their first jobs at major networks. Frank, in other words, has been around the block. Here's his homily to network marketing, which came right at the end of our interview:

> 'I think [network marketing] is potentially the greatest economic opportunity that has ever existed. Network marketing is turning off the spotlight of working for a corporation and turning on the floodlight of the greatness that we all have within us. I love what you're doing in network marketing, because you're creating an opportunity to affect the self-esteem of many, many people. That's the essence of what you're doing; you're giving people hope and providing a launching pad for people to discover their own greatness. You are the future.'

With world-class leaders like Hatch, Turner, and Maguire saying things about us like that, can we really call this "alternative" any more?

Our model works; we've proven it, over and over. Now the rest of the world has begun to realize it. In fact, it's working a lot better than many of the other, more traditional modes of earning a living. Come to think of it, the next time a serious prospect tells you he or she isn't really interested in taking a look at building long-term residual income and financial security with your business model, you might just say:

"You're not? Okay, no problem. But I'm curious... if you don't mind my asking—what's your alternative?"

John David Mann is one of the United States' preeminent writers on network marketing. He was cofounder and senior editor of the Upline journal, editor in chief of Network Marketing Lifestyles and editor in chief of Networking Times. He edited and produced John Milton Fogg's The Greatest Networker in the World (1992), which sold more than a million copies in eight languages; worked with Paul Zane Pilzer writing The Next Millionaires, with Jeff Olson writing The Slight Edge and with Cameron Johnson writing You Call the Shots: Succeed Your Way- and Live the Life You Want- with the 19 Essential Secrets of Entrepreneurship (Simon & Schuster, Jan. '07).

John has been a network marketer for more than twenty years; during the 1990s built an organization of over 100,000 distributors. He is also a concert cellist and prize-winning composer, recipient of several New Jersey State grants for composition and of the 1969 BMI Awards to Student Composers. At age seventeen he founded a private high school in Orange, New Jersey, called Changes, Inc. Visit him on the web at http://JohnDavidMann.com.

JILLIAN MIDDLETON

Myths and Legends

In MLM network marketing, it is all about your efforts and 'who you are.' It is how you show up FOR people and how you show up WITH people that makes all the difference. If you're looking for personal control in your financial life, this could be your vehicle.

Way too often, people have an unnecessary low opinion of network marketing. It is time the real story is told. I can speak about both the merits of network marketing, as well as its "less than stellar" public opinion, because of my own experience.

My early opinions of network marketing were solid... and ugly. I thought people who did MLM were unable to do anything else. I felt this way even though I was introduced to the business the same way many people are, by a friend of many years, Norine Arundel. Although I had every reason to believe her and trust her judgment, my prejudices were so strong I simply couldn't see around them.

If you're looking at network marketing to solve a financial dilemma, like I was, or simply to make a few extra bucks, for heaven's sake, don't let the myths get in your way. Instead, look to the real legends.

It's Time... for Network Marketing

To make sure we're on the same page here, I'll define what I mean by myths and legends.

One of the definitions for myth from dictionary.com is "an unproved or false collective belief that is used to justify a social institution." Two great examples of this kind of myth in MLM network marketing are:

1. Anyone can do it
2. "Gangster money" is available to everyone who decides to work a network marketing business

It isn't a huge leap of common sense to realize that everyone cannot possibly be cut out to do network marketing, anymore than everyone is cut out to be a doctor or hairdresser.

And the notion that "gangster money"... when something sounds too good to be true, it usually is. The worse part of this kind of myth is it gets in the way of the real legends in the industry.

What do I mean by legends? Dictionary.com again: "A collection of stories about an admirable person... a person who is the center of such stories."

So, who are these legends in network marketing? People just like you and me. They have jobs they don't like. Or they have a business that owns them rather than them owning the business. They are often professionals, yet just as often from "blue collar" industries. Some come to MLM with no college, and some come with PhDs.

I consider myself a pretty smart person, but the myths I heard about this industry nearly kept me from one of the best financial/entrepreneurial decisions of my life. My prejudices about network marketing were so strong that even though my construction business of eight-plus years was falling down around my ears, I wasn't embracing MLM any too fast!

> I thought MLM could be described in two words: hokey and unprofessional. I thought if you were in network marketing, you chased your neighbors down the street to sell them soap.

The California economy had been in a huge downturn for about four years, and had thrown everything I had at my construction company: my savings, effort, time, and finally all the credit I had, but nothing could stop the train wreck of business disaster. I was broke and in debt to everyone, including the IRS. Under those circumstances you would think I would be open to something new—especially if a trusted friend brought it to me!

But instead, my stomach turned into a knot and I thought, "If this is where I've come to, it really is the end of the line." I didn't want anyone to know I was doing MLM. The bottom line for me was shame!

It's embarrassing for me to look back on all this. I'm not sure just who or what I thought I was. I'm sharing this with you not because I'm proud of it, but because I've met too many people who think along the same lines as I did. It actually took my friend Norine about four months to bring me to the table. And then it didn't have a thing to do with the business really. It came down to friendship.

When Norine came to the end of her patience with my arrogance, she simply reminded me of who she was. I'll never forget her words:

> " You know, Jillian, I didn't turn stupid last night. If I think there is some value here,

maybe you should take a look."

Reality check: Norine was right. My take on network marketing was a caricature. My view was a misrepresentation of both the people who work MLM businesses as well as the business model itself.

I was so afraid that if I started an MLM business, when people saw me coming they'd look underneath their bathroom and say, "Oh, here comes Jillian, do we need more toilet cleaner?" I didn't want that kind of image.

After Norine's reminder of who she was and her no nonsense "get over yourself" talk, I agreed to drive up to Fresno, California where she lived and go to an event.

Not because of the company or what it represented, but because of who Norine was to me.

The Event

It was a big room—probably a 1000 people, maybe more. And of course, like at any event with that many attendees, there were people from all walks of life there.

There were some people on stage that were just too much for me. They did what my dad would call a "dog and pony act." They had a religious revival meeting feel to them that fit my original negative vision of who did MLM.

But there were two women who spoke that day that caught my attention: an interior designer and a real estate broker. They plunked down their calendar on the podium and showed people exactly how they did the business. Those two, as well as a number of others that day, blew away my image of who I thought did network marketing.

Myths and Legends

> Shock of shocks... there were people doing MLM who were professionals! That was an eye-opener for me.

I mean, I had an image to preserve and beliefs that were hard to crack. Forget that I was broke! Powerful myths! And... not very smart.

Leverage

What I learned that day was MLM is a business that offers leverage.

I understood the notion of "compounded interest," getting paid interest on the interest accumulating in my savings accounts. That's how it is with dollars, but in network marketing my efforts would be compounded.

This isn't dissimilar to a traditional business. If I owned the business and had employees, then I benefited from the work those people did for me.

If I worked forty hours a week alone in my brick-and-mortar business, I only got paid on the efforts produced by my time. But if I hired an employee to work forty hours, now I got the benefit of eighty hours—the hours I worked plus the hours my employee worked. Of course, I also had all the red tape like payroll taxes, and what I'd have to do if they decided to quit or not "perform" up to what was required. Then there were the promotions and evaluations—who gets moved up, paid more, and who's left in place. Good jobs are usually a hotbed of competition.

> In network marketing, I had the same kind of "time leverage." When I sponsored someone into the business and helped them get up and running, the

company paid me a commission. How cool is that?

I help someone else start a business, and I get paid too. If I work my network marketing business twenty hours a week and my new recruit works her business twenty hours a week—then I am in effect getting paid on forty hours of business time!

Another huge difference between network marketing and more conventional types of businesses is that the leverage network marketing provides is built on a cooperative business model, rather than the traditional competitive model.

I wasn't the boss, and the people I turned on to the business weren't my employees. They were independent contractors. We came together in partnership to help ourselves and others grow their businesses in order to better our lives.

> Network marketing was going to allow me to rebuild in my "early middles" much more quickly than any traditional business model, and to do it in a cooperative environment working with like-minded people, rather than climbing over people to get to the top. I liked it. Lots!

The Drive Home
I sound like a true convert to MLM, don't I? Well, I was. I'd found a solid business model that was going to allow me to start over, and it appeared that I was not going to have to work the next twenty years to put my life back together. Cool.

I'd like to say I was cured from my obsession of "What will people think?"—but alas, I wasn't.

I lived in Lake Arrowhead, California and Fresno was about a six-hour drive. That's a long time to think. The closer I got to home, the more my stomach knotted.

Now I would have to tell people I was doing MLM.

Just as I reached the Los Angeles County Line, I pulled over and was physically sick—opened the door and lost my cookies.

How was I going to tell people I was doing network marketing? Suddenly, all the professionalism I witnessed and the powerful leverage I learned about was once again obliterated by those MLM myths.

Talk about buyer's remorse! Classic. The voice in my head told me I was going to look the fool.

It was a terrible dilemma (and drama). I knew there was money to be made. I'd met real people, people that I believed and I could respect. I loved the business model. But the myths kept crowding out my experience. I was afraid of what other people would think of me.

Feature the Problem

If you ever find yourself in this position, there is hope. Here's what I did to get past my initial resistance and fear of looking foolish.

A great way to avoid feeling foolish over something that you "dread" coming up is to feature it.

Whose problem is it? Mine. So, I'm going to get it on the table and take care of it. Who am I taking care of it for? Right—me.

So, I give my person a call and say something like this:

Hey, Julie, how's it going? Good. (I'm also going to say whatever other things that are appropriate for me to say to this person I care about.) Julie, I'm calling because I'd like to set up a time for us to have lunch. I've found a financial opportunity (business opportunity or...) that I'd like you to take a look at. I'll tell you up front that it is out of the mainstream... in fact, it can look a bit hokey or even unprofessional, but once you get into it, it is full of leverage, and the business model is built on cooperation rather than competition. I think it's worth a good look. What's your schedule look like for lunch?

Now think about this for a minute. Who did I make feel better here? Me, you're right. Are you more relaxed when you feel good? Do you show up more like your "authentic self"? You bet.

Do you think others will respond to you more positively when you're in this frame of mind rather than worried about how you're going to look?

So Who Are the Legends?

It's time that all of us in network marketing let people know what the big deal is. It's leverage, and the real numbers are wonderful. We don't need to talk about gangster money. Only a few people are going to make that. If everybody could do MLM as easily as that, there would not be the kind of money available to those who are in the top 20 percent.

Unfortunately, the entire industry suffers because of the MLM myth that "anyone can make it big." Most people can't... and won't....

There's no need for this hype. It is my experience that 60 percent of the people between the 20 percent at the top and the 20 percent at the bottom are making money in this business. Often they make enough to replace their jobs. Many of them replace their incomes and make more money than they did in a regular job—and they have much more control over their lives.

Plus, they can take advantage of many tax benefits that add money to their bottom line and the quality of their life. I know lots of network marketers who write off most of their travel. MLM lends itself to combined business and vacation trips!

> Something very important to remember is that the majority of people who come into network marketing would be thrilled to make an extra $500 a month!

What Do Network Marketing People Look Like?

Well, now I can tell you—they look like me! But they also look like you.

People who do network marketing come from all walks of life. Blue-collar people, pink-collar people, white-collar people are all involved in network marketing.

I was surprised to find so many accountants in network marketing, but then they understand leverage. People with entrepreneurial spirit are often found in network marketing, but entrepreneurial spirit is no guarantee they will embrace the business model. Remember, I could barely get over myself and I'd been an entrepreneur since I was twenty-three!

Another group of people who are fairly common in network marketing are franchise owners. They like that MLM is a "turnkey" business just like in a franchise—you don't have to start from "square one."

And no list of "who does network marketing" would be complete if we didn't talk about service professions. I run into teachers and nurses in this business all the time. Why? Network marketing is more cooperative than a typical corporation or even a small business. It's based on "people helping people."

We end up with all kinds of people in MLM.

The reason we do is that there is nothing here to keep anybody out: Age, sex, race, education, income, past business experience, success or failure... none of that matters here. Network marketing accepts everyone equally.

Bet on the Legends, Not the Myths
The network marketing industry needs to be telling the stories of real people making real opportunities work for them. Not stars in your eyes, pie-in-the-sky hype, but stories about real people.

In network marketing, it is all about your efforts and "who you are." It is how you show up FOR people and how you show up WITH people that makes all the difference.

Real people making a difference, not only their lives but in many, many other's lives as well.

Jillian Middleton is a mentor, coach, and trainer, and the author of the courses 5 Steps to Working Less and Making More in MLM and Setting Up Your Store Hours and Design Your Calendar.

As creator of the Savvy Sponsoring Strategies programs, Jillian trains network marketers and direct sales consultants to use the same strategies she used to build two six-figure network marketing businesses in five years.

Get your free report: The 5 Steps to Work Less and Make Money In Network Marketing at http://SavvySponsoring.com

KATHY MINSKY

Leaders Made Here

Network marketing is THE leadership business. What we do for a living is bring out the best in people. And rather than speak about that as an intellectual concept, I thought I'd show you exactly what we do to make a leader. That's the best way I know for you to really understand.

True leaders don't create followers, they create more leaders.

— Tom Peters

Tonight belonged to Ann.

After eight years in network marketing, supporting her team, attending every training, and participating in all she could in spite of a busy schedule, a full-time job and a hectic family life, she had never been asked to share her story before. Not once! Ann had just joined our team from another company. She is an immigrant to this country and simply lacked the confidence to ask to be heard.

Ann had prepared handouts and knew just what she was going to say. The excitement she felt about being asked to participate for the very first time was palatable. Those of us who knew her could tell she was nervous. Our job was to smile encouragement in her direction.

The small gathering of eight included two first-time guests. Ann's story was an exceptional example of the success of our products. However, it was not the content, or the carefully designed handouts that moved the group. It was the animation and excitement she showed as she shared her story.

Afterward, everyone told her what a great job she had done and how interested they were in the information she presented. The smile did not leave her face the rest of the night.

> Goal accomplished. After eight years of incubating, a leader had emerged.

How could someone not have seen the potential in Ann? Why was she passed over all this time, and more importantly, what changed? Why was she in front of this group, this night?

As the Leader of The Global Success Team, I brought nine years of experience and a strong team to Shaklee in 2004, following the bankruptcy of Excel Communications, my former network marketing company.

After the first year, I became concerned that our team was not uncovering new emerging leaders. Since we brought a lot of proven talent to the new company, we didn't put "beginners" in front of new prospects. Only the "best presenters" publicly presented information. There was no forum for budding leaders. As a result, we were sponsoring a lot of new members, but we were stagnant in producing anyone new in a leadership role.

So, we set out to find new ideas and formats designed to provide every person a forum to become the leader they desired to be. We examined our own process as well as business fundamentals for a solution.

> We did not need to know WHAT to do when you are a leader; we wanted to

know HOW to develop leadership skills in people who did not see themselves as leaders yet.

A look back at my own emergence as a leader helped me to understand what was missing.

Growing up, I was very shy. Sandwiched in the middle of ten children, I followed the lead of my older brothers and sisters and rarely put myself out front. I had a safe place to hide, with no conflicts. So why change anything?

But something inside me was shouting to be heard.

It started with a grandmother who made me feel special every day. It took many years and much patience on her part, but she finally convinced me that I could do anything I chose in life.

My father continued the process as he worked on my character, which was often at the expense of being unable to sit comfortably for a while. He recognized something special in every one of his children and often told me, "You can be the president of the United States one day, if you want to." He offered me experiences in life that told me he trusted me.

What he also taught me was to never lie, steal, or cheat anyone.

If I followed these simple rules and worked hard, I could get along with almost anyone and would be successful in whatever I tried, because people would trust what I had to say.

This turned out to be valuable advice I still subscribe to today.

When I reached high school, I finally decided to stick my toe in the waters of leadership. I was pretty bad at it. In fact, I was terrible. But I had one high school teacher who saw something in me I did not see in myself. Every time I tried, she would tell me, "That was really good. You are going to be a real leader one day."

What was it really that my grandmother, my father, and a very special teacher gave me? I have to boil it down to two things: experience and confidence.

You see up to that point, I had not succeeded, because I had never really tried for fear of failing, or worse yet, being laughed at.

> You cannot consistently perform in a manner, which is inconsistent with the way in which you see yourself.
> - Zig Ziglar

So, where does that confidence come from? We boiled it down to three ingredients:

Know what you are talking about.

Not everything about it. Just enough about the subject you will be sharing for the time you will be speaking. When you listen to great motivational speakers, realize that most of them give the same speech over and over. They are great, in part, because they know their subject inside and out.

Practice. Practice. Practice.

If you have done it well in front of the mirror or a friend, you know you can do it.

Begin with people you trust.

A small group of friendly distributors is a great beginning. Eventually (after you know you are not going to die when you speak in front of a group), you can expand your subject matter and then gradually expand your audience.

I started my network marketing career in Fairbanks, Alaska. Being the very first distributor in the state, there was no local support of any kind. What seemed to be a disadvantage at the time proved to be a valuable lesson in leadership. Not knowing where to begin, I just started inviting people over to my house and we tried to figure it out together.

We laughed much more than would be acceptable in most networking circles today, but more and more people kept joining the team.

> We shared the leadership role, and everyone took part on a rotating basis. We didn't take ourselves too seriously, so mistakes were not only permitted, they were expected.

By the time we were able to get a network marketing "pro" from our upline to come up to Alaska, our team had grown in excess of 200 people. He told us we had been doing it all wrong and that only the BEST speakers should present and the rest of us were just there to support that speaker.

Eventually, after trying the suggestions of the professional, our team stopped growing. It nearly killed our business. So we went back to our less formal meetings, and the business began to grow again.

I'm not promoting disorganization. We were using a structure that allowed everyone to participate at the level they sought and provided a forum for them to do so. Of course, when we conducted a big citywide meeting, we put the best presenters in front of the room. And you know how they learned to be the best.

Now that our team understood the problem, how were we going to develop a comfortable atmosphere that provided confidence-building experiences, so team members would begin to see themselves as emerging leaders?

We have team members in fifty states and four countries, so it had to be duplicatable at every level and circumstance. We decided on a two-pronged approach.

> Create a program that offers an opportunity for new distributors to practice their leadership skills in a friendly environment.

> Start them in a small group format and continue to build confidence in their ability to lead a growing team.

We devised a weekly meeting plan that was intended to be used for small in-home meetings, where a simple and duplicatable agenda would give every representative who was interested an opportunity to lead a short portion of the meeting and practice their speaking and leadership skills.

The outline was flexible and designed to last about fifty to sixty minutes.

There would be up to five presenters, each following the agenda for time and content.

Our agenda went as follows:

- Personal Story of Host or Team Member – 5 minutes
- Recognition – 5 minutes
- Product Introduction – 10 minutes
- Opportunity – 20 minutes
- Motivational Talk – 10 Minutes
- Close

Each portion is given by a different person each week so that eventually each distributor learned the six components that compromise a complete meeting. We encourage fun and laughter, and when someone makes a mistake, we have them just tell the guests...

" See, anyone can do this business."

Not long after learning all six segments, people are encouraged to consider hosting their own event and start building emerging leaders on their own personal team. A more experienced upline leader is encouraged to attend and support their new meetings for the first few weeks, if needed.

Since these are conducted in home environments, there may be only five to ten participants, so there's no need to be nervous about the size of the group.

Usually 50 percent of the audience is comprised of people they know, like, and trust who are experiencing the same training, so they are very supportive of one another.

After the meeting ends, the rest of the team makes sure to lift up each speaker. There is no place for criticism, and each person feels like they contributed to the success of the event.

The outcome speaks for itself: We are, again, bringing out new business leaders on the team. It is most heartening to see names that have been around for over a year all of a sudden breaking out in one or two months time after starting their own meeting.

They know what to do. They know how to do it, and they are in an environment friendly to their learning process.

Now it is up to the individual to decide whether they want success enough to move out of their comfort zone.

You'll be pleased to know that Ann is starting her own meetings. I have complete confidence that she will be a great leader, because she understands the goal is not only to gather customers and team members for her business, but to offer leadership opportunities to all those who want them.

> Life's battle does not always go
> to the stronger or faster man;
> But soon or late, the man who wins
> is the one who THINKS he can.
> - Author Unknown

Kathi Minsky is a Master Coordinator with Shaklee Corporation. Over the past seven years, Kathi has successfully trained over 30,000 distributors to communicate, duplicate, and train using online tools. She can be reached at her website here: http://TheGlobalSuccessTeam.com

What if...

corporate America was suddenly turned upside down- the end of organizational politics? What if your success would not be hindered, but furthered, if you helped every person in your department contribute at a maximum level with no limits?

Imagine you are a corporate executive with five direct reports in your department. You bear significant financial responsibilities to your family and to your own future, and you fervently desire promotions and pay raises. You envision recognition for rising in the hierarchy, along with the accompanying admiration.

You know that the single overriding factor for your success in this equation is the way your superiors in the organization perceive you and your accomplishments- in a word, politics.

Sure, you and your department must perform, but you know that your promotions and pay are solely the prerogative and even at the whims of your superiors.

You've watched the true hotshots in the organization blaze trails and walk through all barriers to contribute to the growth and profits of their department and to the company. Yet often these high performers were mysteriously blindsided, torpedoed, backbitten and driven politically from the organization for the crime of becoming threats to others who coveted the positions these superstars seemed destined to command—if they were allowed to succeed politically.

You watched how the organization rewarded and promoted yes-men, those who always seemed to get into the right social circles or go to the right church, who belong to the right country club and, here's the key—those who get credit for others' successes.

So, you are ever vigilant of the need to keep your head down at the right times, play the politics of getting noticed and approved of without becoming a threat to the wrong people.

You learn to toe the mark within the rules of the game that have been followed by surviving organization men and women worldwide throughout history.

Today, a new hotshot is joining your team. Personnel sent over his folder with notations: "Highly qualified... Has top management potential."

So, you ask yourself, how will you train and manage this new superstar?

Will you teach him EVERYHING you know as fast as you can, including all the "secrets" you have learned in ten years about how to score big successes and how to rise in the organization and how to set new records without stepping on any political landmines?

What if...

Will you inspire him to have a burning desire to be promoted to your level in record time, so that every day he comes to work on fire to pursue this goal?

Laughable to even ask...

You will carefully feed him just enough information to do well enough to make YOU look good. You hope and pray that he will NOT be recognized as a star rising faster than you are.

You have learned the nature of the "logjam" of candidates for promotions to higher levels in the organization, starting with your boss who wants to survive long enough to move up behind his boss in five or ten years. So, you're already desperate to get personal recognition for any accomplishments your department has.

For you to rise up in the organizational chart sooner than the slow timetable of your superiors, you will have to take risks and step out of line to get the visibility to be recognized and promoted faster than usual. Without, of course, alarming your boss or his boss that your higher level of accomplishments may benefit you and not solely them, much less threaten their positions directly.

Should one of your direct reports develop into a rising star too soon and garner the credit for the successes of your department, your chances for the next promotion are out the window.

That new member of your department may be a threat. So, you say a silent prayer that he is not connected by relationship to anybody in top management or to company ownership.

But...

What if... your organization was turned upside down and you could be certain that your success would not be hindered but, instead, be furthered if you helped every person in your department contribute at a maximum level with no limits?

What if... you and others were certain to be recognized and RECEIVE CREDIT solely on the basis of accomplishment instead of politics?

What if... the "age-wage" curves that define the limits of salaries based on "years since receiving your BS degree" were thrown away and anyone could be recognized and paid WITHOUT LIMITATION strictly on the basis of true contributions, instead of on the politics of managing the perceptions and preferences of top management?

What if... you could actually focus on being a rising star and mentoring and serving others, and what if you could eliminate all the wasted time, effort, and stress involved in mastering the maze of maneuvers and manipulation demanded by the reality of the primacy of politics in the organization?

What if... you had immediate, unlimited earning potential based on accomplishment?

What if... you were allowed to identify and mentor others to follow in your productive footsteps and be rewarded accordingly, on a permanent basis, for their success, without fear that they would replace you?

What if... you received a small monthly percentage of the earnings of all those you identify, nurture, train, and mentor to contribute to the company's success?

Oh yes, and...

What if... there was no limit, now or in the future, on your upside success and income?

Imagine the burst of growth, productivity, and successes all this unleashed energy and creativity would produce. Sure, the political "bigwigs" who knew how to play the game and how to take credit for others' work would suddenly be naked, and they would have to contribute and truly serve and train others with all they knew, instead of putting most of their waking efforts into polishing their image and protecting their turf and position.

There would be no more politics.

Individuals would succeed solely on their accomplishments personally and, more importantly, on mentoring and serving others.

If you identified, trained, and mentored many others who became more successful than you yourself had, you would continue to receive a leveraged, residual percentage of all the sales volume created by those individuals and their organization, for as long as they remained members of the organization, with no limits. Why not, since you were the causal factor in their joining, learning, and following in your footsteps, hopefully to the point where they took this foundation you provided and went beyond your accomplishments? Do you suppose you would continue to champion them, long-term?

And think expansively, without limits, that you would further be rewarded for teaching your leaders to serve and to teach other leaders, with you receiving additional tiers of override compensation for this extraordinary, increasing success.

What if this utopian business model could actually be implemented?

It's Time... for Network Marketing

It has been. It's called network marketing. How does it look to you?

Warren Nelson is a Royal Ambassador in FreeLife International. He was introduced to network marketing while at the helm of an electronics company via an MBA degree from Harvard Business School. He is unique in the Networking industry in having a "batting average of 1000"—three and ONLY three companies joined, all still in business, and top pin levels achieved in all three. Warren's pin titles were Blue Diamond, Crown Diamond and now, Royal Ambassador in FreeLife International.

Warren and his wife, partner, and best friend Mary Nelson, have trained thousands across the country in their seminars on "How to Create an Obscene Income in Network Marketing" as well as having been featured trainers and speakers at numerous networking company conventions. They have been featured as Master Networkers and have written articles for many networking magazines and books, including Networking Times Magazine', The Network Marketing Magazine, Upline', The New Entrepreneurs, and others.

The Most Remarkable Business

I don't believe that anything in this world is perfect, but network marketing is as close to the perfect business as I think you will ever find.

Del was sixty-two and three years from retirement when he walked into my sales and marketing class. He had done what everyone told him and socked away a nice nest egg in his company's 401k plan. Del and his wife would be able to live quite nicely for the rest of their lives.

Well, at least that was the plan. Then his company went bankrupt, and he lost everything.

That day, Del asked me how to rebuild his mid-six figure retirement plan within the next three years. I told him that there was only one way- network marketing.

Patti was a single mother of six children living in a rural town with a population of only 8,000. She had just lost $75,000 in her business. She had researched all kinds of traditional businesses and franchises, but there seemed to be only one type of business that would enable her to stay home with her children, quickly pay off the debt, and earn a nice six-figure income within the next five years—network marketing.

Collette was a single mother of five children, two of which were chronically ill and required regular medical attention. She was deeply in debt and could only work part-time as a secretary. The medical bills were piling up, and the future looked very bleak.

That was when she was introduced to a fantastic home-based business by her brother. At first Collette didn't think she could be successful, because she had never operated a business before and had no sales or marketing experience, but this business was different. It seemed to be her answer from God—network marketing.

What makes network marketing so remarkable? The incredible, almost unbelievable stories—and these are just three of the thousands and thousands and thousands.

Network marketing is truly a life altering business. How many other types of businesses can you say will radically change your life?

I certainly haven't found any others. I mean really, name another type of business where a twenty-three-year-old carpet installer with an injured shoulder and no money or a seventy-year-old butcher could become millionaires within a few years. Only in network marketing.

Here I am, ranting and raving about how amazing network marketing is, and you're probably wondering what happened to Del, Patti, and Collette.

Well, Del did rebuild his retirement plan in three years, but he was having so much fun, he didn't retire.

The Most Remarkable Business

Patti has stayed home with her children, paid off her debt, earns a nice six-figure income, and now several of her children have joined her business.

Collette continued to work part-time building a network marketing business, and she is now the top income earner in her company.

> Network marketing is the most remarkable business I've ever seen- and since I've been a business consultant for many years and have thoroughly researched thousands of businesses, that's quite a statement for me to make.

It is the only business I've ever seen that enables the average person, regardless of age, gender, financial situation, past experience, education, knowledge, or even language to start a business with little or no money and in a few short years literally be living the lifestyle of the rich and famous.

> I don't believe that anything in this world is perfect, but network marketing is as close to the perfect business as I think you will ever find.

Consider these advantages over other conventional businesses: Low start-up investment, proven turnkey system, high quality products and services, outstanding training and support, quick compensation, movable, unlimited growth, no employees, very little overhead, can be operated from home either part- or full-time, and produces long-term residual income. Those reasons alone (and there are more) are why you should seriously investigate this truly remarkable business.

It's Time... for Network Marketing

> Once you find the right company, then there is just one secret to success in this business- WORK!

I know, you were hoping for that get rich quick deal. Well, get over it. That doesn't exist.

Network marketing is a real business, and it requires work: prospecting for people interested in your products, services, or business, giving presentations, answering questions and handling objections, doing follow-ups, sponsoring, training, and supporting. If you do these things well and treat it like a real business, in time you will be successful.

Who knows, perhaps some day you will be like Del, Patti, Collette, and so many others who are enjoying true financial security and the time freedom to really enjoy life.

Yes, network marketing is the most remarkable business. My question for you is: Will you do your research to find the right company and then work hard and smart so that some day other people will share your "incredible, almost unbelievable" story, too?

Rod Nichols has been involved in the network marketing industry since 1979, as a company founder/owner, distributor, consultant, trainer, and author. His books, Successful Network Marketing for the 21st Century and Would You Like to Dig in My Goldmine? were industry best sellers for several years, and his newest book, The Ideal Business has quickly becoming a must read. His latest book The 12 Power Secrets for Network Marketing Success, will be out in early 2007.

Even though Rod retired from network marketing for three years, he continued to earn a full-time residual income. Recently he decided to come out of retirement and is now actively building his business once again.

Rod and his wife, Karen live in Washington State. They have five children and four grandchildren. To learn more about Rod, visit his website: http://RodNichols.com.

SHELLEY PENNEY

It's Not the Marketing... It's the Network

The best thing about network marketing isn't the money; it isn't the time freedom, and it isn't being released from the nine-to-five drudgery. The best thing about network marketing is the ability to reach out and make a difference in the life of someone else... many, many someone elses.

"There are no strangers in this world. Only friends I haven't met yet."

Like just about everything I have learned on my "working at home" journey, that paraphrased quote is not my own, but it resonates deeply within me. After ten years in network marketing, if I were to take inventory of all my accumulated assets, my "friends" would top the list by a landslide.

When I started my very first business I was excited, but like most people I was a wee bit insecure. I found that while I wanted to shout to the world when I was at work in my office, as soon as I found myself in front of someone, I became all tongue-tied and shy.

Now REALLY! Imagine me... SHY! This had me completely baffled! I've never been shy—ever!

I was the four-year-old who was brought to the customer

service department in Woolco by a stranger lady with oh so pretty shoes that I had followed around for half an hour. I was the eight-year-old singing off-key at the top of her lungs in the third grade recital. I came in first in the public speaking contest, participated in "Reach for the Top," and danced all alone (heaven forbid) in my own world if I liked the music.

I have NEVER missed an opportunity to stand in the spotlight and shine, and I have never been one to worry about looking silly to myself or anybody else. So, I couldn't understand this unwelcome reluctance to share with the world the new excitement in my life.

It took me a while, but I finally figured it out.

> It's not what you can get, but what you can give that makes the difference.

When I REALLY got what this whole "networking" thing was all about, I was overjoyed, and my business skyrocketed. I realized that the reason I was freezing up and scaring people off was that I was so focused on what I needed in order to be successful—more customers, more sales, more recruits—that all of the conversations that I used to have effortlessly with people had become a burden.

> The minute I saw someone to speak with, I immediately evaluated them for what they could add to my business.

People had become a commodity to me, and this was so against who I was as a person that I became miserable, insecure, and failing.

Put the "NETWORK" back into network marketing.
One day I simply decided that this business was too difficult,

and I wasn't going to talk about it any more. So, I simply went about my daily chores. As I was waiting in line in the grocery store, there was a young mother ahead of me with a cooing toddler smiling and batting his eyes at me while we waited to pay. He was the most adorable little guy, and I quickly told the mother so. We started to talk. She told me his name, how he was big for his age, and already starting to say a few words. I told her about my own children (then in elementary school) and we commented on "how fast they grow."

She told me that she was working nights at a local convenience store when her husband was home so she could spend time with her son during the day, and in that way she could keep him home and away from babysitters... but oh, how she wished she didn't have to work.

Then she asked me what I did for a living. I began telling her how I was a nurse at the local hospital and that I had recently started a home-based business because I really had a dream to stay with my children. I didn't want them to be "latchkey kids" anymore. I found myself just sharing a conversation, telling a stranger about my hopes and dreams, asking her about hers, and simply enjoying the socialization. A remarkable thing happened.

> She said very simply, " I would love to be able to work at home. Could you come by for coffee at naptime and tell me more about that?"

Of course, I agreed, and we set a time to meet. Later, I sat in my car and went over what had just happened, and I had an epiphany.

> It's not the marketing,
> It's the network.

It's Time... for Network Marketing

I had been so hung up on the marketing aspect of network marketing that I didn't understand a very simple concept. Network is the first word in that phrase, and it was the networking part that spoke to me and to who I really wanted to be as a person... who I already really was.

All of a sudden, I was on fire! I didn't have to be anybody different. I didn't have to be special. I didn't have to look for people to sell to. All I had to do was be myself. What a huge relief! What a release!

That day changed my life and my path.

> I started to view my business as the vehicle that allowed me to meet the people who needed me, instead of meeting people that I needed.

Over the years I have found homes for kittens, helped a family to a shelter, and took a woman in labor to the hospital because her husband couldn't get home in time, and stayed and breathed with her until he arrived.

I helped a young man find a job, gave a mom advice on a wayward teenager, and recommended a daycare center for a single parent. I taught people what I had learned about communication, money, and business, and I did it all without selling a thing. I developed a six-figure income and never sold anything any day in my business life.

Now, I know on the surface that many of those things appear to be unrelated to business, but that is what is so wonderful about this business. You see, each one of those people became a part of my business over time. They remembered me for the networking, not the marketing, and when the time was right for them, they each, on their own, came to me with questions about my business.

It's Not the Marketing... It's the Network

After ten years of simply reaching out to people—networking in the true sense of the word—and making a difference whenever I saw an opportunity, I have developed a list of friends all through my community and all over the world.

The very best thing about network marketing is the NETWORKING!

If you take the opportunity to really understand what that means, and if you get good at it, then not only will your business explode, but you will attract the kinds of people into your life that will become your lifelong friends and supporters.

The principle and practice is simple:

> Whenever you meet someone, practice great communication skills. Talk with people openly, ask them questions that are of interest to you AND them. Listen for ways that you can offer assistance or add value to their lives.

Something very exciting happens when you remove yourself from the center of the picture and focus on someone else.

The first thing that happens is that you stop being self-conscious. You see, when you are aware of being "nervous," you are automatically thinking about yourself. Nervousness or shyness are self-indulgent feelings that keep you from developing meaningful relationships with others.

Once you get good at it, people are drawn to you like a magnet, and the Law of Attraction is at work. The people who network for the sake of others are the happiest and most magnetic people on the planet.

You see, it is truly IMPOSSIBLE to be unhappy when you are

100% focused on how you can serve. It is impossible to feel insecure, nervous, shy, or self-conscious when you are on a mission to better someone else's life. And the simple act of taking the light off of yourself and shining it on another actually shines it back on you in the nicest of ways.

> The best thing about network marketing isn't the money, it isn't the time freedom, and it isn't being released from the nine-to-five drudgery.

The best thing about network marketing is the ability to reach out and make a difference in the life of someone else from the purest perspective of giving unselfishly, understanding that the Law of Attraction will be at work in your life, fervently returning the energy to you that you so freely send out. When you abundantly and unselfishly give, you can be neither unhappy nor poor, and when you truly embrace the concept with crystal clear vision, your business, your personal life, your social life, and your bank account will be overflowing.

Shelley Penney retired from her full time nursing career ten years ago after just ten months working her home business. She is a mentor to many, and works with a servants heart and a philosophy of abundance. Aside from her own personal successes in network marketing, Shelley is co-founder and master trainer of Prospex (http://YourProspex.com) a company that teaches home entrepreneurs the principles of success. In keeping with Shelley's belief that every success is important, regardless of company affiliation, Prospex training is free for everyone. Shelley is also loving wife of Jim, and they are raising Justin (17 years old) and Alyssa (16 years old) from their home on the beautiful Saint John River in Canada.

an interview with **PAUL ZANE PILZER**

The Next Millionaires

> More than any other industry, direct selling/network marketing is about changing people's lives from whatever position they are in life to something better; it improves their marriages, it improves their relationships with their children, and of course, it greatly improves their ability to do business.

Paul, in 1990, the world was, economically, "going to hell in a handbasket." The other economists were saying we were doomed, and you predicted just the opposite. You were right; they were wrong.

You predicted that Japan, the then leading per capita economy, was actually going to go down the tubes. The experts were screaming recession and depression, and then we had a really explosive economic decade. Now talking about the extraordinary number of new millionaires and a period of growth and wealth like we've never seen before. Are you going to be right again?

I would phase it a little differently. In 1990 I predicted roughly a forty-year period of economic expansion, effectively the end of the business cycle—the quadric cycle of boom/bust in every industry. We're in the fifteenth year of that expansion, so that, to me, has been straight on.

We had a minor—which I can say now in 2007—aberration called 2001-2004. But by 2004, the stock market was higher

It's Time... for Network Marketing

than it was in 2001, but it's about more than the stock market—the real estate market and the most important market called "household wealth," barely took a hit.

Because in 2001, when the stock market went down, real estate went up a proportionate amount, so we're in a solid fifteen-year trend here going on a straight trajectory, fairly steady and going up, in both the United States and Western economies. And I still don't see any end in sight. I want to be correct in saying that I still don't see that we cycled down and now we're back to where we were.

Here we are looking forward to 2007, just taking stock, particularly when we look back on the last fifteen years.

One of the things we learn in economics is that history is the best and only thing we really have for predicting the future, but you must heavily weigh recent history in analyzing the data.

> So the last ten years are probably as important as the previous thirty or forty in predicting the next ten.

Paul, what's responsible for this sustained growth?
Technology. And coupled with technology, democratic ideals that have become worldwide, or perhaps the democratic ideals have spawned the expanse of technology... it could be a chicken and the egg issue.

But it's a combination of technology and effectively, universal entrepreneurialism worldwide.

Paul, what are the technologies that you see having the greatest impact?

> Information technology. It's amazing what we're starting to do and we're just at the

beginning of the information technology explosion.

Information technology is just getting started and that's been the greatest impact in the last fifteen years. Information technology has just taken what I call world civilization, and catapulted it forward.

Let's go back 5000 years: 5000 years ago we lived in a pretty poor, agrarian economy. What happened? Sometime between five and ten thousand years ago writing came. With writing we could take the technology that somebody invented, like a better way of farming, and where before he could only teach it to his children, now he could write it down and pass it around and whole civilizations could be built on this shared information. How to build buildings, how to build sewer systems, how to farm much better, and then we had this HUGE explosion called the printing press which took the writing of information and just exploded it worldwide. And that's the last 500 years of civilization.

> And then came the Internet, which is much bigger than the printing press and in ten to fifteen years has started to have an impact on the production of goods and services that's equivalent to the printing press, or perhaps the invention of writing itself!

The Internet has just ratcheted it up because now, every time you want a new part or component or need a better method you discover someone has already made it! Find it's in a different language? No problem, push a button and translate the web page. Oh, translate the order form, let's go buy it. You see how quick we've united the world? Instead of one mind, a hundred minds, a million minds... we really have a billion minds connected on the Internet, solving issues.

And how does this affect our business of direct selling and network marketing?

We've seen an enormous democratization of entrepreneurial opportunity at a level in our lifetime that no one has ever seen before.

When I graduated Wharton, I went to work at Citicorp because they had the best technology of any bank or financial services company who had entered in the technology area. I think in those days a used IBM 360 cost $1.1 million, so if you couldn't come up with several million dollars for support and the buildings to house a computer the size of a room, you couldn't play at the table and deliver efficient products to your customers.

In almost every field I saw that happening.

> Little did I believe that only a few short years later the unit of technology would fall from a multimillion-dollar IBM mainframe to an IBM PC that cost originally $2000! Today $200 or less...

What we saw as the unit of technology, this power, shifted from the giant mainframe commanding a building of 10,000 people to the individual who can now communicate virtually instantly with anyone in the world.

So, consider that the best and brightest minds of almost any industry have always been the toolmakers. A toolmaker is often nothing more than the farmer, network marketer, or doctor, who make tools for themselves to do the job better. And then it occurs to them that they should sell the tools to others who do those jobs instead of continuing to do that job themselves, because they can see a greater need for the tool to be produced than what they were producing before creating the tool. They see that they will make more money selling the tool that will help the others make more money producing the food, or saving the life. That's what a toolmaker is.

And the toolmakers used to make tools for giant mainframe computers. Today they get up every day and they think of the individual at his or her desk, because that's the new unit of productivity. So they say, "He's got a PC, he's got a Treo 700 handheld. What can I do to make that person even more efficient?"

The spin-off is that individual entrepreneurs can just take off and take off well, because now the best tools are available for them.

The second part of your question is direct selling in particular. The one thing we always used to have was that people liked brand names. What's a brand name? What's a Sony? What are Levi's? It's a synonym for a five letter word called TRUST. People like brand names. And that's always been a problem for individual entrepreneurs, or anyone just starting out with a product.

Well, what's amazing about direct sellers today is that their products have become brand names. These are billion dollar companies who had the money to spend on R&D to produce the best products, but instead of selling them in a store, they sell them to individual entrepreneurs who build their own business and effectively give them brand name goods.

How much of that has to do with the democratization of everything that you've mentioned?
A huge amount, because the individual entrepreneur has a level playing field. I always thought, "Wouldn't it be nice if we could level the playing field?", that anybody could start in a business regardless of who their parents were, where they went

It's Time... for Network Marketing

to school, or how much money they had. I just wanted to level the playing field so that individuals who didn't have the opportunity or inclination to go to great schools could participate and succeed.

I wanted a level playing field! Well, in my lifetime, now as my children are growing up, it's actually not level.

> It's so unfair for the employee of the large corporation.

The individual entrepreneur, particularly if he aligns himself with name brand products and takes advantage of the tools given in a network marketing or direct selling organization, doesn't have a level playing field.

> The direct selling entrepreneur has a great advantage over the person working in a large company.

Better technology, being able to work his or her own hours, he has name brand products and here's the most beautiful part, if he doesn't like what he's doing, how fast can he switch? And that's what keeps these network marketing companies so sharp, and why we have these multibillion-dollar entities. It's unbelievable how fast they find out when they make a product that's inferior.

Let's be honest. Not every product works, not every marketing plan works. Do you know how long Proctor & Gamble takes to figure that out when they launch a product? They do test markets and they go to focus groups, but in the case with network marketers you're distributor is your customer! How fast do they figure out when the package doesn't work or there's something wrong in manufacturing? It's instant!

Network marketers give such amazing feedback up the supply chain.

> And the most beautiful part is when a company isn't doing well, or the management is not up to par, people leave! They join another network marketing company! That is so phenomenal!

That ultimately keeps the companies so sharp and on their toes. It's real time feedback from a worldwide consumer base.

Do you see network marketing/direct selling as a profession?
Yes, I would say that. Or it's emerging into a profession.

It's interesting when you use the word profession, because it's so new. We have to take a look today at the wealthiest people in the world; it's pretty interesting. I've been spending a lot of time on that in my latest research.

> Today, of the top ten people on the Forbes 400 list of Richest Americans, nine of them were born poor/middle-class and nine of them didn't finish college.

The "professions," as we used to define them, created licenses for themselves and effectively priced out other people in the market who wouldn't pay you the dues, which just meant lots of time to price-fix the market.

And along came the computer business and the network marketing business in the last two decades. They grew so fast that while they were having meetings to decide, "What should we license a computer programmer to be? How should we regulate that business? How should we define these as professions?", Microsoft and these other companies grew so big that they became the wealthiest people in the world, and they couldn't be controlled.

And you found that all of these people, who didn't fit in the licensed environment; they just couldn't sit through law school—it was too tedious. They really wanted to help people, but they found everything was wrong when they started out in med school. All these people found a home in the computer industry and now the network marketing industry.

So I use that word "profession" and find it often means a lot people that get together and pass laws and licenses to put people in jail who do what they're doing unless they pay the dues over many years.

We see this explosive growth in the computer business of people who couldn't play by the rules, meaning they just couldn't be bored enough to get through the schooling it takes to get to a profession. The same type of person is now joining the network marketing industry.

> Network marketing is so exciting because, just like computers, it lets anybody join, there is no ticket of admission, you don't have to have gone to this school for this many years and waited these many years until you could, " take the test." You can take the test, meaning jump into the market, the day you start!

Paul, speak more to me about why you believe, so strongly, in direct sales and network marketing.
Anyone can show up and join, and these are new rules—the person who recruits you for network marketing doesn't make money until you make money.

Because that's the way network marketing and the new rules work, primarily promoted by the direct selling association and good companies worldwide. They don't allow people to make money just signing up people or taking their life savings from them to start a new business.

Another reason I like network marketing so much is the training. I was discovered by the network marketing industry in 1989 when I wrote Unlimited Wealth and started doing research and started giving speeches for network marketing companies. Now I hear from people who heard me speak back then.

One type of people I meet say, "Paul, I heard you speak about unlimited wealth years ago and that made me leave my job and now I'm free and I want to thank you!"

The second type of people I meet—and I've been fascinated by this group, I've been doing a lot of research, and I've collected about ten of these people and I'm now analyzing them—are people who have become very rich and successful from what they learned in network marketing, but didn't do it in network marketing.

These are people who got into network marketing and for the first time somebody told them about what's possible for them. Somebody retooled them, in effect, from whatever their lifelong problems were; whether it was overcoming their shyness, teaching them how to speak, or whatever. And for whatever reason they didn't "make it" in their network marketing business, but they took what they learned and who they had become and started a different business successfully.

Network marketing retools people. It's had an amazing, amazing effect on our U.S. economy.

Not just for the people that succeed in network marketing, but for the people that become better people, better

It's Time... for Network Marketing

residents of the planet, because now they know how to improve the world and they have the confidence to act.

Those tools come from being in a network marketing organization. Because, ultimately, that's what they really train, while of course they also train you on their specific product and service.

Paul, in Unlimited Wealth **you spoke about how, prior to 1990, fortunes were made in manufacturing and then a big shift came and fortunes were being made in distribution. Do you see a relationship between network marketing/direct selling and the distribution of information?**
You know, ultimately, information is the most valuable product, but at this point in our world economy, very few people have found the model that would optimize making money on the distribution of information.

The newspapers went online, but the moment they tried to charge fifty cents for a copy like they do when selling paper, people didn't want to buy it. Because there's another person in the world who will offer the information free online. So the distribution of information has not become that successful as a business model primarily because people are used to getting information for free and because in our competitive world there seems to always be a company who will take similar information and distribute it for nothing. The distribution of information for pay, direct by the user, is not currently a viable model.

Now, that said, the most successful company in the history of the world, which is far eclipsing Microsoft, is currently Google and Google is in nothing but the distribution of information business.

Google has found the model for distribution of information paid for by the person that supplies the information, but that also gives you free information.

By that I mean, when you do a search on Google, what distinguishes Google from all the other information sources is they give you what they call the links based on an algorithm of, roughly, the most popular links, under the theory that the most popular links are good because the most people are going to those links. But they also give you paid links on the right and top of the page, clearly identified as paid links. So Google has found the business of distribution of information that has clearly made it the most successful company in the history of the world.

Next point on Google— they have new search engine algorithms that are just coming out in this decade, they have phenomenal impact for network marketers. Specifically, one of the last things an individual entrepreneur couldn't do was buy a Super Bowl ad. Most can't afford the $3 million price tag, but even if you could run the ad, what would you do with eight million leads? You really only want one, two, three, four maybe ten to work on and then ten to follow up with when you're finished with the first ten. That's what Google does!

Google says, "Instead of charging you $8 million for the number one ad on the top of Google, for a period of time, maybe one second or one click, I'll put your name ($8 million translates to something like $1.20 an eyeball or an impression) up there for a price." So you tell Google you'll pay $1.30 or $1.40 for an impression. Or you tell them you'll pay $15 for ten clicks whenever someone enters your keyword, be that "vitamins" or "work from home" and you're okay about letting others buy a share of the clicks.

> You see what happens; you now have the same marketing/ advertising power as the person who can afford a Super Bowl ad but you've done it just by purchasing it per click.

And that is going to allow entrepreneurial businesses to take off in another huge way. And notice, this new technology like all the new technology, focuses on the individual, not the large organization. It's based on providing more tools and services to the individual in their own business.

Short-term, long-term, what do you see for the future of direct selling/network marketing?
I see direct selling as the main strength, or growth area. And direct selling meaning person-to-person education about products and services that will improve another person's life.

I see that growing exponentially from where we've been, even though we've had exponential growth in the industry, because there's a backlog in the technological world, because we're still inventing far more products and services, from biotechnology to better ways of teaching people with educational tools, than we have ways of distributing them.

And because that bottleneck is increasing, that will increase direct sales, because direct sales is currently the best method we have in our economy of efficiently educating people about products and services that will improve their lives.

So I consider direct sales in any method to be growing at a very, very great level. Network marketing, or how you recruit the people for direct sales, or multilevel marketing is the compensation method and for now that seems to be the best way for recruiting other people into the network.

> But that also may change. We may see large direct sales companies in the future, where we use mass media to recruit people.

The market will determine the best way to recruit people, but it's the direct selling—that the ultimate product is distributed by one person who uses the product, who is talking to another person about the product—that's the core strength I see in network marketing or direct selling that's going to grow exponentially.

So you see a bright future and lots of new millionaires in network marketing/direct sales.
Right! And we've also just so expanded the playing field. Today you might be sitting in America talking to someone in Taiwan. You are able to build and manage an organization from anywhere in the world. Today companies really are international for the individual distributor, when you look at just the communication costs alone.

Is there anything you see, Paul, which we should be doing that we're not doing?
I'd like to say, things you could do better. And that's a different response for each company. Every network marketer himself, as well as every company, can probably do things better.

> Generally I would say all of us, including myself, can retool ourselves more frequently.

In my book, Unlimited Wealth, I say that every six months you've got to stop and look at your computer, look at your method and ask yourself, "Is this the best way to keep going?"

Today, you no longer can wait six months to reexamine your service. You've got to wait, maybe, three months, maybe only one month. Just because you bought something new doesn't mean there might not be a better one or a better way a month or two down the road. We need to accelerate the time and analyze what we're doing on a more frequent basis because technology is changing faster. And all of us can do that now.

> We can all take more time away from

It's Time... for Network Marketing

> what we're doing to ask ourselves if there is a better method to do what we are doing.

I think what I'm probably most excited about with network marketing is that point I brought up about how I'm meeting people today who succeeded in network marketing and were introduced or motivated by me fifteen years ago, as well as meeting people who have succeeded outside the network marketing field by using the information they gained from network marketing.

> I've come to realize that what direct selling is really about is changing people's lives and reeducating people into doing something they never believed they could do.

> More than any other industry, direct selling/network marketing is about changing people's lives from whatever position they are in life to something better; it improves their marriages, it improves their relationships with their children, and of course, it greatly improves their ability to do business.

Even if that business is outside network marketing! And that's where I look back and say, "I'm really proud to be associated as an educator in this industry."

I get up and speak, people listen, initially thinking they are going to become a better distributor of their weight loss product because of listening to Dr. Pilzer, but ultimately they become a better person. Because someone is giving them the confidence to believe they can change. Network marketing is the one area that just parades people in front of others as living examples of what can change for the better.

Paul Zane Pilzer is a world-renowned economist, multimillionaire entrepreneur, college professor, keynote speaker and the author of five best-selling books including Other People's Money, Unlimited Wealth, The Theology of Economics: God Wants You To Be Rich, The Next Trillion, The Wellness Revolution and The Next Millionaires.

He lives with his wife and four children in Utah, where they are avid snowboarders, mountain bikers, and chess players.

To learn more about Paul Zane Pilzer, please visit his website at http://PaulZanePilzer.com.

The Next Millionaires, by Paul Zane Pilzer, is published by Momentum Media (2006), a division of Video Plus, 200 Swisher Rd. Lake Dallas, TX 75065. Contact Reed Bilbray: 1-800-752-2030, via email: rbilbray@VideoPlus.com

MIKE POTILLO

The Key to Success

You've got to have a coach, mentor, or guide to teach you exactly what to do to build a thriving, long-term, international network marketing organization. There is no other way.

I've eaten ramen noodles—for weeks. I've slept on an air mattress—for months. I've driven 1000s of miles to attend a meeting—one person showed up. I went broke—twice. All because of network marketing.

So why in the world would I... could I... do I... think that network marketing is the most remarkable and the greatest opportunity in the whole world?

Very simple. All those bad things happened to good ol' me because I tried to do network marketing alone, all by myself, on my own. Hey, I'm a big boy and a smart guy. I didn't need anybody else.

Wrong!

I didn't have a coach, mentor, or guide to teach me exactly what to do to build a thriving, long-term, international network

It's Time... for Network Marketing

marketing organization.

Well, I've got to tell you, once I figured this ball game out, I went from struggling in the minor leagues of networking to major league network marketing success, OVERNIGHT!

How did I do this?

I started listening to the real deals, the authentic, intelligent, sincere, and serious people who were actively building thriving network marketing businesses in TODAY'S marketplace.

Methods, tools, and techniques change, but the essential core principles on HOW to build this business always stay the same.

I learned exactly how to get the hype and hustle out of the way and laser focus in on what to do... what to say... and how to say it.... And that has not only made me a fortune, but it's making fortunes right now for the 1000s of people in business with me around the world.

I believe network marketing is so remarkable because...

It's the only business I know of where you start with dimes and turn them into dollars, literally and figuratively overnight.

It's the only business where you can simply do a couple things right consistently over a short period of time and have long-term success.

Here's the thing that's amazing to me: If you get your "mind" right, you can make a fortune in network marketing.

All you need (as in it's required, mandatory, a must-have) is a coach, someone that's actively and successfully building their business today. He or she can show you exactly how to build your business and "compress the success" time frame for you. Someone who can show you the REAL things you need to get right BEFORE you start actually building your business.

Let me tell you a quick story.

I was having a cup of coffee with a new affiliate on my team, and the questions started flying. What do I do first? Where do I find people? How do I prospect on the phone? How do I achieve the goals I have set?

All great questions, but I had to stop him because we had to cover the first things first.

> The secret to success in network marketing doesn't lie in any of that. The secret lies in YOU and how you program your mind for prosperity.

Sounds hokey, right? It's not.

I used to think that if I could just get a couple of things going right in my business, everything would be OK and success would just... POOF... happen. Well, I got those things right, and guess what? It didn't.

Then I finally found someone who told me the truth about how to be successful in network marketing.

I changed my thinking. I started reading the right books, getting around the right people, putting pictures of my goals all around the house, and I started programming my mind for prosperity on a daily basis. Guess what happened then? Everything else just fell into place. Now, isn't that interesting....

It's Time... for Network Marketing

Before all the retailing, prospecting, and sponsoring starts, we must get ONE main thing straight:

Your business will never grow larger than you do.

Repeat that, please.

Your business will never grow larger than you do.

Sound funny? It's a fact, and if you really want to build it big, you just have to get comfortable and committed to that statement.

Find somebody in YOUR COMPANY that is having success with a their system. Go see them—right away. Fly there, drive there, I don't care HOW you get to them, but go see them now.

Camp out on their doorstep... spend a weekend... sleep in the garage, mow the lawn, do their laundry—do whatever it takes to have that person help you put together a game plan for YOUR business.

That's the key. There isn't any other. That's the one that unlocks the door to success.

Network marketing can truly be remarkable for EVERYONE, if they just find the right person to help them achieve their dreams.

Mike Potillo is an international major league networker and the author of the Major League Networking Newsletter and the creator of the NEW audio series How to Go from Minor League Networking to Major League Networking.

Mike says, "It's, not the money, but the person you become... not the 'things,' but the people you can help... and last but not least, not making the sale once, but doing it right one time and getting paid over and over and over."

To learn more about Mike, visit his website at: http://MikePotillo.com.

PAULA PRITCHARD

Stay the Course Long Enough to Discover the Magic for Yourself

Years ago, I uncovered four levels of what I call 'pursuit' in network marketing. Each one leads to greater appreciation and a higher consciousness: Money, Freedom, Helping People, and Changing the World.

William Barclay said, "There are two great days in a person's life; the day we are born and the day we know why."

For me, I thought my why was to teach the teachers in order to impact more students. That is why I pursued a career at Kent State University. I was partly right. My why was to teach the teachers, but little did I know it was in this amazing, crazy world of network marketing. I know in my heart that I was always destined to be here. It is the one place I always felt I truly belonged.

Network marketing for me was no cakewalk. Anyone who knows my story knows how much I struggled the first fifteen months.

But when I finally cracked the code, I was unstoppable.

It's Time... for Network Marketing

The pursuit was always exhilarating, and over the years I learned to identify and experience the different levels of achievement; I discovered how each one would take you to an even higher level of maturity and understanding of how truly miraculous network marketing really is.

Few people actually stay the course long enough to discover the magic of this business, but once they do, they will never contemplate doing anything else.

Years ago, I actually uncovered four levels of pursuit in network marketing; each one led to a higher consciousness and a greater appreciation. The first was all about money.

> When I figured out how to build a network marketing business, I was passionate about paying off my bills, getting a new car, building a house, and doing things for my family. I quadrupled my teaching salary. I was on fire.

After my financial needs were met, I moved into level two, which was the pursuit of freedom. There's no question that teaching at a university is a fairly free existence. I like change, so teaching new students every ten weeks, with a break in between for good behavior, was about as close to perfect as a job could be for me.

But the idea of being totally free and never using an alarm clock again was extremely appealing. Most people never contemplate being totally free. It is an amazing existence to be able to live where you want to live and do what you want to do.

We live in a free society, but until you are financially free, you are never truly free. Someone decides where you live, since it must be close to your job. The size of your house, the schools

Stay the Course Long Enough to Discover the Magic for Yourself

you send your children to, the vacations you take, and the length of time you are away—all of this is dictated by your location and the size of your paycheck. Your life is controlled by your job.

Being totally financially free means you can live in any state, in any house, vacation where and when you want, and send your children to the college of their choice. The pursuit of freedom is a worthy goal.

The third level of pursuit is the most exhilarating.

Once I had made enough money to be free, helping others do the same became my focus.

> Helping other people change their lives and reach their goals is so much more rewarding than anything you do for yourself.

Many of you will not believe me until you've experienced it.

I have helped people leave unpleasant jobs, move away from unpleasant circumstances, and take control of their lives all because of network marketing. I've had the opportunity to watch people change their attitude, their self-esteem, and become believers in their own gifts. Many of them have gone on to become leaders, motivational speakers, and successful business owners. Many became millionaires. Because of network marketing, I have friends all over the world.

One particular case is near and dear to my heart. Years ago, I spearheaded a company into Europe. While in England, I called a friend named Laura to see if she would be interested in working with a new company. I was unaware of the fact that she had purchased a beautiful home and had become financially drained after a divorce.

The same day I called, she had just received a letter from the bank suggesting that she file for bankruptcy. She was extremely distraught and didn't want to. We decided her only option was for us to roll up our sleeves and build this new business together.

Within that year, she became the first person in Europe to make it to the top position with that company. Within eighteen months, she was highlighted in a major newspaper as one of the top 100 women income earners in the United Kingdom. She was number seventy. We were totally blown away.

> It was one of the most exciting accomplishments in my network marketing career. It was much bigger than anything that I had ever accomplished just for myself.

The fourth level of pursuit is pretty lofty and revolves around the essence of network marketing as the leading edge of free enterprise.

Network marketing has the ability to change people—to change the way they think and the way they act.

I have seen network marketing create amazing teamwork, camaraderie, and esprit de corps among individuals working together to reach their common goals.

I have seen network marketing unite cultures and help people rise above race, gender, social, economic, and political differences.

I have seen network marketing create hope and optimism and empower people to take control of their lives.

Stay the Course Long Enough to Discover the Magic for Yourself

Network marketing is a gift, and in the right hands, it can change the world. I know this from firsthand experience.

In 1994, I was on my way to Paris, France, to speak at the launch of an American network marketing company. A couple days before the launch, I was doing a meeting in Antwerp, Belgium. At the conclusion of the meeting, I was told that there was a gentleman waiting in the lobby who wanted to speak to me. I will never forget his story.

He was Croatian, and it was during the time when there was a war in his country between the Serbs and the Muslims. He was involved in another network marketing company, and he was looking at joining our company.

He proceeded to tell me about an organizational meeting that he had attended a few nights before in order to recognize and congratulate one of his distributors on their advancement. This meeting was in Croatia, where he had to cross a border and risk his life to enter into a very dangerous part of the country. Snipers were killing people there every day.

The meeting was held in the basement of a house in the war zone. Everyone that attended was risking their lives. Every day, they were smuggling their products across the border to build their businesses. But what was amazing was that at this meeting there were Serbs and Muslims, all sponsored by one another and all hugging and congratulating each other.

What a paradox:

Outside, there was war, hate, and destruction. Inside, there was peace, love, and harmony... and it was because of network marketing.

It's Time... for Network Marketing

I saw clearly at that moment that this business was about so much more than just money. It was about bringing people together. It was about an unselfish commitment to help someone else become successful. It was about looking for the good in one another instead of the bad. It was about free enterprise and helping to change the financial status of one family, then two, then three. It was about bridging the gap between different cultures, religions, and ethnic backgrounds.

For the first time, I truly saw what an impact network marketing could have around the world.

And today, when I think about singing the praises of network marketing, I think about that Croatian man and his sacrifice to fulfill a dream. Then it becomes really clear. To those that embrace the power of network marketing, it ceases to be a business. To them, it becomes their life, and their life is magic.

Paula Pritchard was pursuing her doctorate degree while teaching at Kent State University when she was introduced to Amway. Out of a million distributors at the time, Paula was the first single woman in the United States to reach the coveted Diamond level. Since Amway, she has risen to the highest possible position and income levels with a number of network marketing companies, building organizations of over 200,000 distributors, in more than fifteen countries, producing hundreds of millions of dollars in business. Because of her success, Paula has also consulted with both established and new network marketing companies in both the United States and Europe.

As one of the most consistent top performers in network marketing, Paula has proven time and time again that her business building methods work. Her techniques for building large successful organizations have created many successful leaders in the industry and have been well documented in her book Owning Yourself and the CD audio training series What You Need to Know to Build a Profitable Network Marketing Business. Today Paula is known worldwide as one of the top network marketers, trainers and leadership developers. Additional information is available on her website at: http://MLMMadeSimple.com.

a conversation with **BOB PROCTOR**

The Network Marketing Success Puzzle

You've got to love helping people. You've got to love helping people realize their dream and understand that they are capable of achieving their dream in network marketing.

Bob, why is success in this business a puzzle for most people?
The puzzle exists in the fact that people know what to do and they don't do it, and they don't know why. There are two areas of the mind. The educated or intellectual side of the mind knows what is required to be successful in network marketing. But that isn't the side of the mind that controls our behavior. The side of the mind that controls our behavior is not programmed for success with a network marketing model.

We're programmed genetically and environmentally. Paradigms are not just a buzzword. Paradigms are really the cause of all kinds of problems for all kinds of people. Paradigms are nothing but subconscious conditioning. We're conditioned genetically—that's why we look like our relatives—and then we're conditioned environmentally by the people that surround us in our little life.

We've moved into a new economy. Network marketing is truly the

> distribution system of the new economy-there's no favoritism, there's no nepotism.

In the old economy there was waste, favoritism, and nepotism; therefore the cost of doing business skyrocketed. It had to come to an abrupt halt.

But in this new economy, we are working with the wrong programming. We're living in a different world; the Internet has changed our world... that little chip has altered the world we're moving in and if we don't adapt to the new world... we're sunk.

So what are some of the pieces that put the puzzle together, Bob?
First of all, I think the major understanding is that givers gain. The law says, "as you sow so shall you reap." Whatever you give, you're going to get. Well, there are people out trying to get somebody into the business; they're trying to get a bigger check, and they're not going to win.

> You have to literally fall in love with the idea of network marketing! It's one of the most phenomenal concepts I have ever seen in my entire life!

You've got to love helping people. You've got to love helping people realize their dream and understand that they are capable of achieving their dream.

Now I know you hear this all the time, but in most cases it's shallow rhetoric; there's no real energy behind it. You hear people say, "I really love giving," but the truth is they are trading, they're not giving at all.

A person is an expression of the Universe. You're dealing with the Universe, you're not dealing with John, you're not dealing with Bob, you're dealing with the Universe and when you put good energy out (and you can put it out all kinds of way, it might be a thought, word or an action, but it's good energy out) the Universe will always send it back! It has no choice in the matter! That's the law of our being.

So, you give to get... what else with network marketing?
In network marketing, most people coming have an employee consciousness. In network marketing, you're an entrepreneur. As an employee, somebody tells you what time you have to go to work, and so you go.

In network marketing nobody says you have to go to work. You have to make the choice yourself, and most people make the wrong choice. They're really up to date on The Price Is Right or Wheel of Fortune or what's going on in the news, but they're not disciplining themselves to work consistently for a certain period of time. The wild part about this is, if you only put in a small amount of time, but you do it consistently, and you only follow through on certain suggestions consistently, the success that you can achieve will be way beyond your wildest dreams.

What else do we need to change from the employee mindset to the entrepreneurial mindset?
I don't think it's that there is so much to change; it's putting in the time to change it. We're programmed along a certain line of learning and we never really learn that much, we gather information. But if people would have learned more, they would have demonstrated it in their results.

My life changed like night and day. It was shocking to me and everyone who knew me. My income went from $4000 to $175,000 and then to over a million, and I really didn't know what I was doing. It took me nine years, but I did very well at it. Now, I was reading the same book every day and I am still reading it... it is sitting right in front of me. It's Napoleon Hill's book, Think and Grow Rich, and I've been reading it all this time. Then I got a hold of Earl Nightengale's condensed narration of the book and that led me into other recordings that he had and I would listen to them over and over. I literally got to the point where I could go word for word with Nightingale on that record.

And you know what? This didn't make any sense any sense to me, didn't make sense to anyone who knew me. They thought, "He's listening to some guy on a record who is saying the same thing over and over—he's really losing it!" I made everyone listen to it every morning and some people began to hate me for it. But they also got reprogrammed.

It's repetition that programs us, and it's repetition that will change the programming.

The problem is that it is totally illogical. We've been programmed to read a book once and put it away. Maybe we read a paragraph out of it a couple of times, but logic would say, "You've already listened to it; you already know it, so why would you want to or need to listen to it again?"

It's the "un"-logical, it's the uncommon thing, that changes the paradigm. And if a person doesn't change their paradigm when they come into network marketing they are going to be miserably disappointed. Napoleon Hill calls it the graveyard of dead hopes and the front porch of opportunity, and you know something? It's both!

So what other paradigm changes do we need to make to be successful in this business?
One of the first paradigm changes we have to make is how to change a paradigm. Learn what a paradigm is and gain an understanding of what it is and why we do what we do.

If you had someone follow you and had them log or journal every move you make, and maybe record everything you say, you would discover that almost everything you do you are unconscious of doing, you just automatically do it. When we sit down to eat we don't ask ourselves, "Hmmm, how am I going to get that into my mouth?" We just automatically start to shovel it in.

We have to learn how to focus on what we are doing, and we've got to understand why we are doing what we're doing. We've got to see the power of paradigms. They control our life!

And changing paradigms requires....?
It requires understanding. We have to understand the mind and how it works. Most people say, "Well I read those books. I understand all that." Listen, I talked to a man this morning, he's in network marketing and he is earning nothing, nothing! He's been in it for about five years. His wife works and earns around $75 - $100,000.00 a year, and he's asking me what he has to do.

I said, "Tell your wife to quit work!"

And he remarked, "Well, I don't want to go right into the deep with this."

So I said, "No, you want to sit home and play around worrying about what other people think, while your wife keeps you. You have to look at the reality of this until you get so disgusted with what you're doing that you will change your paradigm."

This is a true story. He's a nice guy. He's a bright guy. But you know what he's concerned with? He's concerned with what other people think when he phones them and they find out it is network marketing.

> I told him he wants to be so darned excited when they ask him if it's network marketing he'll shout, " YES! Yes, it is!"

That is exciting! And if somebody starts to laugh at you, just say, "Wait just a minute. Do you understand it? Explain it to me. Because if you don't understand it, then you're advertising your ignorance."

We are programmed to be concerned with what other people think. When we were little kids, doesn't matter what we did, the concern was, "What would the neighbors think?" Well, I found out what the "neighbors" think... they don't! Terry Cole-Whittaker wrote a great book entitled, What You Think of Me Is None of My Business.

I gave this man a question: "To respect and love me, who would I really have to be?" Then I told him to sit down and write out an affirmation:

"I am so happy now that I am _____"

And then, staying in present tense, write out who you would have to be. Then I said, "Go and BE that person."

Bob, how do you go "be that person'? It's very simplistic without adding, "and here's how you do that."
If a person is a mature individual, and they're not earning what they want to earn, they're not living the way they want to live and they're unhappy... what is their problem? It s how they see themselves.

If you're not doing a good job, if your wife or husband is 'keeping' you, you can't really respect yourself. And if you don't respect yourself you sure aren't going to love yourself. To respect and love me who do I really have to be? That runs very deep!

> We think in pictures, and we have a picture of ourselves that is programmed into the subconscious mind. It's our self image.

Maxwell Maltz in Psycho-Cybernetics said it was the greatest discovery of his generation.

To respect and really love yourself, who would you have to be? Write out a description of that person and then be that person. That's not going to be an easy thing to do.

That's what I was addressing, Bob. How do you go about being that person?
An hour at a time, a day at a time, because, you see, if I'm concerned with what you think of me, then I'm lost. I have to be concerned with what I think of me. And I better really like me because I only have one life.

> This is about lifestyle and I want to enjoy this one life. I want to enjoy my family, I want to enjoy my health, I want to enjoy wealth, I want to enjoy my work, and I want to enjoy my day!

If I don't love and respect me, I'm not going to enjoy much of anything. And I think there are a lot of people running around in network marketing that fall into that category. It's too bad, because they don't have to be there.

The beautiful truth is in network marketing you can change on a dime! I don't have to satisfy somebody I'm working for and be on probation for six months. I can change right now. I don't need anybody's permission, I don't need anybody's approval and if I change right now, I'm going to be compensated immediately for it; both from a psychic and a material perspective.

So, are there any other "to do" action steps? The hour a day one day at a time?
Napoleon Hill said, "You've got to have a definite purpose." Your purpose is why you're living. Then you have to have a vision of how you are going to execute your purpose. A vision as a long range view of a multiplicity of goals. The further you go down the road the wider it becomes and the more beautiful it becomes. When you've got the vision, then you set a goal.

It's Time... for Network Marketing

The goal is to take the first part of the journey and commit to it.

Bob, what's the best thing about network marketing?
The best thing to me is its openness, its inclusiveness. It's not exclusive it's inclusive; everyone can be a part of it. There is no discrimination.

There is always something we can give. There is always something we can do. In The Science of Getting Rich, Wallace D. Wattles says, "Leave everyone with the impression of increase." It doesn't matter who you come in contact with, make sure their life is a little better because you've come in contact with them. There are so many ways we can do that.

And you don't share in order to get something back. You do it to help someone. The Universe will reward you because it all comes back. So another thing you can share is that network marketing is open. And it's open to everyone. We should understand that and mention it to as many people as we can.

Bob Proctor, is a speaker, author and coach, and for forty years he has focused his entire agenda around helping people create "lush lives of prosperity, rewarding relationships and spiritual awareness."

In 1960, Bob was a high-school dropout with a resume of dead-end jobs and a future clouded in debt. One book was placed in his hands—Napoleon Hill's Think and Grow Rich. In just months, and with further support from the works of Earl Nightingale, Bob's life literally spun on a dime. In a year, he was making more than $100,000, and soon topped the $1 million mark.

Bob went to work for his real-life mentors, Earl Nightingale and Lloyd Conant. After rising to the position of Vice President of Sales at Nightingale-Conant, he established his own seminar company. Bob Proctor now travels the globe, teaching thousands of people how to believe in and act upon the greatness of their own minds.

You can learn more about Bob Proctor's live seminars, best-selling books and recordings at his website here:
http://BobProctor.com.

LORNA RASMUSSEN

What if...

> network marketing is the absolute best way for women to take control of their lives, to be there for their families and their communities, and most importantly, to be valued for who they are and what they bring to the table?

Perhaps you have, like me, asked the question "What if..."

What if I had said yes?
What if I had accepted their offer?
What if I had started earlier?

Life is filled with "What ifs." These are usually idle speculation or musings over lost opportunities. However, my "What if..." was about an opportunity I HAD taken. I wondered aloud what would have happened if I hadn't. "What if I had not joined a network marketing company twelve years ago? What if, like my husband, I still ran a traditional business, or worse yet, had a job?"

Those "What ifs..." were prompted by a situation that no one ever thinks will happen to them—a fire that destroyed my home and all its contents along with my home office. Two weeks later my husband's business partner of nineteen years decided he wanted out of the partnership, and a month after that, we were putting my husband's mother in a nursing home and attempting to figure out how to get my son qualified and off to college.

> What if I hadn't decided to take an honest look at network marketing and give it a try?

What if I had not stuck through the challenges of starting in a new industry, learning a whole set of new skills, and going through the trials that eventually led me to success?

What if I had turned my back on an industry I once thought of as beneath me?

I had always been enterprising and hardworking. I had taught at a number of prestigious colleges, I had run my own film production business, and I had bought a training franchise. I had, in other words, tried every way possible to make a living. I was successful (my walls were decorated with my awards), but I had never made the money I wanted and felt that I deserved. On top of that, I seemed to be working all the time. As I grew older (moving into my early 40s), I began to think that I would never be able to retire and if forced to stop working, I dreaded the lifestyle awaiting me.

> But twelve years ago, I finally looked at the business of network marketing and to my surprise, found everything I was looking for.

I felt, eventually, that I had found the absolute best way in the world for women to make money. I felt I had found the solution to the balancing act I had tried to manage as a wife, mother, and business owner.

I immediately saw that there was an opportunity to make as much or more than I had ever earned before. And finally, I saw a way to make a good living while having the time to enjoy it. I could also see that the leverage it created—coupled with the power of residual income—would eventually allow me retire in comfort.

While I mainly saw men in the leadership roles, I truly saw this as a business that solved a lot of issues for women. Growing up during the early days of the women's movement, I thought that I was going to have it all—a family, a career, a great lifestyle. But I didn't have a clue how to achieve it. Traditional business, the corporate world, and even academia did not allow for the flexibility I needed to have a family. I waddled into class just a week after delivering my son via a C-section, because I was afraid I would be fired if I didn't show up. I often found myself faced with a choice between a great job and looking after my child. Even when my husband and I ran a company together, somehow an unequal portion of the household tasks landed in my lap. I didn't mind them—I just couldn't figure out how to manage them and my work outside the home. One or the other was always being shortchanged.

Finally, I saw a business that I could work around my family and my life, instead of trying to make my life fit into the needs of my business.

> And it paid me what I was worth! It paid me for exactly what I put into it. It paid me for the skills I developed and, best of all, it paid me for helping others.

Suddenly, I found myself earning double what I had ever earned, and then doubling that. One day, my company sent me a congratulatory letter saying I was being honored for having earned over a hundred thousand dollars in one year. And I had earned it from home, "part-time."

I had earned it while attending outings with my son and taking time to visit my family over 3,000 miles away.

I had earned it while looking after my needs and making certain that we had a comfortable home to live in.

I had earned it without sacrificing either myself or my family.

And I had earned it without stepping on the backs of others. Indeed, I had earned it because I had helped others earn a good living and improve their situations.

> But the real test of my networking business came when I lost my home. Had I been in one of those traditional businesses or worked at a job for someone else, it is clear to me I would have lost one or the other.

Or worse, I would have lost my mind.

Instead, I stopped working completely for more than three months. I devoted every day to solving the numerous problems we faced as a family. I had to buy and replace everything we owned, I had to set us up in temporary housing, and I had to fight the insurance company to give us what was fair. I did all this while dealing the emotional stress that such a trauma causes.

> I did the lion's share of the work because my husband owned a traditional business, and he had to go back to work or risk losing everything he had worked for. I did the lion's share because I could.

When things were reasonably settled, I returned to work my business on a part-time basis, mostly supporting the work that was being done by my team. For eleven months, I simply held on and my business continued to pay us, even more than it had paid us when I was working full-time.

In the final analysis, when I thought about what might have happened if I had not built a successful network marketing business, I was left with a great feeling of having done the right thing for myself and for my family.

I had no idea when I made the decision to enter the industry twelve years earlier that it would be so critical to my future.

I had no idea that it would save me from bankruptcy and allow me to end up in a better situation.

I had no idea that it would be such a perfect match for my talents and abilities.

> All I knew was that I had tried everything else, and nothing else was working for me as a woman and as a wife and mother.

There is no glass ceiling in network marketing.

There is no one telling you to sacrifice your children in order to get ahead professionally, or to sacrifice your career to have children.

There is no one telling you how hard you have to work, or what they will pay you for the job.

> For the first time in my life, I felt the freedom to name my price and achieve it within my time frame.

It's Time... for Network Marketing

If my family needed me, as they did last year, I was free to be where I was needed for as long as I was needed.

I believe that network marketing, as a profession, is the absolute best way for women to take control of their lives, to be there for their families and their communities, and most importantly, to be valued for who they are and what they bring to the table.

I remember telling my husband about my day one evening at the dinner table. When I finished my excited recounting of what I had done, his only comment was "Wow, someone has made a business just for you." And he was right, to a point.

It is the perfect business. Except "someone" didn't make it for me. I did.

Lorna Rasmussen, is a Platinum Jacket and Six Figure Ring Earner with Pre-Paid Legal Services. She began her professional life as an award-winning documentary film producer. Lorna taught at universities in Canada and the USA and ran a commercial film production company with her husband, George Hornbein. She is the co-author of a book about women's history; a contributor to Build it Big, a how-to book by the Direct Selling Women's Alliance and co-author of the recently released Absolute Best Way in the World for Women to Make Money.

To learn more about Lorna, visit her website at:
http://AbsoluteBestWay.com

KIMBERLY RHODES

A Level Playing Field and a Great Game to Play

This country was built on free enterprise, and that is what MLM offers. Network marketing is more consistent with the original 'American Dream' than just about anything else you can do to make a living and a life.

MLM legend Mark Yarnell says that network marketing is "the greatest opportunity in the history of capitalism." I couldn't agree more. In this business, you can truly have many of the things the corporate world promises, but rarely delivers: From work/life balance to full and fair compensation and the feeling of accomplishment and satisfaction you get as a result of your efforts and creativity.

I've spent a fair amount of time in corporate America. I had a career that was even rewarding at times, but there were always several things that left me knowing there was more to life.

Whether it was the glass ceiling, the politics, discontented coworkers... there were always reminders that this looked nothing like the "American Dream" I grew up believing in.

Network marketing offered me the three things I yearned for

that no other job could guarantee me:

- A level playing field (no glass ceiling)
- The opportunity to create my own definition of success
- The opportunity to truly win by helping others

My female colleagues in the corporate world and I were forced to make hard choices between careers and families. Some women had even opted not to have a family at all in favor of pursuing what they thought would be rewarding careers.

It's like we are being punished for wanting success. The more we "go for it" in our careers, the more give up at home. It may be time with our spouses and children, missing private lessons, recitals, games, or not being able to prepare the kinds of meals we know our family should have.

Whatever it ends up being, we are faced with the decision to either have a great family life or a great career.

But network marketing gives us the amazing opportunity to have that wonderful family life and a rewarding career. Countless women have proved that this business provides an environment for them to truly reach their goals in a way that makes them happy, fulfilled, and balanced in all areas of their lives.

So many businesses today talk about providing a "level playing field," but MLM truly delivers on that promise—and not only for women, but for many men as well.

There is neither a glass ceiling nor are we bound to office politics or "the good old boy network." We are paid in direct proportion to our service, value, and the contribution we bring to each person we sponsor into the business. What's more, the entire MLM model is built on personal and professional development. So, the better you become as an individual and a leader, the more you are rewarded by your business success.

Another important benefit of network marketing of particular interest to women is that for once you get to design your business around your life, instead of the other way around.

> You can literally "tailor" your work to exactly what you want to put into it, what you want to get out of it, and how you want that to fit into the rest of your life.

If you choose to stay at home and raise your children, you can do that. If you only want part-time income to add to your household, you can do that. If you want a bustling business that makes a nice living, you can do that. And if you want to be a high-powered CEO running a multimillion-dollar company, you can do that as well.

What's best is that all of these options are available without you having to sacrifice your home life or being looked down upon for not being "ambitious" enough or "setting back the women's movement," simply because you want to be a mom—or even simply a stay-at-home woman (for all you single ladies).

> A network marketing career is all about having a CHOICE!

In addition to work/life balance and a pressure-free environment, there are so many other personal benefits of being a network marketer. One that matters most to me is that you get to design your business in keeping with your own personal values and beliefs. In corporate America, you may end up working for a company whose integrity and business practices are in direct conflict with what you believe is right.

In MLM, you can choose a company whose founders are

consistent with your beliefs and values. You can market a product or service that you truly believe offers great results. You may even choose a company because you are inspired by their mission. And best yet, you can choose to join AND recruit a team of business partners that you not only work with to become wealthy, but that you just flat-out enjoy being around.

Who could ask for more? But there IS more!

While the news media is filled with stories of jobs being downsized, CEOs jumping out with golden parachutes, and average employees' pensions being dismantled and disappearing... it might leave someone to think that all is doom and gloom.

That may be so with business as usual, but thousands of people every day are building what we call their " retirement insurance policy" using network marketing.

Do well here, and you'll be rewarded over and over. The luxury of leverage—residual income from compound effort—will always be a better deal than trading your time for dollars.

Women naturally like to work together on teams, and the collaborative culture of MLM provides an excellent forum for that.

This is why MLM is something that we just tend to be hardwired to do and do well, and for that reason, women make up nearly 80 percent of this business!

I love the fact that when I am working with a distributor on my team, I get what I want by helping them get what THEY want. That's true "win-win."

I love the opportunity that introducing someone to this industry provides me. People come to network marketing with their hopes and dreams in fragile glass jars. Often, their ability to dream has been shadowed by the disappointments they've had in life. However, there is no price you can put on the feeling you get when someone you introduced to this business has the light switch turned on.

> This is an industry that inspires and encourages you to become your best self and live your best life; when we all use our natural talents in a team environment with a common vision, magical things happen.

Everyone wins!

This country was built on free enterprise, and that is what MLM offers. Network marketing is more consistent with the original "American Dream" than just about anything else you can do, because it operates from the same premise that made our country great: Dig in your shovel right where you stand and create a life you love!

One remarkable woman who has done just that is my good friend Sharon. Before coming to network marketing, she was a divorced mother with four kids. She had spent ten years working in an advertising agency trying to reach the level of partner. Sharon was a six-figure income earner, and her job was 50 percent travel.

Although her career would be wonderful by most people's standards, it didn't measure up to Sharon's.

While she was on the road or in meetings, trying to provide her kids with a "good life," she was completely missing out on their lives.

It's Time... for Network Marketing

> Like many working mothers, Sharon justified the situation by promising that she would give them more quality time later, but in her heart she knew that she was missing out on her children's best years.

She had to choose between being a provider or being a mother who was there for her children. She desperately needed (and wanted) to do both, but she found that the corporate world did not provide the flexibility and freedom that would allow a woman to wear both those hats.

Then Sharon was introduced to network marketing.

At first, she worried about what her friends would think. She had spent years vying for partnership in a prestigious firm. How was she going to explain giving up her lofty corporate goals for MLM? Several people she knew actually thought she was going through a midlife crisis. Why would she give up a fabulous career to do some "pyramid thing?"

Despite the naysayers, Sharon made the decision to forego chasing the never-ending corporate carrot and build a part-time network marketing business.

What she found on the other side was literally everything her heart desired—the perfect balance between work and home.

> Sharon found a level playing field where no one could limit her level of advancement, and she was able to choose the life she wanted on her own terms.

She met other single mothers and began to share her vision.

A Level Playing Field and a Great Game to Play

These women related to her story, because it mirrored what so many of them had been through. Something clicked in Sharon that was literally like catching fire. She became passionate about helping other single moms use this business as a way to be at home with their children. It became her mission to help as many as she could to choose freedom.

As a result of persistent effort, extra money started to roll in from her MLM business. She took that as a supplement to her income and stopped taking on extra projects. Instead, she opted to start attending some of those events with her kids that had hurt her so much to miss out on earlier.

Sharon started to build a team of women who helped each other build their businesses, pick up one another's kids, and provide a complete "mom's" business network. They even took turns having sleepovers and parties for each other's kids!

They had done it! They were both moms and successful businesswomen by working cooperatively toward the true American Dream.

And Sharon had the opportunity and blessing of being the one who had originally offered the gift of freedom and choice to all of these women. Working together, they had literally changed each other's lives for the better forever.

This never would have happened in corporate America. Sharon was leading a team who created a blueprint for success, and she could choose to run as hard as she wanted, when she wanted, to obtain whatever level of success she wanted.

More importantly, Sharon was able to help numerous women just like her do the same thing.

It's Time... for Network Marketing

There was no job description, they worked when they wanted, and best of all, they were creating lifetime relationships that were helping their professional, financial, and social lives improve dramatically. And no one was changing the terms of success midstream, like so many experience in the corporate world.

Sharon found that her team was like a family. That was something she had never experienced before. The best part was that she did not have to sacrifice to have it.

After four years in network marketing, she replaced her six-figure corporate salary and left the advertising firm.

There are countless stories like Sharon's in network marketing. It's women like her—and like the woman who may be reading this—that makes network marketing the best game to play!

Kim Rhodes is an author, speaker, trainer, coach, and internet marketer. Her passion for helping women in business inspired her to create http://MLMSecretsForWomen.com.

Kim started her professional career in corporate sales over twenty years ago. She transferred her to the MLM industry and rose to the top levels in two companies. She currently is columnist for the Personal Wealthy Journal and the creator of http://IHateCorporateAmerica.com, a site developed for those who want to create passive income without a job. She's the author of Hey Boss You're Fired! 5 Actions Steps to Escape The Rat Race & Build Wealth From Home and contributing author to Buiding A Championsihp Sales Team. She lives in Pasadena, California.

KATHY ROBBINS

My Best Decision

Nineteen years ago I sold my ownership in an investment firm to my partner and left the business permanently for network marketing. It was the best decision I have ever made.

During my years as a financial planner, then as the manager of the tristate office of a national firm, and finally as the owner of my own investment firm, one of the hardest things I ever had to do was to sit across the table from an individual or couple and tell them they did not have the assets to accomplish their dreams.

Sometimes it was retirement; other times it was a new home, college education for a child, or a change in careers.

The standard cliché of financial planners is that these people didn't plan to fail... they failed to plan.

I found that that is not always the case.

Many did plan and worked hard to achieve those plans, but life got in the way. Someone lost a job, became sick, or simply didn't make the amount of money they needed to make their dreams a reality. For many, there is too much month left at the end of the money, no matter how hard they plan.

Network marketing is a perfect answer, whether for the young couple just trying to get ahead of today's bills or trying to find a way for one spouse to stay at home with the children, or for the baby boomer that now faces retirement with apprehension instead of anticipation.

I came to network marketing through a client, Paula Pritchard. She was already very successful in the network marketing business. Paula was unaware of the fact that while I had great success in the investment business, I did not enjoy it. I felt trapped.

I had a bachelor's degree in education and could not imagine where else I could go and make the kind of money I was making as the owner of an investment firm. I watched Paula for a number of months, I knew what she was making, and I became convinced that I could do what she was doing. I began part-time, as many others do, and in six months I was able to leave the investment business permanently.

It wasn't just my ability to leave a career I didn't enjoy that drew me to network marketing.

> It was all those people that I had sat across the table from and told they couldn't achieve their dreams. I saw network marketing as a solution for them.

Many people are unaware that this nation was founded and developed by individual entrepreneurs. We were a nation of small businesses and small farms. Each of these people took responsibility for their own success.

My Best Decision

Our current system of thousands of people working for large corporations has really only taken place in the last 100 years. When the shift from entrepreneur to employee occurred for large numbers of Americans, people typically went to work for one company and remained at that same company their entire career. That is no longer the case. Employees change jobs regularly; sometimes voluntarily, sometimes not.

Whenever you work for someone else, they control your destiny. Network marketing returns us to the world of entrepreneurship, self-responsibility, and control of our own destiny.

I find it amusing when someone talks about network marketing as if it is some small, little, somewhat "shady" business in which only losers become involved. People who believe that clearly have no understanding of the business as a whole.

The direct sales/network marketing profession is a $30 billion business in the US alone, with over 14 million people involved. Some people make little or no money, while others make better than six figures a month.

I know the second is possible, because I have done it. The first is also possible, because we are a business of independent contractors and there will always be a large percentage of people who simply cannot or will not do what it takes to be successful. In between, there are huge numbers of people who make a few hundred to a few thousand dollars every month.

> The business we developed generated $100,000 a month in earnings and created over $3 million in sales every month in our organization alone.

That is a small business, but not a little business.

As for the concept that network marketing is a little "shady"; there are people in every business that fit in that category. Think Enron. Think Wall Street. Think real estate, government, medicine, law... can you think of any business that doesn't have its share of unethical people?

Here's what I believe: There is no better way for a young couple, a single mother, a parent with college age children, or an individual ready for retirement to supplement their income and potentially build a full-time income with almost no risk than in network marketing.

The keys are finding a good company with a good product and a fair compensation plan that will be around to pay you long-term, and a commitment on your part to put the same focus and energy into your network marketing venture as you have in your full-time job.

What do you have to lose except a little time and money? Compare that to what you can gain:

Freedom from financial worry, a sense of self-respect and self-esteem, and the ability to help others find the same.

I will be forever grateful that Paula walked into my office and showed me a different path. I have traveled all over the world and lived a life I could only imagine. The same opportunity is available to you. You just have to reach out and grab hold and make it yours.

Kathy Robbins began her business career as a high school teacher. She loved teaching, but left to become a financial planner and later became the manager of a tri-state office for a national investment firm. When Kathy first took control of the office it was ranked 126th in the company. Eighteen months later it was number fifteen.

My Best Decision

While Kathy found financial success, she didn't have any time to enjoy it and lacked the freedom to travel.

In 1987 Kathy decided to pursue network marketing part-time. Eight months later, Kathy had replaced the six-figure income she was making in the investment business, and became a full-time network marketer.

You can learn more about Kathy and her work at: http://MLMMadeSimple.com.

TERESA ROMAIN

It's Not the "Big" Money. It's the "Little" Money...

Network marketing and direct sales offers an alternative way of life for anyone and everyone who is willing to let go of the 'victim mentality' and embrace their power to create a life experience for themselves that's fulfilling, free, and abundant.

What makes network marketing and direct selling great is that it gives people an opportunity (unlike any other I know of) to reclaim their power over their lives—especially financially—and to create the life experience that most fulfills them.

While it's true that every human being has the power to create the life they want—it's more difficult to recognize that potential when you're working 40-60 hours each week at a job that pays you a fixed salary or an hourly wage over which you have minimal control. When this is your reality, it's far too easy to get caught up in the "not enough money and time, too much work, and I better be happy with what I have" syndrome.

> When you are in a job where to a great degree someone else determines what you need to do, the hours you must work, and how much money you'll make- it's

> easy to feel powerless and fall victim (no pun intended) to what is known as a "victim mentality."

You may think you have no power or control, so you go along with life as it is and make the best of it and/or you blame others (your employer, the government, other people) for what's not working in your life. It's also easy to give up your dreams.

Network marketing and direct selling blow powerlessness and a "victim" mentality out of the water!

> Network marketing reawakens people to their dreams and desires, because it gives them a vehicle through which they can see how to make those dreams and desires a reality!

For a relatively small investment of your money, time, and energy, you can increase your income, become debt-free, and start "growing" money at a rapid rate! You can experience freedom and choice like you've never experienced before!

After all, you are the one who decides what you do or do not do with your business. You choose when and if you will work—as well as how many hours you'll work on your business.

You choose how fast or slow you want your business to grow.

You choose your own company from among the hundreds (even thousands) available to you.

You even get to choose the sponsor you work with.

> Bottom line, what makes network

It's Not the 'Big' Money. It's the 'Little' Money...

marketing direct selling great is that you're in " the driver's seat" of your own life and work!

You choose the actions you do or do not take, and thus, you are ultimately and completely accountable for the results you have—and the life you live!

Granted, many network marketers and direct sellers still try to play the "victim game" when things aren't working out.

They'll blame their company or compensation plan.

They'll blame their upline or downline.

They'll blame their prospects or customers or the new product or the marketing materials...

And they can play this game all they want—but that's just what it is, a game.

It's a game, because what you can achieve in your business is 100% up to you.

It doesn't matter how much or how little you start with.

It doesn't matter if you're the first distributor in your company or the millionth—the same opportunity for greatness, prosperity, and abundance is available to you.

You've always had the power (even if you didn't recognize it) to create a life of maximum fulfillment and complete financial freedom. With network marketing and direct selling, you have the vehicle that makes this potential undeniable and 100% achievable!

Best of all, you don't have to make thousands and tens of

thousands of dollars each month to create this lifestyle, to fulfill your dreams, or even to experience financial freedom.

> What makes network marketing most exciting and empowering is that almost anyone- no kidding- who enters this business with the intention to experience greater fulfillment and freedom (especially financial) can do so.

For example, if you can make as little as $300-$500 profit each month in your business AND you are willing to learn some new ways for using that money (ways that are based on principles of abundance instead of scarcity), you can achieve financial freedom more rapidly and with greater ease than you may realize.

Consider that the average American household carries an outstanding credit card debt of roughly $8200. Add to that a couple of car payments, and a small $125,000 mortgage, and you—or any person in this industry—could easily have total personal debt of $150,000 (or more!).

Let's say that you are that "average American," and you've got a network marketing or direct selling business.

> Do you realize that if you build your business so that it generates $400 profit each month, you could use that to become completely debt-free (mortgage and all) in less than nine years?

In the process, you could save anywhere from $80,000 to $120,000 in interest!

Imagine that! Imagine the freedom, the ease, and the fulfillment you'd experience no longer having to worry about making your car payments or mortgage payments! Imagine how enthusiastic you'd be about your business!

Imagine the possibilities that would open to you and the prospects you'd be talking to!

For example, once you're debt-free, you could invest the money you had been paying towards debt (including the $400 you make in your business) and, over the next fifteen to twenty years, accumulate assets ranging from $750,000 to $1.3 million or more! That alone could give you a passive income (pretax) of $7,000 to $10,000 a month or more!

How's that for exciting?

Far too often, network marketers and direct sellers think that they need to make "big money" in order to live the life of their dreams and become financially free. While making "big money" is absolutely possible in this industry, what network marketing and direct selling does best is that it makes freedom (financial and otherwise) and unprecedented levels of fulfillment possible for everyone who's willing to invest a small amount of money, time and energy over a period of time.

Bottom line, network marketing and direct selling offers you an alternative way of life. It's available to anyone and everyone who is willing to let go of the "victim mentality" and embrace their power to create a life experience for themselves that's fulfilling, free, and abundant.

You have the power- and the opportunity- to access and experience more abundance than you might have

ever dreamed possible.

In the process, you'll discover that who you are is much more powerful and magnificent than you ever realized.

And that, my friend, is what makes network marketing and direct selling more than simply great—it makes it a great gift... for yourself and many, many others!

Teresa Romain is the founder of Access Abundance, an organization committed to transforming scarcity on all levels of life and work into truly abundant being, doing, and having in the World.

AccessAbundance offers a variety of excellent products, programs and both individual and team coaching, including the Access Your Abundance! Collection, Abundant! Network Marketing, Revitalized! Network Marketing and What If Money Really DOES Grow on Trees? Teresa also offers an abundant series of teleclasses, including: Money, Freedom & Abundance for Network Marketers! and her life- and business-changing LIVE! 3-Day Workshop, **Inside-Out Abundance!**

You can learn more about Teresa on her website at: http://AccessAbundance.com. And be sure to sign up for Teresa's free newsletter(s) when you visit her site.

Passive, Recurring Income and Leverage

Network marketing is the simplest and easiest way for the average person- the average person who has an above-average desire for positive change- to get into free enterprise, take control over their earning abilities, and start generating profits in a reasonable amount of time.

Let me tell you how I got here.

I'd just gotten home from a job I hated. From a commute I hated. To a house I hated.

And one too many times, I slumped down onto the couch, and I heard myself say, "Something's got to change."

I was living—with my wife and two kids—in a cinder-block house about twenty-five miles away from the town where I worked. We had one vehicle—a 1992 Mazda MPV minivan, which required timing belts and transmission work as often as oil changes.

Man, when my car broke down... my life broke down.

The last winter we lived there, I realized that I'd really messed up. We ran out of heating oil—does anyone remember heating oil?—and because I hadn't paid my bill from the previous year, they wouldn't bring me any.

So, for several weeks in a row...

> I would get up about an hour before my family, go to the kitchen and turn the oven on "broil" and leave the oven door open. That way the kitchen would be a bit warm when the kids got up to eat their cereal.

Later I found a propane camping stove in the basement that I would put in the bathroom each morning so that we could get ready without freezing to death.

Wow.

What a difference network marketing has made in just a few short years....

I'm writing this from the balcony of my room at the Hilton Waikoloa Village on the Big Island of Hawaii. We flew here a few days early, before our company event, and we'll stay a few days late. We chartered a yacht to do a sunset cruise. The boys want to do a helicopter tour of the volcano and swim with the dolphins.

And, if you'd told me way back then that I'd be writing a chapter in a John Milton Fogg book while looking at a Hawaiian sunset... well, suffice it to say that I would've asked what you were smoking. And if you'd told me that I would have just spent more on first-class airfare than I used to earn in six-to-eight months, I would've called you a liar. (I believed that first class was for idiots who were willing to pay more to get there ten seconds faster. Boy, did I have a lot to learn.)

So, how does network marketing work such magic?

The answer is two terms that every networker marketer knows and loves: passive, recurring income and leverage.

Network marketing offers you the unique ability to get paid over and over for work you've done once... and the ability to earn that same kind of income from the efforts of others as well.

The fact is that the twenty-four-hour day is "The Great Equalizer."

We all get the same twenty-four hours. It's what we DO with those twenty-four hours that determines whether we get rich.. or whether we go broke.

Network marketing is the simplest and easiest way for the average person—the average person who has an above-average desire for positive change—to get into free enterprise, take control over their earning abilities, and start generating profits in a reasonable amount of time.

All without having the huge start-up costs and hassles normally associated with traditional business ownership or franchising. Think about it: where else can the average person have the opportunity to earn an executive-level income by working from home? Without having to go to college for years, pile up tons of student loans, and climb a corporate ladder that they don't even enjoy?

And because of passive, recurring income and leverage—oh, my, I do love those words—you're not just working for a paycheck. You're building an asset that will continue to pay you for months and years to come.

> And it's not even about the money. It's about what's under the money... and that's freedom.

The ability to finally get enough money flowing into your life so that you can spend more time doing the things you want to do, when you want to do them... with the people you're in love with.

That is the real power of network marketing.

Last night, we were walking back to our room from a black-tie dinner and my sons (Will and Pate—Easton is too young to talk) both said, "Dad, thank you for making enough money so that we can come to places like this."

I was amazed. They're ten and eight, and they already notice that our lives are vastly different from those of their friends. When their friends are all going to local Myrtle Beach or Panama City for vacations, they're going to the Caribbean, Hawaii, or Sydney, Australia.

They notice that I'm the only dad on the field trips, and that unlike many of their buddies' fathers, I'm home when they wake up... and when they go to sleep. And they know that the only alarm clock we have is when they come running into our room and jump on the bed to play in the mornings.

What a great life this business has provided me!

> Network marketing is an opportunity to learn to live your life on purpose, so that your life is full of exciting possibilities that you create.. not just circumstances

Passive, Recurring Income and Leverage

that " happen to you."

I like what Richard Brooke once said: "Network marketing is a leadership factory disguised as a business opportunity."

Make no mistake about it: the money is important. The money is fun. (Whoever said that money doesn't buy happiness can't have had much of it.)

But, the real value of learning to create a large income in network marketing is what it will make of you to achieve it. Learn to earn $50,000 a month by working from home, and you'll find that obstacles in every other area of life just don't seem as large as they did when you were earning that much in a year.

I remember once hearing Bob Proctor ask, "What would your life look like if you turned your annual income into your monthly income?" I was stunned. Such a thing seemed too hard to even imagine. Was it possible? Were people doing this? Could I do it?

And the answer is "Yes, I can." And I did. And you can, too.

Network marketing is the greatest industry in the world. I believe it's given more hope and freedom to people than any other occupation. But remember this:

Network marketing is an opportunity, not a guarantee. Your results will be in direct proportion to your goals, your drive, and your persistence.

Let me close with this story from Earl Nightingale...

> A pastor was driving one day, and he saw a farmer tending a beautiful garden. He stopped to talk with the

275

farmer and asked for a tour. The farmer showed him the beautiful flowers, the bushes, the waterfalls, the landscaping, and all that the garden offered.

The pastor, not wanting the farmer to be prideful, would nod and smile and say, 'Yes, God had blessed you with a beautiful garden.'

Finally, the farmer looked at the pastor and said, 'Yes, God has given me a beautiful garden. And I'm very grateful. But you should have seen this place when God had it all to Himself."

The moral to Earl's story (as it applies to network marketing) is clear: Whether you're considering network marketing as a career or whether you're already involved and setting goals for a magnificent life...

Network marketing really IS the best opportunity in the world to create your life by design.

Millions have. I did. You can, too.

Tony Rush is a full-time, home-based entrepreneur living in southeast Alabama. He's one of the real characters of the home business industry, earns a significant six-figure income that he uses to indulge his passion for family travel. You can find him online offering practical, "what it really takes," nuts-and-bolts business-building strategies coupled with a keen understanding of the mindset that's required to attract abundance and prosperity into your life at http://TonyRush.com.

TIM SALES

Network Marketing Is an Organic Business

In the ideal network marketing model, one human being asks another human being what will help them- and then helps them achieve whatever it is they want. That's organic business- one human helping another.

Network marketing is an organic business.

The word organic means:

1. Simple, healthful, and close to nature
2. Resembling a living organism in organization or development; interconnected

The reason I have chosen to focus my life's efforts in network marketing is because I feel it's a true organic business. One human being helping another human being is as organic as it gets.

Why does food grow on planet earth, other than to help other life to grow?

Why are humans on planet earth, other than to help other life to grow?

There is only one real business on this

277

planet- the business of making someone's life better.

Let's imagine for a moment that you and I live on an island, just the two of us: I'm a fisherman; you're a farmer. One day I say to you, "If you pick a little extra corn today, I'll catch more fish, and we can exchange them with each other this evening. That way you don't have to eat only corn and I don't have to eat just fish."

Through that exchange, we've made each other's lives better.

Now, a new person comes to our island that can make shoes. He makes us both a pair of shoes, and we give him food in exchange. He's made our life better, and we've made his life better.

That's organic business—one human being helping another.

In the ideal network marketing model, one human being asks another human being what will help them- and then helps them achieve whatever it is they want.

I'm not talking about just getting the product they need, but the solution they're after. If a person wants to lose body fat, you don't just sell them a product. You keep working with the person until they lose the body fat they want to lose—that's real help.

If a person wants to spend more time with their family, you can help them spend more time with their family through helping them replace their income. If a person wants to achieve financial freedom, you can work with them to perfect their skills until they achieve financial freedom.

Network Marketing Is an Organic Business

In most situations I've experienced in my network marketing business, someone (the prospect) wants something that they can't get on their own. How do I know they can't get it on their own? Because if they could have, they would have. So, they need help—that's where I came in.

Normally it wasn't someone just needing a great business "vehicle"—they needed to develop their skills and sometimes learn completely new ones. This in turn caused me to have to learn how to train that new skill. I made their life better and they made mine better, because now I know a new skill, too.

And with each new person that I helped to develop skills, I got more wealth. That allowed me to contribute to various charity programs, like funding a medical team to go into Sir Lanka just after the tsunami, or donating to an organization that helped get over four million kids off drugs, as well as other large donations. See the cycle? People helping to make other people's lives better.

As I said, this is the ideal MLM model. It doesn't always happen this way.

Often network marketers (and all marketers) get caught up in profits and other distractions and forget what the basis of all business is about- helping people.

That is why I've devoted my life to helping the MLM industry.

I created a video to help people explain what this industry is, and what it's not. I created a training program to help people learn how to communicate better because, quite frankly, what else could limit someone's ability to market a product, a service, or a business other than poor communication?

It's Time... for Network Marketing

If you've chosen this great profession or are investigating it as a possibility, please decide the kind of person you want to be now. I recommend you be a person who keeps the real essence of business in front of you—helping people.

Also be a person who realizes there are some things you don't know—and be willing to study and perfect your skills.

I've observed that there's no such thing as a born leader, a born salesperson or a born public speaker. Just go into any maternity ward and try to select the baby who will be great at any of those things some day!

No, each of those professions (along with network marketing) involves using skills you need to get good at. Just get good at them, and by becoming good at them you will grow—organically.

And as you grow, the rewards will be remarkable.

I promise.

Tim Sales is an author, speaker, trainer and a six-figure monthly income earning leader in network marketing. In 1989, near the end of an eleven-year tour with the US Navy Underwater Bomb Squad Team, Tim answered an ad in the Washington Post newspaper that led him to his first and only network marketing company. Five years later his network marketing income rose to over $150,000 per month with over 56,000 people in his organization.

His most noted contribution to the network marketing Industry is the Brilliant Compensation presentation—the single most watched presentation in the history the industry. Tim's latest, is the equally brilliant training package, the Professional Inviter. To learn more, visit the website with our affiliate link, here: http://ProfessionalInviter.com

In addition, Tim is a teacher at the university-affiliated Network Marketing Certificate Seminar sponsored by the University of Illinois at Chicago. To learn more about Tim and subscribe to his FREE! newsletter, visit his website at http://BrilliantExchange.com.

TOM "BIG AL" SCHREITER

So, How Ugly Can Your Relatives Be?

We provide choices and opportunities for people. They can pick and choose what they want out of network marketing. It's not all about the money. Yes, the money is fine, and you can buy some happiness with money. But life is wonderful when you enjoy what you are doing.

So, how ugly can your relatives be?

Ugly. Real ugly.

And depressing, negative, small-minded, and they can even have bad breath.

That's why my friend, Bob, joined network marketing.

He was tired of socializing with relatives and friends who discussed and reviewed every negative story on their 24-hour news channel.

Bob wanted a new group of people to associate with.

He was looking for positive people who were moving ahead in their lives.

Hey, if you have to live, why not live with positive and

friendly people?

"I turned eighteen and decided that I had learned enough."

Sound like some of your friends?

Let me tell you about another one of my friends, Alisa. She is different. I met her only six months ago. For her, network marketing is all about self-development. Alisa spent eighteen years of schooling memorizing facts and never once learned about the power and satisfaction of self-improvement. Now she starts every morning with fifteen minutes of positive reading, and her days are filled with positive experiences that she creates.

> So many networkers have improved and changed their personal lives with the power of self-development.

They read books, listen to CDs, and attend workshops while their high-school classmates watch reruns of the television show Friends. Guess who is getting more out of life?

"But my boss is a jerk, I am underpaid, the day care ignores my children, and I hate the traffic back and forth to work."

I bet you have a friend or two who repeats this complaint every day. For them, network marketing provides enough income to stay at home with their children and create a real family life. You don't have to earn a lot of money in network marketing to drastically change your life.

So why don't more people use network marketing to replace their jobs and create the lives they want? Well, they just don't know. All of their network marketing friends are keeping it "top secret." Hmmm, there is a lesson here for us.

So, How Ugly Can Your Relatives Be?

"Okay, I got the house, the car, the boat, the vacations, the lifestyle..."

Yes, some people take their network marketing business to the top level.

That's okay too.

I do know that when you earn more, you can give more. That should be a good enough reason for people to earn more than they can spend.

And network marketing provides that income and freedom for many people.

That's what makes network marketing attractive to people who desperately want to make a big change in their lives.

So what is right with network marketing?

A lot.

We provide choices and opportunities for people. They can pick and choose what they want out of network marketing.

As you read the articles in this book, remember this: "It's not all about the money."

Yes, the money is fine, and you can buy some happiness with money.

But life is wonderful when you really enjoy what you are doing.

Tom "Big Al" Schreiter is a legend in network marketing. In over thirty years in the business, he has created more successful network marketers than any other single individual. Under the name of "Big Al," he has authored and sold more books than anyone, and his travel and speaking schedule (once described as 397 days a year) has Tom meeting, learning about, and teaching more networkers around the world than anyone else as well. John Fogg has called him The Greatest Networker in the World, because, well, he is. Tom provides many free training resources at his website: http://SponsoringTips.com

BO SHORT

Network Marketing Can Provide a Venue for You to Become a Great Leader

People from all walks of life, with varied education and income levels, have an opportunity to develop leadership skills in this business that will assist them throughout their lives, regardless of whether or not they continue to be involved in network marketing.

There are so many opportunities to achieve financial and personal success in this world. I believe that opportunity maintains a constant presence in our lives. Our ability to be ready and take advantage of it... that is the challenge we all face.

"The future belongs to those who prepare for it."
— **Ralph Waldo Emerson**

Investing in real estate, the stock market, starting a traditional business, or rising through the ranks of a corporate structure are various ways in which individuals achieve. All have merit. In fact, I have taken advantage of each of them. Network marketing is another avenue through which people can seize opportunity and create success.

I have been an outspoken critic of many aspects of this profession. In spite of voicing my concern and criticism, I still maintain that this industry offers individuals an opportunity to achieve great successes in multiple areas of their lives.

The opportunity to associate with like-minded people that care about their families and their country, and who are willing to help you navigate your way through a business model you may be unfamiliar with is only one of the many benefits of network marketing.

Learning how to lead as you follow someone that places your success above their own is yet another.

Taking time to sit down with your family to share goals and aspirations while collectively working to achieve them is still another of the many benefits of this business.

Facing failure... failing... and standing up once more to go again is probably one the greatest lessons you will learn. This particular lesson—because it helps define who you are—is an important aspect of laying claim to your ultimate success.

> "Mistakes are easy, mistakes are inevitable, but there is no mistake so great as the mistake of not going on."
>
> — William Blake

These are but a few of the benefits of network marketing. Of course, you can experience these in other business endeavors. In fact, you should.

However, network marketing can offer you the opportunity to experience them in an environment where your failures are

Network Marketing Can Provide a Venue for You to Become a Great Leader

cushioned and your successes are celebrated much more so than in a conventional business setting.

It would be unwise to presume that all network marketing companies are similar. Nothing could be farther from the truth. In my fifteen years in this industry, I have seen what I consider to be the best and the worst. It is crucial that you do your due diligence, as you would before investing in a stock or buying real estate or entering into a partnership with someone. Do not let the emotion associated with an opportunity meeting be your deciding factor.

You must understand the role that products/services, corporate leadership, field leadership, compensation, and timing play in your potential success or failure. Don't let your unfamiliarity with these issues keep you from investigating them. While this book is not really designed to address these issues, I believe they are worth noting. Follow your instincts, as they will be instrumental in helping you find the right place to be.

In my opinion, the greatest benefit of network marketing is the opportunity it provides for leadership development.

People from all walks of life, with varied education and income levels have an opportunity to develop leadership skills in this business that will assist them throughout their lives, regardless of whether or not they continue to be involved in network marketing. Never underestimate the serendipity associated with opportunity.

In order to take advantage of this aspect of network marketing let me offer you the following ten suggestions:

Understand that great leaders are great followers.

They simply show better discernment for who they follow.

Having had the great fortune of interviewing some of America's greatest success stories, I've learned that each one of these leaders was also a follower. They always talked about their mentors—the people that impacted their lives and their decisions.

Never be afraid to follow... just pick wisely, as your future can depend upon it.

Serve your team and your customers.
Of course you are working to attain your goals, but you can only do so long-term by serving your people. In a conversation I had with Admiral Thomas Moorer, former Chairman of the Joint Chiefs of Staff, he told me, "You win leadership when you serve your troops... not your superiors. If you are serving your troops honorably, you are doing likewise for your country and your leaders."

When you want to quit... do not.
While this is easier said than done, I believe it is one of the great separators of people in this industry. One of the obvious differences between those people that claim success and those that do not is the ability to fail and then reengage.

> Since the "price of admission" in network marketing is generally low and you usually have another primary source of income, it is easy to quit when things are difficult. Simply put: do not.

Stop looking for courage.
So many people are waiting for a magical moment in which they will find the courage they need to act. Please understand that courage finds you, not the other way around.

Courage finds people that have practiced sufficiently enough to proceed. Get in motion as quickly as possible, so that courage knows where to look for you.

Take responsibility for your failures and give credit for your success.
Great leaders always bare the brunt of missteps and give credit to their team for the victories. As a leader of people, you must be willing to set aside personal acclaim for the benefit of the people around you. Remember, your success is incumbent upon them finding value in their own individual businesses. Make sure your actions will facilitate that.

It's not what you say... it's what you do.
One of the greatest downfalls of people in network marketing is that their words and their actions are not consistent with each other.

> While proper planning and consistent effort will allow you to build a successful, independent business, the strength of your character will determine the real intrinsic value of the business you have built.

I have witnessed so-called leaders create a tremendous amount of sales volume. Unfortunately, since they displayed poor character, they were never viewed in an admirable fashion. Their journey in this industry is stained. I would suggest that they will never feel the emotional gratitude that comes with true leadership.

"You are never as good as people say you are, and you are never as bad as they say either."
This advice came from my dad. He was the chief of staff for the oldest and longest-serving senator in the history of the United States. As I began to experience success in my life, he told me

that success brings with it both allies and foes. At their extreme, they either raise you higher than you should be or they bring you down lower than you should be. Neither is correct.

Stay grounded, appreciate your success, and never believe the glowing things written about you in the press. None of us are that good.

Cast your vision farther than you think you can.
People have a tendency to set goals that are below their potential, because they are afraid of failing. Great success stories are filled with more failures than victories. Your success will be no different. If you are going to work diligently you might as well set goals that require great expectations.

> I know something about you that your family already knows: when you give your best effort long enough, doing the right things, you will succeed. It might as well be for something magnificent.

Read books.
Learn from other people. Read about other people's struggles and ultimate success. You will realize that your struggles oftentimes pale in comparison to theirs. You will be reminded of why you must finish what you have begun.

It is not simply about making money. In the right environment that will happen. It is about reaching beyond who you think you are and finding out whom you can become.

Measure Up!
When I was a child growing up in Georgia, I lived about eleven houses away from my grandparents. Each day after school I would go to their house. During the course of the day my grandmother would always look me in the eye and say,

Network Marketing Can Provide a Venue for You to Become a Great Leader

"Measure up. Live up to your potential. Do something great with your life."

The network marketing profession, probably more than most, offers you the opportunity to do just that. At this point, it is not simply about products and services; it is about you. What is your legacy? What will your example teach your children? This is much bigger than the particular business you represent.

Network marketing can provide a venue for you to become a great leader.

Assuming you are associated with the right business and are willing to work, you will make money.

The greatest joy will come as you look around and realize that people are following you, because of the type of person you have become in the process.

Please know in advance, I look forward to applauding your success. I will leave you with words from my second book, Living to Win.

**Dare to step out,
Dare to achieve, and
Dare to do something great with your life.
Life is too short and too precious to settle
for second best.
Live your life to win!**

Bo Short is an author, speaker, radio personality, and leadership expert. Among his MLM credits, he was an Amway Diamond, an MLM company owner, and achieved the rank of Diamond in Univera

It's Time... for Network Marketing

LifeSciences faster than anyone in that company's history. He has been featured on the cover of industry magazines and highlighted in a Wall Street Journal best-selling book about network marketing. As an industry advocate, Bo played a critical role in a Dateline NBC expose that uncovered and discussed specific problems that had been limiting the success of many faithful, yet fledgling network marketers. He also serves as president of the American Leadership Foundation and sits on boards and committees for numerous national nonprofit organizations.

Bo has spoken around the world to more than 1,000,000 people in twenty-one countries. He shares his leadership insights with corporations and universities. For a FREE report that will help you explode your personal network, visit http://BoShortOnline.com and download Bo's FREE Report, **Foundation for Success: the 5 Pillars of Leadership Power.**

ROBERTO TORRES

Lifestyles of the (Virtual) Rich and (Not So) Famous

In network marketing, it's easier to produce $5,000 dollars a month residually than it is to come up with one million dollars to invest at a 6% return. (If you can find a 6% return....) That's the power of residual income.

The Business Model

Six years ago, I did not believe in network marketing, but I knew that I wanted financial freedom and time freedom. I knew that working, as a police officer was not going to do that. So, even though I had approximately six years to go before retirement, I decided I would look for something different.

Having practiced martial arts since I was eight years old and teaching it privately since I was seventeen, I opened up a martial arts school. While my family and I were excited about this, my initial investment a little over $30,000—just to get in the door. Added to this was everything else that comes with running a traditional brick and mortar business.

> But the real kicker was... we lost our time freedom.

With the police department I had sixty-four days off a year and my weekends free. Well, that was gone now. We were at the school seven days a week until 10:30 or 11:00 pm.

The school grew very fast and was giving us a great income... but it owned us. Then one day one of our students called and invited me to take a look at of those things my wife Cleta was telling me for years we needed to get into.

My immediate reaction was " No way!"

At the urging of Cleta, and out of respect for my friend, we end up going to the meeting. There are all kinds of fancy dressed people. Some I can tell are making some money. In addition, they are all so positive and excited.

So, the meeting starts, and they start to speak about the product, and I say to Cleta, "Hmmm... this sounds interesting." Then they presented the network marketing business model— a model that I knew I could never duplicate with my martial arts school. We were in!

Education
Network marketing can provide you with a great education. Not only on how to build your business, but how to be a good speaker, a leader, and how to get organized. But for me, the best thing I have learned is how to negotiate. I have used this skill for everything from purchasing and designing our new dream home to buying a new car.

In fact, this one skill alone has become so powerful I used it to generate a six-figure check in less than twenty-four hours out of thin air!

Recognition
"Babies cry for it and grown men die for it." People love

recognition. Big or small people like to be recognized, and in network marketing there is no lack of it.

Unlike at a job, in this industry you are being recognized constantly for building your business. From your upline, your downline, crossline members, the corporate side of the company, and so on.

> I love the idea that people who never got recognition, in school, at work, or from their family can now receive all kinds of recognition.. many times in front of large groups of their peers.

Lifestyle of the (Virtual) Rich
My favorite part of network marketing is the lifestyle you can achieve.

> By creating a residual income, you can actually live the life of a millionaire.. and catch this- you don't have to make a million to do it.

Here's how.

First, realize the power of residual income. You do the work once, and it keeps coming in month after month. As long as customers keep buying your products, you keep getting paid. You don't have to resell those customers over again each month.

So, here's how to get the millionaire lifestyle. Once you get your residual income check to $5,000 a month, you take that money and start paying off your debt. Once you are debt free, you use that $5,000 a month for whatever you want. Travel, a new car, braces for the kids, or taking your spouse on wonderful weekend getaways.

> You see, when you are making $5,000 dollars a month in residual income, it's like having a million dollars in the bank.

Now, you are probably saying, "Roberto, I don't know what kind of math you are using, but my math tells me that's $60,000 dollars a year; where's the million?"

Okay, here it is: For you to produce $5,000 a month in income that keeps coming in whether you get up and go to work or go to the beach with your family, you would have to put one million dollars into an investment that gave you a 6% return!

> Now, my question to you is how many people do you know that can go to the bank and put one million dollars into their account? I would dare say very few.

In network marketing, it's easier to produce that $5,000 dollars a month residually than it is to come up with one million dollars to invest at a 6% return. (If you can find a 6% return....)

By following this principle, today we live in a beautiful 5,000 sq. ft. dream home we custom built in Florida. We have all the time we want to travel and be together as a family. I have more recognition than a hero would get on the police force. And I've had the personal growth and leadership development education of a lifetime.

You see, an average part-time person in network marketing can truly have the "Lifestyles of the (Virtual) Rich and (Not So) Famous." And there's actually nothing "virtual" or "not so" about it!

Roberto Torres retired at the age of forty-six from the Suffolk County Police Department in New York State after twenty years of service. He is a martial arts grand master and has appeared on the cover of Inside Kung Fu magazine. He lives with his wife Cleta and their four children, Sarah, Raquel, Kristina and Keila in Dunnellon, Florida.

Roberto currently mentors people sharing his keys to winning in network marketing based on his seven years in this industry. To learn more, visit his website http://KeysToWinning.com.

TY TRIBBLE

MLM Goes Mainstream

While you were busy trying to convince your brother-in-law that network marketing was a viable business, the business world was busily adopting the concepts behind network marketing, labeling them Word of Mouth, Buzz Marketing, and Viral Marketing.

A word-of-mouth marketing company, BzzAgent will deploy 1,000 word-of-mouth agents in a twelve-week campaign for $85,000. Companies send BzzAgent a product, and BzzAgent sends the product to its agents who then tell others what they think about the product.

Seth Godin, the best selling author of Permission Marketing and perhaps the number one marketing blogger in the universe, has written an entire book based upon the concept of "remarkable products." The book is titled Purple Cow—because cows are basically boring, but a purple cow? That would be something.

Network marketing has always been about marketing great products through word-of-mouth, and the mainstream is starting to catch on.

The Essence of Network Marketing
Networking with great people and marketing remarkable

products sum up the essence of network marketing.

In its most authentic form, few can argue whether or not network marketing is a good, strong business concept.

Remarkable Products

Network marketing begins with products, and network marketing companies have been producing these cutting-edge, innovative, and remarkable products for decades.

The first multivitamin sold in North America was sold person to person and friend to friend through word-of-mouth referrals.

> Carl Rehnborg was not only a pioneer in the vitamin and nutrition industry, he also pioneered a revolutionary business structure called MLM (multilevel marketing), or network marketing.

Today, network marketing companies are on the leading edge of biotech and nutritional science.

Word of Mouth

When Carl Rehnborg first began producing nutritional supplements, he gave them away to his friends to learn what results they got. Carl's son, Sam Rehnborg, describes what happened:

> After a certain length of time, Dad would visit his friends to see what results had been obtained. More often than not, he would find the products sitting on the back shelves, unused and forgotten. It had cost them nothing and was therefore, to them, worth nothing... It was at this point that Dad rediscovered a basic principle—the answer was merely to charge something for the product. When he did, his friends, having paid for the product, used it, liked it, and further, wanted their friends to have it also. When they asked my dad to sell the product to

their friends, he said, "You sell it to them, and I'll pay you a commission when they buy."

There is some debate about whether or not authentic word-of-mouth can involve a commission reward structure. I believe that compensation is not really the issue. The issue is honesty and integrity.

When someone is recommending a product or service and will gain from the successful sale, people appreciate an upfront approach with full disclosure about the commercial relationship.

Today, big brands such as Coca Cola and Sprint/Nextel are adopting word-of-mouth as a way to market their products. As these large companies embrace the core concepts of network marketing, the lines between traditional marketing and MLM will continue to blur, and the perception of the network marketing industry will change dramatically.

MLM Goes Mainstream

Warren Buffett's Berkshire Hathaway, Jones Apparel Group, Citigroup, Hallmark Cards, Jockey, The Body Shop, Time Inc., and Vanity Fair are just a few of the mainstream companies that have ventured into the network marketing arena.

You can expect to see many more companies utilizing the network marketing model as social commerce continues to evolve.

MySpace is a good example of social commerce. Instead of traditional Web sites, many bands now have MySpace sites. Even mainstream movies now have a MySpace URL instead of a traditional .com address.

It's Time... for Network Marketing

I expect other mainstream companies to leap into network marketing in the near future. Once businesses figure out that the new version of network marketing is just like the readily accepted and high performing affiliate programs, but on steroids, the floodgates will open and people will be actively seeking out network marketers.

The Challenge

As traditional marketing inches closer and closer to network marketing, our challenge will be to embrace to authentic, intelligent, and credible network marketing more fully.

People are (still) tired of expensive products, slick MLM pitch artists, and hotel hype sessions.

> Yet today, more people are open to the idea of word-of-mouth, affiliate marketing, and earning a commission for recommending products and services than ever before.

So what do we do about it?

We lead. We follow. Or we get out of the way.

We tell our authentic story about the products and companies that have made such a positive, powerful difference in our lives... and we tell it often and well.

Ty Tribble is famous for his "one line bio": Husband, Dad, Entrepreneur. Ty is an entrepreneur who lives in Federal Way, Washington with his wife, Richelle and two children, Emma and Tyler. He hosts a number of top-ranked weblogs including: Multileveler (http://Multileveler.com) and the MLMBlog (http://MLMBlog.typepad.com/blog).

The Business of Hope

I was a new mom, looking to stay home with my newborn son. I wasn't really looking to get rich, or even set the world on fire- although I did allow my mind to dream a little about what that might be like.

Network Marketing. It's a term that typically conjures up strong emotions, on one side or the other. It deserves a chance to be accurately defined, that's for sure. There are many misconceptions about what this business is and does.

When I decided to join the ranks of network marketers, I was only looking for a few things: A way to generate some income to stay home with my children... Some flexibility around my hours... Adult interaction, or a way to keep my foot in the "grown up" world while being home with toddlers

That was really about it. However, what I got was a list quite a bit longer. Here's what network marketing has given me so far:

- Generated enough income to allow me to stay home, and for my husband to stay home as well if he chooses
- Funding to invest in other income-producing assets
- Self-funded Retirement and College Tuition Programs
- Total flexibility around the hours I work, my workdays, and with whom I work

- Great adult interaction and a business my kids enjoy, too
- Coaching and listening skills
- Communication skills
- New friends, beyond my wildest dreams
- Personal success
- Business success
- The greatest self-development course in the world

When I first started looking into the home based business arena, I was convinced of one thing—I needed to steer clear of that thing called "network marketing."

> I wasn't exactly sure why, but "they" all said it was bad; a scam; something to be avoided.

Why was it, then, that everything I was looking for in a business kept directing me back to the business of network marketing?

I'm forever grateful for the day that I put my skepticism aside and decided to find out for myself what this business really is—and more importantly, what it isn't. That day ultimately changed my life. I hope you'll create a day like that for yourself, and allow this profession to transform you and your life.

That was nearly thirteen years ago, and today, I am able to put so much of what network marketing offers into words, feelings, and experiences. One phrase that sums it up best for me is that it is the business of hope.

> This industry provides hope in so many ways.

My story is similar to many and may ring a bell with you.

I was a new mom, looking to ensure that I would be able to stay home with my newborn son, and any other children who might come along. I wasn't really looking to get rich, or even set the world on fire—although I did allow my mind to dream a little about what that might be like.

It wasn't long before my mind expanded to embrace the possibilities available through network marketing and I went about doing some serious goal setting.

Seeking to secure our financial future outside of the airline industry, my husband and I began our network marketing journey together, working side by side. My vision was that he would do the "list making," the prospecting, show the plan, do the follow up and sign them up. I would assist with training, and of course, cash those big, fat paychecks.

And that's a lot of how it went for the first three years. Although I carried out a few of his "duties," he did the bulk of the work. That is, until he came home one night and announced that he was worn out... and done with network marketing. He could not work his full-time job, have time for his family, and also work this business. "But," he announced, "I will support you all of the way if you decide to continue."

> Wow, thanks a lot, I thought. Now, how was I ever going to get to those big, fat paychecks?

That's when I first realized what everyone meant when they said this was a business about personal growth and development. If I really wanted to create the success I desired, I was going to have to go to work on myself first.

See, deep down, I wanted everything that network marketing offered, but I didn't really want to be the one to stretch myself and go after it. I was content to walk across stage on my husband's arm, looking adoringly at him, flashing my diamond ring.

That illusion was shattered when my husband said, "No more!"

I had to make a decision.

Change or abandon my dreams.

That's when I realized the importance of personal growth, development, and working on myself. I found mentors and empowered myself to lead my own changes... and my own business.

It wasn't long before I realized that I really did have the ability to chart my course and create my own history the way I wanted. I had the ability to shatter glass ceilings and earn more as a woman than I had been able to before.

The best thing about the entire process is that there were many people along the way to cheer me on, to assure me that I could reach my goals, and to support me in moving ahead. It was so different than corporate America, where climbing up the ladder of success almost always meant stepping on or over someone else.

So, what specifically does it take to succeed and how does this differ from conventional business?

Many people (myself included) make the mistake of wasting a lot of time and energy looking for the "secret" in this business, the Holy Grail that's going to make the difference between failure and success.

They waste time looking for that perfect "script" to say to people, or that perfect "sizzle call" to dial their prospects into, or some elusive something they have not quite grasped yet that's going to change everything.

The real secret to this business is... there is no secret.

The Holy Grail that does exist is that of working on oneself; understanding what skills and beliefs are required and spending time every day working on your mindset and your ability to attract exactly what you desire.

Once I began to work on myself, amazing things started to unfold for me. Prospects began to call me... people signing up were a consistent weekly occurrence... attrition rates dropped, and I began my rise to the top of my company's pay plan.

How I went to work on myself really came down to a few simple things:

Focusing on feeling good and expecting success to come my way ALL THE TIME.

I stayed tuned into my "positive meter" and made sure that I did not make calls or speak to people if my attitude and mindset were not at a ten or above.

I did these things by spending time—twenty minutes in the morning and twenty minutes at night—focused on exactly what I WANTED to have show up in my life, and focusing on what I knew that would feel like once it arrived.

And, like magic, I began to take inspired action. I would wake up knowing what I wanted to accomplish for that day and what steps would be required to have that happen. I went about taking these steps joyously in anticipation and expectation of what would show up.

It really was as simple as that.

So, that's what I mean when I say network marketing is a course in self-development. Yes, we have awesome products and a great moneymaking opportunity, but beyond that...

We are committed to assisting YOU in being the best you can be in all areas of your life.

The skills I have developed have prompted me to now focus on creating a win-win in every relationship I encounter. It's no longer about "getting the sign-up." It's about seeing how I can serve another person and what I might bring to the table to enrich each person's life through the business and through a connected relationship.

I simply cannot imagine my life without network marketing.

I cannot imagine not being able to have the interactions with all the positive, like-minded people this business has placed in my life.

What are you seeking to find in your journey through network marketing? Are you looking for financial freedom... time freedom... to learn great new skills... to have great new relationships?

You are surely in the right place if your answer is yes. Even if you only seek one of those things, stick around and you'll find that you won't get one without all of the others.

Jackie Ulmer, a veteran home-based business owner of thirteen years, has coached and trained thousands of representatives both inside and outside of her own sales organization of 7,000 ScentSations representatives. Her primary goal to help others succeed has propelled her to become a Platinum Director (a new position created for her as she went higher in her program than anyone had before) and a six-figure income earner. Jackie and her husband Mark have two children, Justin, 13, and Lexi, 10. They live in their dream house in Lake Arrowhead, California.

You can learn more about Jackie and sign up for her free newsletter at: http://StreetSmartWealth.com.

DR. DENIS WAITLEY

The Biggest Business Trend in Business History

This unparalleled economic trend will enable you to be your own boss, in your own business, and earn based on your own efforts, integrity, and relationships. You will have the freedom to be the master of the future security of you and your loved ones.

I've spent much of my thirty-year-career studying champions in every field from Apollo Astronauts to Superbowl and Olympic athletes; from Fortune 500 top executives to small business owners. As I travel throughout the world, lecturing on "The Psychology of Winning" and how to become a 21st Century leader to multinational corporations and entrepreneurs, many of these individuals learn of my involvement as a board member of a publicly traded network marketing company. Some are surprised; some are impressed. Recently, however, their questions have changed. Many of these achievers are sensing the opportunity and they're asking what I think of the future of network marketing.

My answer is simple and straightforward.

Unless you are networking, you soon may be "not working." Network marketing is not just becoming mainstream, it's emerging today as the dominant market trend. It's a trend that can't be, won't be stopped.

The real question is, how can you benefit?

Let's look at the trend itself.

At any given time, there are several emerging trends in society. Some drive the next product or products that will be successful. For example, aging baby boomers practically ensure the success of the health and wellness and financial services industries. Similarly, emerging technologies will continue to fuel product opportunities online and through telecom sectors. These trends, and others, are all relatively young and they're emerging together.

Although the elements of these trends have been around for years, the trends themselves emerge only when the timing is right... when several factors come together.

The health and wellness industry has been with us for centuries, but it took the convergence of aging baby boomers with advancements in medical science to create the critical mass of an emerging trend. The telephone has been a primary mode of communication for over a century, but utilizing our phones to trade stocks, receive photographs, and surf the Internet is a new market trend as a result of synergistic technologies.

The "networking" trend I have been witness to is not so obvious, and, as a result, many will miss its significance.

> The opportunity it offers, however, could be even greater than the two trends I just mentioned. Those "early adopters" and innovators who catch it now will be rewarded handsomely.

The Biggest Business Trend in Business History

The trend is a fundamental change in the way we conduct our business—in the way goods and services reach the consumer. Today, the consumer is increasingly "going direct"—purchasing goods and services based upon a direct relationship with the provider. The middlemen—from wholesalers to retailers—are being bypassed.

Moreover, as the products we consume become more sophisticated and complex, consumers are demanding a quality relationship with the provider of these goods and services. They want to know what they are consuming. They want speed, variety, customization and choice. They want the products to deliver what the advertising promises.

Educated consumers going direct is the essence of network marketing. More importantly, it's the natural thrust of today's market economy.

Why? Let's explore three major reasons:

First, the Internet and low telephone costs have leveled the business playing field. Communicating with prospects and customers—communicating direct—is now something anyone can do. If you have a question concerning almost any product, you get on the phone or go online, and you get answers.

Answers direct from the supplier in a matter of seconds. It's an entrepreneur's dream! It no longer takes thousands of dollars to get your message out. Instead of being tied to an office, you take your office with you. Web pages, e-mail networks and intranets have placed quality, inexpensive marketing and sales tools in the hands of anyone willing to use them. Small business owners have been empowered to compete with the bigger players, and these same tools complement network marketers perfectly.

It's Time... for Network Marketing

The second factor is a sobering reality we must all face and should already know. Different from the past, we are responsible for our own financial security and that of our families. No longer can you go to your place of business day-to-day, safe and secure that your organization will take care of you.

> Seniority no longer means security. It signifies vulnerability. Instead of a steady job with guarantees, you are now a free agent whose contract is always a week-to-week proposition.

Cost-cutting, downsizing and outsourcing will continue well into the 21st century.

At the same time, as a society we are increasingly returning to the concept of family and family values. This is impacting our employment by demanding that it be more responsive to family needs. We want flexibility, control over our workload and hours, and the ability to conduct business from anyplace we desire—most importantly the home.

Network marketing offers the ability to earn additional streams of income part-time or full-time, without a large capital investment and the necessity for hiring and managing employees.

Don't misinterpret what I'm saying: As with every other business, network marketing is focus- and effort-intensive.

> Treat it like a hobby and it pays you like a hobby. Treat it like a serious business investment, and it pays you serious money.

The third factor behind network marketing's emergence is a byproduct of the ever-increasing complexities of our postindustrial society. We can't be experts in every field.

The Biggest Business Trend in Business History

On the one hand, we need counsel and advice about the products and services we need and want. On the other hand, we don't know who to trust. Oftentimes, the marketplace appears to be just one huge "infomercial" over-promising and under-delivering. This means that we must have more direct contact with manufacturers and providers, and it also means that we most likely will rely even more on traditional relationships such as family and friends whose opinions we trust as being in our best interests.

> Not surprisingly, another term for network marketing is "relationship marketing." Its very foundation combines trust and an intelligent referral.

Quality network marketers take the time to know both their products and their customers—right in step with the demands of today's consumers.

Network marketing is not a new phenomenon. Most emerging trends are innovative, but not necessarily inventive. The Health and Wellness movement didn't take hold until the baby boomers came of age. Telecom opportunities burgeoned as a result of technological advances with a device we've utilized daily for generations. Going direct, through referrals, certainly is a seasoned concept. But the opportunity for financial rewards via direct global networking is enormous and immediate.

A number of young entrepreneurs have already spotted the trend. I recently spoke at a dinner meeting in Hong Kong sponsored by Dell Computer Corporation for its "Fortune 500" customers. Michael Dell, the founder and chairman—one of the wealthiest and most admired executives in America—has a philosophy that is brilliant, uncomplicated, and right in line with this emerging economic trend. He creates a relationship directly with the consumer and sells high performance products only through this channel. Following the trend, Dell sells

It's Time... for Network Marketing

approximately $40 million per day direct to the consumer, with no retail distribution, and creates customer loyalty better than the competition.

> A growing number of "Fortune 500" companies are jumping on the direct and relationship bandwagon.

Network marketing, by its very nature, is designed to help you develop a lifetime of residual income. If you work the business, it's going to work for you. As an employee, regardless of your salary level, when you stop working the income virtually stops. Most retirement programs are totally inadequate to meet your future needs and that includes Social Security. With network marketing, when you stop working, your business continues to pay you. In fact, you can provide for your children's future, or better yet, bring them into your business with you.

Another advantage of network marketing is being your own boss. In the traditional company, there is always someone over you to decide your future and someone under or around you who may want your position.

> In networking, individuals who join you don't want your job or to become your boss or supervisor.

They want to build their own organizations and, in that way, build even more success for you as well.

In the traditional business setting, there is a lot of talk about teamwork and winning together; however, in reality, it is rampant with politics, competition, and the survival of the individual in the face of market uncertainties.

> With network marketing, you are

> surrounded by individuals whose success is your success.

When you share your experience and knowledge, it will most likely advance your own career as well, not be used selfishly to compete with you or replace you.

Network marketing throws out the Law of the Jungle and survival of the fittest philosophies for a working environment where you are rewarded for team play as much as individual effort.

Network marketing in the new millennium has entered the mainstream and is destined to become perhaps more prolific and popular than franchising. There is risk in network marketing but far less than there used to be. And, unlike franchising, you're risking your time and effort, not your fortune or a mountain of debt.

With network marketing, you don't need inventories and you don't need to create and manufacture the goods and services. You are the "direct" in going direct.

> So when an industry leader asks me what I think of network marketing, I don't talk about networking in the new millennium, I say that network marketing is the new millennium.

As with any opportunity, timing is half of it and execution the other half. You have no control over the former—the trend will emerge without you. The jet is leaving the ramp, and you can either be on it, or miss the journey. If you take the risk, the execution is all up to you, by the effort you make to place yourself in a position to capitalize on the trend.

Network marketing is a major step forward in the evolution of

It's Time... for Network Marketing

our free enterprise system.

We are entering an era of giant killers! Individuals today have as much power and knowledge accessibility as corporations! Instead of being a victim of change, you are now in a position to be a change agent.

The main subject of this offering was supposed to answer the question, "What do I personally love most about network marketing?" But that answer is too simple and concise for more than two sentences, which is why I saved them for the end.

What I love most about network marketing are the people in the business. In the majority, they care more about win-win relationships than any other group I have encountered throughout my career.

I firmly believe my earlier quote, "Unless you are networking, you soon may be **not** working." The new power is not in your position in an organization, but in your relationships with other people who share the same passions and goals.

Dr. Denis Waitley has been one of America's most respected and beloved authors and keynote lecturers for over twenty-five years. With over 10 million audio programs sold in fourteen languages, Denis Waitley's CD album, The Psychology of Winning, is still the all-time best-selling program on self-mastery. To order this best seller or his newest release, The Platinum Collection, and to subscribe to the free Denis Waitley Weekly E-zine, visit his website here: http://DenisWaitley.com.

Never, Ever Quit

Find a product, a company, and a sponsor you believe in and go to work. Don't look back. Keep moving forward. If you do this, you will be very thankful as you become truly free and successful.

I've been around this business long enough to have had my share of failures and successes. Yet I cannot imagine ever doing anything else.

Network marketing is the ONLY way I know whereby the average person can grow a business of their own, allowing them the freedom to do what they want the way they want.

If people only understood that, they would not get discouraged or give up so easily. Many people start in our business, knowing nothing about it. They make a few bad choices, run into the wrong sponsor, or even join a company that makes so many mistakes it's forced to go out of business. They "give up" before they ever have any success. Of course it's difficult. Tell me one worthwhile thing that isn't?

I'm thankful I learned before it was too

It's Time... for Network Marketing

> late that there is no security in working for someone else.

It took me long enough, and I had my share of challenges and difficulties along the way; however, network marketing is the ONLY career in the world I know that truly works and lets us be free. I somehow knew that instinctively when I started, and vowed to take time to learn and NEVER QUIT, so when the going got rough, quitting was NEVER an option.

If you think about it, when you go to work for a salary, you are working to make someone else rich. You trade your hours for dollars, and if you need more money, you take a second job or work more hours.

> In network marketing, everyone has a chance to build true residual income, so they can one day be free.

With residual income, you leverage your time as income is built by helping others become successful.

The more people you help, the more successful you will be.

It won't happen overnight. It won't make you rich while you sleep. You won't get wealthy joining those things that appear too good to be true, or those things that tell you that you will get rich by just "joining."

It will take more than just signing up. It will take work. Work isn't a bad word... work is a great word. If you will find a product you believe in, share it with others, and teach them to do the same, you will build a successful business over time. And yes, at times, it will be difficult.

Make up your mind to get involved in network marketing and

vow to NEVER quit. I've seen so many people over the years that had much more talent than I ever had give up on their business. They did not stick around when the going got tough. It got difficult. They quit. I find that very sad.

> No one can promise you that the road to success will be easy, but in network marketing, we can promise you that if you stick it out and work and build, it will be worth it down the road. More worth it than you can imagine now.

Long ago, someone sent me this article. I never learned who wrote it. I don't even recall who sent it. I wish I knew so I could send a "thank you" card. In my opinion, it says it all.

Difficult! Difficult!
Is a home-based business difficult?

It is difficult when you must produce a report on a Saturday afternoon and cannot attend your son's football game.

It is difficult hearing the mobile phone ring on a birthday morning and you cannot see the excitement on your daughter's face as she feverishly tears into another box.

It is difficult knowing the rust bucket you call a car is eating you alive in maintenance, but you cannot afford a new one.

It is difficult to go to your annual performance review, and even though you have worked hard for another year, you come away empty-handed.

It is difficult knowing that you shop by sticker, rather than whether the garment looks good on you.

It is difficult knowing that you married a wonderful person and promised them the world, and for the next thirty years, you look at balancing the budget and figuring out what sacrifices must be made.

It is difficult reciting, "If we get this, we cannot have that."

It is difficult always lowering your dreams to meet your means.

It is difficult knowing that you have spent forty years of your life working for someone else only to realize that you will be retiring on a third of what you cannot live on today.

It is difficult when your children move out and you cannot visit them, because traveling costs too much.

It is difficult knowing that the fish are biting this week and you cannot drop what you are doing and take your dad fishing.

It is difficult watching the spark in your partner's eyes fade, because both of you realize the house you have been wanting is just a dream because someone else is controlling your finances.

It is difficult waking up one morning and realizing that your children, the most precious thing imaginable, no longer need bottles, diapers, have tea parties, eat things found under the sofa, are shorter than the baseball bat they are trying to swing, but are grown and starting their own families and you missed all of that, because you agreed to be locked in an office for twenty years by a boss who watched his children grow up.

It is difficult dropping your one-year old at the nursery, because you have to be at work by 9:00 am to stand by the Xerox machine or handle irate phone calls and realize someone else is going to watch your daughter take her first step or have your son say "dada" to the playground teacher.

It is difficult knowing that you have diligently worked only to be given an early retirement.

I will tell you what is difficult. It is real difficult realizing it is too late and that time frittered away can never be retrieved. It slips through our fingers one second at a time.

What are we doing with it? We have nasty habits about rationalizing, procrastinating, and skirting important things rather than facing the issues. Too often we allow others who do not pay our bills, who do not share our dreams, to direct our future.

We have absolutely no freedom as a child.

We rebel in our teen years and scream for freedom.

We will die for the right to be free.

We fight wars to have the seemingly innocent ability to choose.

We reach adulthood and we relinquish freedom, because we think it is too difficult.

We do not want to take responsibility.

We do not want to make a wrong decision, so we obligingly give that awesome power to someone else.

We feel it will take too much time. Then we have the audacity to complain when the decisions made were not what we wanted.

We wake up too late. Phrases like: "I wish I had only... " "If I could only have that time back... " etc.

I believe the majority of people want to sing, but die with the music still inside. Face the music and shoulder some responsibility. You cannot have that time back.

You have chosen your direction. If you have not spent your time wisely, too bad.

You have no one but yourself to blame. You had the chance. Perhaps the opportunity was presented many times and each time you elevated the trivial to a higher priority than yourself. Is a home-based business really difficult? Is it so traumatic to show someone an exciting product or idea? Is it so difficult to understand that if you work this marketing idea for a couple of years, you might not have to confront some nasty options?

Would you work real hard for a year or two so you could put your family in the home of their dreams?

Would you work real hard for a year or two so you could send your children to college chosen by excellence rather than one chosen by price? (The same criteria you used for clothes shopping.)

Would you turn off the idiot box, the soaps, the talk shows, sporting events, or Lost for a year, so you could take dream vacations several times every year?

Would you apply yourself for a year or two so you would have the freedom of being able to roll over, yank the covers over your head and wake at the crack of noon because you wanted to?

Would you work really hard for a couple of years to mold a lifestyle of your choosing so your family could live a lifestyle of their dreams, rather than trying to live how someone else thinks you should live?

Can you identify with the words "next time"? How many "next times" will you have? What will it take to get you off dead center?

Will it be knowing that people are physically deteriorating when you have a product that will help them but are afraid of someone thinking you are taking advantage of that person and are just out for the money? Gosh, I hope not.

Will it be knowing that people are agonizing through bankruptcy, realizing they only needed a couple more hundred dollars per month, not $50,000 per month, but you procrastinated once again?

I hope not.

Realize the awesome power you have in your hands with this opportunity. This business you have chosen has the ability

to change lives.

IT cannot do anything. But YOU can change lives with IT. YOU are the one with the life changing ability. What are you waiting for?

What will it take?

You will pay a price for your actions.

Which one do you choose to pay?

— Author Unknown

I've often read that article over, especially when things were "difficult." It's been a blessing. And yes, I have paid the price.

I'd do it again, gladly, because today, I have solid, residual incomes from my network marketing businesses and I am free.

I'm thankful that I never gave up when the going got tough. I'm thankful I stuck it out long enough to learn. And I am confident that if I can realize success, anyone can!

I no longer have to get up to a blaring alarm clock when it's still dark outside to go to a job that owns me.

I no longer have to be told I HAVE to work mandatory overtime.

Never, Ever Quit

I no longer have to drive a car that is bottom of the line. I drive the car I want.

I no longer have to worry about giving up eating to pay for gas.

It's not always been easy getting here, but it has been so worth it.

You, too, can reach all your wildest dreams, if you're willing to step up to the plate, and go to work for it. Give up the boob tube. If you miss a show, someday, when you're on a cruise, you can catch the reruns. Give up reading and listening to negative news. If something earth-shattering happens... your neighbors will tell you anyway.

Take that time and invest in YOU. Read positive motivational books. Go for a walk and listen to a CD. If you're still driving to work, get some good audios to listen to and develop yourself. Learn to look for the bigger picture, and what's right with things, rather than focusing on negatives.

Network marketing has changed for the better over the years. You no longer have to build a business dragging people to the Holiday Inn after work. You can truly work from home, with a phone and the Internet, so you can work in your PJ's, any hour you choose.

Find a product, a company, and a sponsor you believe in and go to work. Don't look back. Keep moving forward. If you do this, you will be very thankful as you become truly free and successful.

> Network marketing is the only business I know of that you can be free to work when you want, where you want, and not

have to report to a boss. YOU are the boss. Just vow at the very start to NEVER, EVER QUIT.

I recall a quote I read a few years ago that said, "Quitters never win and winners never quit!" We all have a choice.

What will you choose?

Think about that and choose carefully, as it is a life changing decision. It may be difficult at times, but it is more than well worth it. Find something that works for you and get started today, so you can be truly FREE!

Diane Walker, "aka MLMBlonde" is a professional network marketer who has built her business using the power of the Internet. She has two grown children and five grandchildren. She can and does work from any place in the world, where and when she chooses.

She has also developed multiple income streams and is committed to helping others reach their dreams.

' The key to success is helping others be successful. That way, you never have to worry about yourself. Think about the BIG picture. Where do you want to be tomorrow? Tomorrow starts today. What will you do today to change your tomorrows... ? '

WENDY WEISS

Is Network Marketing Selling?

Most network marketers are honest, ethical, and believe in the value of their products and their opportunity. And that is what they should focus on. And that is sales.

I looked up the word sell in the dictionary. This is what it said:

To persuade (another) to recognize the worth or desirability of something.

This definition assumes value. It assumes that you recognize the value of whatever it is that you are selling. Inherent in the definition is the concept of worth or desirability.

I also looked up salesperson, saleswoman, salesman, sales clerk, and my favorite, sales talk. The definition for sales talk was "a line of reasoning or argument intended to persuade someone to buy something."

Whenever I do a workshop or teleconference, I frequently ask my participants, "What are the words that come to mind when you hear the word salesperson?" Invariably, I hear back words like "manipulative," "dishonest," "unethical," and "sleazy."

In the dictionary, however, when I looked up all of the above sales words, none of the definitions referenced "manipulative," "dishonest," "unethical," "sleazy," or anything particularly negative. The language in these definitions was actually quite neutral, and several of them spoke of value.

Unfortunately, in our culture, the words sales or sell are viewed with disrespect. The words no longer simply mean to persuade someone of the value of what you are offering. Instead they carry the baggage of images of untrustworthiness and deviousness. This is a misconception that does an enormous disservice.

> Far too often, network marketers buy into this stereotypical image of sales and see the activity of selling as negative and untrustworthy.

They feel that if they are selling (or being perceived to be selling), they are doing something that is not quite right, or that has the potential to be not quite right. It's as if there is a line drawn someplace, but they don't know where that line is—or when they've stepped over it. It causes them to be cautious and careful and worry about how they are perceived.

This anxiety puts network marketers, in their own minds, at a disadvantage and on a lower level than their prospects and customers. This is a difficult place to be. And it stops many network marketers from taking action.

> The reality is, network marketing is selling. Network marketing is persuading people to buy your products and persuading people to join your team. It is persuading them of the value of your products and your opportunity.

Is Network Marketing Selling?

So, I looked up the word persuade in the dictionary. It said:

1. to prevail on a person to do something
2. to induce to believe; convince

Again, nowhere in that definition do we find the words, "manipulative," "dishonest," "unethical," "sleazy," or anything particularly negative. As with the word sell, the language is quite neutral.

The bottom line: Network marketing is persuading and convincing people to buy your products and persuading and convincing people to join your team. That persuasion is based on value.

> If you cannot persuade and convince people to buy your products and/or to join your team, then you do not have a business.

If you believe that selling is manipulative, dishonest, unethical, and sleazy, this belief will not support your ability to build a business. It is very difficult to sell (persuade and convince) while believing that selling (persuading and convincing) is wrong.

> It is time for network marketers- and the world they serve- to change their beliefs about the words selling and sales.

The truth is that most professional salespeople are honest, ethical, and they believe in the value they have to offer. And most network marketers are honest, ethical, and they believe in the value of their products and their opportunity. And that is what network marketers should focus on.

It's Time... for Network Marketing

Here are some questions that network marketers should ask themselves:

- Do you believe in the value of your products?
- Do your products provide a benefit to your customers?
- Do you believe in the value of your opportunity?
- Does your opportunity provide a benefit to your downline?
- Are you doing the best you know how to ensure that your customers get what they need?
- Are you doing the best you know how to ensure that your downline gets what they need?

If you have answered yes to the above questions, then you are proceeding with integrity. If you are proceeding with integrity, then obviously you are not being manipulative, dishonest, unethical, and sleazy. You can persuade, convince, and sell with your head held high.

If you answered no to the above questions, then get out of the business. It's not a fit for you. Find something else to do in which you can believe.

The ability to persuade and convince is not something that everyone is born with. Some people have that skill more naturally than others.

Most people, however, no matter what their natural abilities or what level they have attained in a company, can improve their skills. The really good news is that selling is communication.

Is Network Marketing Selling?

Like any communication skill, selling skills can be learned and improved upon.

Improving skills is a process. It's not something that happens overnight, but instead it is something that builds over time with study and practice.

Because so many network marketers have negative beliefs about selling, it is difficult for them to gain the skills they need to persuade effectively. They are bombarded with the message that selling is a negative activity.

> They are also frequently told that they are not selling. If they are not selling, how do they persuade and convince?

Because of these contradictions, the idea that there is skill involved, or that they could learn and improve their persuasive abilities is foreign to many. They are paralyzed to take action and sell, and they are unable to improve their skills. Even when they try to improve their persuasive skills, their belief of selling as being negative frequently gets in the way and keeps them from moving forward.

What's the solution?

Let's reclaim the words sell and sales. Let's redefine the words to mean

> " to persuade and convince with integrity."

Let's remember that value is inherent in the definition. Then network marketers could understand that as long as they proceed with integrity, and as long as they believe in the value of what they are selling, then selling is an ethical and moral act.

This would free so many network marketers (and people

considering becoming one of them) who are paralyzed by not wanting to sell. It would now be possible for them to align their positive intent with their positive action. It would make it easier for them to learn the skills they need to be effective in the business.

Looking to the future, I envision a world where network marketers say with pride, "I sell because I believe in my company's products and opportunity."

Wendy Weiss, "The Queen of Cold Calling," is a sales trainer, author and sales coach. She helps entrepreneurs, business owners and sales professionals gain confidence, reach more prospects, close more sales and make more money. She started her business fifteen years ago, representing clients on the telephone and setting new business appointments. While Wendy no longer "dials for dollars" (except for her own business), all of her workshops, seminars, products and individual sales coaching are based on practical, real-life, hands-on experience.

Wendy's clients include Avon Products Inc., ADP Inc., Arbonne, Sprint, Newmark Real Estate, and thousands of entrepreneurs throughout the country. She has been featured in BusinessWeek, Entrepreneur Magazine, Selling Power, Target Marketing, and various other business and sales publications. Her e-mail newsletter, Opening Doors & Closing Sales, has an international readership and her columns are syndicated to 168 different print and Internet publications.

Wendy is the author of Cold Calling College and Cold Calling for Women: Opening Doors & Closing Sales.

To learn more about Wendy and receive her free newsletter, visit her on the web at: http://WendyWeiss.com

LISA M. WILBER

The Power to Amaze Yourself

What other business is about personal growth but disguises itself as a product sales industry? The amount I earn is in direct relation to the amount I learn.

I'm sure you've heard the Curves International motto, "The Power to Amaze Yourself." I think network marketing could use that slogan with equal conviction. Each year I am amazed when I look back and see how my business has grown and how I have grown as a person.

What other business is about personal growth but disguises itself as a product sales industry? It seems to me that personal growth IS our number one product.

Sure, we all provide products and services that people use and love. Most of us love our companies and love our product lines. But the main thing we are doing in this business is becoming.

Becoming more educated.
Becoming better friends and partners.
Becoming more tolerant.

Becoming more assured.
Becoming more amazing people!

I started my direct sales business like most people I know. I needed some extra money, and I remembered a direct seller coming to my house showing samples to my mom when I was a young girl. I thought this seemed like a good way to earn extra money, and I already knew and liked the products. So, I paid my $25 for the starter kit, and I made extra money for many years.

Fast forward to 1987. I was working as a full-time secretary at a computer company in Bedford, New Hampshire, when our whole department received pink slips shortly before Thanksgiving.

Even though the country was in the middle of a recession, we were all in shock. Unable to find another secretarial job (I even applied at a temp agency and got turned away because I didn't type fast enough!), I turned back to my direct sales business in desperation.

Could I possibly earn enough money to replace my secretarial pay and benefits?

With limited options, I dove in headfirst and started working full time, and the first year was miserable....

I had to reinvest much of my profits, and I was disorganized and unsure of myself. I gave up more than once, even taking a teller job at a bank for six weeks during one especially disheartening stretch.

It was the bank job that opened my eyes. Between the dress code, the forty-five-minute commute, and the small salary I received after paying for downtown parking, I had had enough. I refocused on my direct sales business and got to work.

The Power to Amaze Yourself

Our company came out with their network marketing option in 1990, but I didn't go for it. I had heard many negative stories about this selling style and was completely unconvinced I could benefit from it.

It took three years of investigating to change my mind. I read books about network marketing, subscribed to Upline[1] magazine (THE network marketing magazine at the time) and snuck in to other network marketing company's meetings to learn what it was all about. I finally signed up for my company's network marketing program in January of 1993.

The first year of working the network marketing part of my business was just as hard as it had been when I went full-time in direct sales.

I was disappointed and discouraged often, but I kept reading and learning. I made an agreement with myself that I would work my way to the top of the pay plan with my company (they call that position "Senior Executive Unit Leader"), and only then would I decide whether it was worth it or not. I vowed not to quit until I made it to the top.

After fifteen months, I made Senior Executive Unit Leader! The day I found out, I was so unbelieving... I made the lady that called to tell me from our corporate headquarters FAX me a copy of her computer screen with my name and my title showing! It was a moment I'll never forget.

Had it been worth it? You bet!

In the months and years that have followed that amazing day, it has just gotten better and better and better. I've earned almost twenty all expenses paid trips from my company to places like Puerto Rico, Cancun, Hawaii, the Bahamas, Los Angeles, Washington, D.C., and Alaska.

It's Time... for Network Marketing

I've been receiving our company's car allowance since 1994 and paid for three new vehicles with it.

My personal earnings passed the $2 million dollar mark in the spring of 2005.

Because of my accomplishments with my company, I have also started a speaking business "on the side," earning my professional status with the National Speakers Association; I have given over 200 seminars nationwide. I'm the author of three books and an audio tape set. My story has been featured in magazines such as Empowering Women, Dreams, Upline, Fortune, and Executive Female. The books Wave 4, Dream Achievers and Avon, The Company for Women, among others, have also featured my story. I even had a Nashville recording artist write and record a song about me entitled, "Have A Dream Come True." Amazing!

I think the most amazing part is that I continually feel like I am just starting out at the beginning of my journey, with new worlds to discover and new skills to learn.

I am aware more and more that anything is possible. One of my biggest personal goals is to read and listen more than anyone else I know. I know that the amount that I learn is in direct relation to the amount I earn.

Direct sales and network marketing has done all of this for me, and it continues to change my life in ways I could not have imagined for myself. Truly, this profession can give you The Power to Amaze Yourself!

Lisa Wilber has been selling products and recruiting new representatives for Avon since 1981 when she was eighteen years old. She worked her Avon business part time until 1988 when she got

The Power to Amaze Yourself

downsized out of her secretarial job. Her Avon income dramatically increased after 1993 when she joined Avon's multilevel marketing program called Leadership. Lisa is multimillion dollar achiever, currently the #4 money-earner in the country with over 2000 representatives in her downline.

Lisa has been written about in the Upline Journal, Home Business Connection, Wave 4 and New Hampshire Business Review. You can visit Lisa on her website and take advantage of all her free resources at: http://WinnerInYou.com.

DENNIS WILLIAMS

Network Marketing. It Almost Sounds Like a "Fairy Tale" ...

Changing people's lives is what really drives this business— average people who decide not to live an average life and find this tremendous vehicle of network marketing to make it happen.

After graduating from college, I worked as a manager for a large corporation, and my wife Ruth was an elementary school teacher. Like so many people, we were living paycheck to paycheck, trying to get the promotions, save some money, invest some money, and looking forward to retiring some day. Work hard! That's what we were taught.

My brother first introduced us to network marketing in 1975, and one year later, network marketing became our full time business. We worked very hard with that first company and enjoyed the freedom we were experiencing, but we never really became financially independent. About ten years later, our children were starting to enter college and we needed more income—so I got into the car business and worked on a straight commission, basically seven days a week for five years.

In 1991, we were introduced to our present company, but for six months, we rejected the idea of ever getting into network marketing again. Finally after seeing some dramatic product results with my sister and talking to a very successful consultant who had been with this company for about a year and a half, we became independent consultants. Eight weeks later, I was full-time in the business.

When we tell people about our business, it almost sounds like a "fairy tale." As I sit in my home office overlooking Puget Sound with Mt. Rainier and the Cascade mountain range in the background, ships and sailboats are cruising by and a pair of bald eagles are soaring overhead.

All the while I'm thinking to myself.. "Well, here I am at work."

Ruth and I have introduced our business to six people outside the state of Washington, where we live, but in fifteen years, our business has expanded to every state in the country and we now receive royalty income from over twenty different countries on four continents. The organization we developed generates millions of dollars in revenue each month for our parent corporation, and we do it with virtually none of the common business concerns. We have no overhead, no employees, no inventory, and no paperwork.

People often ask us... "Well, what do you do?"

We simply became customers ourselves and then referred other people to the company.

Our company's mission statement says it all: "To inspire individuals to discover a whole new way of life, and provide them the opportunity to live it by changing their lives through improved health and financial well-being.' The word "inspire" is the key. There is nothing in that mission statement about selling anything. That's one thing we love about this business. We are truly offering a gift, not begging a favor.

Network Marketing. It Almost Sounds Like a 'Fairy Tale"...

We enjoy the freedom! Freedom to choose when, where, how, how much, and with whom we spend our time and work with. Freedom to catch a matinee in an empty theater, enjoy the show and still be "employed" when we return back to the office; freedom to go camping in the middle of the week, when everyone else is at work; freedom to take a vacation once a month, if we choose to do so.

This business also provides the greatest "Insurance Policy" in the world. In our fifth year in the business, I had a major health challenge. Maybe because I didn't eat properly, didn't exercise, had some bad genetics, or for whatever reason—I was unable to "work" for the last three months of that year.

If I was unable to show up for work when I was in the car business, who would have sold a car or a truck for me? Answer: Nobody! In this business however, our business partners had become really great friends, just like family. In your own family, I'm sure that if someone has a challenge, others would rally around. This was no different.

> When the word got out that I had a problem, there was an outpouring of love and compassion I can hardly describe.

Our home looked like a florist shop, and so many cards and letters came in, they were over the weight limit I was allowed to pick up for the first few weeks.

At the end of the year, I looked at our 1099 and remarked to Ruth, "Isn't this amazing? I haven't been able to do anything for three months, it's only our fifth year in the business, but if I was to earn the same amount of money that we were paid this year working at my previous job, I would have had to work there for an additional thirty-seven more years!"

Can you imagine an insurance man sitting down at your

kitchen table and saying,

> "We've got a great new policy here... If you can't work for three months, no worries... we'll simply give you a check for thirty-seven years of your annual income to tide you over."

Of course, there is no such thing, and if there was, nobody could afford the premium. What was the premium we paid? We spent a few hours every week... "inspiring individuals to discover a whole new way of life, and providing them the opportunity to live it by changing their lives through improved health and financial well-being.'

Changing people's lives is what really drives us. So far, we've helped thirty-seven of our friends become members of our company's "Millionaire's Club," and thousands of others earn substantial part-time or supplementary income. Someone once described this industry as a "personal development program masterfully modeled into a business." How true that is.

> Everyone has an equal opportunity to become as unequal as they possibly can.

We can't think of anything we would rather do. Changing the world for the better, helping ordinary people achieve extraordinary wealth while improving the quality of our lives and the lives of others... What a way to make a living! It doesn't just sound like a fairy tale—it IS a fairy tale. Only this one came true.

Dennis and Ruth Williams are seven-figure annual income earners and have created thirty-seven career millionaires in their networking organization. To learn more about Dennis and Ruth (and take a virtural tour of their magnificent home), visit their website here: http://ybhurtn.com.

MARK YARNELL

My Passion for Network Marketing

Bonding is what atoms and people are driven to do. That's what makes us passionate and vitally alive. Professional networkers are bonding with others for a living, while most other people are laboring in alienation.

I find myself more passionate about network marketing today, in 2007, than ever before, but my reasons may surprise you.

No point in trotting out the age-old advantages of working at home, no boss and time freedom, because those are so obvious.

No point in rehashing the wonder of logarithmic growth, passive residual income, or any other subject that most first graders already know about our profession.

To be fair, those are all significant advantages over most industries, but they no longer excite me.

> What floats my boat is the ability to rescue people from their bondage to electronic focus splitters and introduce them to the magic of human contact.

It's Time... for Network Marketing

To understand my passion for network marketing, you must understand my roots. My early years were filled with human interaction, wonderful neighbors, creative childhood games, and outdoor functions. None of the parents in our neighborhood in Springfield, Missouri locked their doors at night, and everyone's home was always open to everyone else. Everything was human, and reality was real, not virtual.

Everybody knew everybody else on a first name basis, and although there were a few who had pen pals, communications were face-to-face and verbally demonstrative. I grew up in a community of wonderful human interaction devoid of pedophilia, kidnappings, guns, or digital isolation. Mine was a world of bonding at the deepest level.

Call me old-fashioned, but I find myself sailing towards the autumn of life missing many things that meant so much in my early years.

Pushing buttons on video games doesn't do it for me. Sending e-mails brings me no fulfillment. I don't like cubicles that separate people, and I'm not impressed with celebrities who became heroes because they inherited money or starred in a couple of movies.

Simply put, I'm passionate about our industry because it's good, old-fashioned, word-of-mouth selling. It's people helping people and big business without lawyers or huge malpractice premiums.

I believe network marketing is more than just the last bastion of true capitalism. I believe it's the last field in which people actually win by building relationships and engaging in human interaction at its most desirable level.

My Passion for Network Marketing

I was horrified recently to learn that a huge US company had slipped so far into the cesspool of digital inhumanity that they had actually terminated several hundred loyal employees by e-mail. Horrified, but not surprised, given the direction of corporate insanity now commonplace outside our industry.

In networking, my associates are also my friends. I want them to succeed, and when they do, we both win. I care about the success of all who choose to enter our field no matter which company they choose, because they are kindred spirits. I would go so far as to suggest that should our industry ever go away, it would be a bleak day for all of capitalism.

Until such time, I will remain passionate and committed to a wonderful industry from which anyone with the motivation to do so may rise to levels of greatness so long as they can make friends, keep their word, and care sincerely about the success of others.

> I think that the greatest attribute of network marketing is that it allows an increasingly alienated population to rediscover the wonder of actual human connection.

Of necessity, those who tend to succeed in our industry are ultimately forced to return to their human roots and bond with other human beings. Believe it or not, like atoms themselves, we humans are bonding entities. There are only about one hundred kinds of atoms in the entire universe, yet there are gazillions of life forms, masses, and minerals. Put a few atoms together and, poot, you have water. Put a bunch of those together and, poot, you have an ocean. The more they bond, the greater their diversity.

We the people are neurologically hardwired to crave bonding and operate in synergistic ways. While many industries are oriented towards alienation and separation, our industry relies on human contact.

Karl Marx may have been delusional, but he did advance one concept that seems to be happening. His grand socialistic plan was a flop, and capitalism is brilliant. However, he suggested that if we capitalists were not careful, we would evolve into an alienation of labor followed by the labor of alienation.

Enter the electronic focus splitter (EFS). Today, most people communicate, work and play on digital devices, alone and alienated from others. EFSs come in many forms, including cell phones, computers, televisions, iPods, and DVD players.

Consider the first one: the cell phone. A guy can be sitting in a restaurant, about to propose to his beloved, when his cell phone rings and immediately his focus is shifted from his future wife to someone else. Or let's get more serious. Every sixteen minutes, another cell phone-related traffic fatality occurs in North America. Some driver is focused on guiding a three-ton piece of metal at 60 MPH, and his cell phone rings. He swerves while reaching for it and takes out a family of four.

EFSs are brilliant technological innovations often misused by society. A handful of companies earn billions by luring people into their constant usage with the mistaken notion that focus on any intended goal is secondary to engaging in digital conversations or observation.

> I'm passionate about network marketing because I can help people wean themselves from allowing EFSs to rule their lives.

Mindless net-surfing and overuse of cell phones serve no purpose to an individual who sells products and recruits people through relationships based on human dialogue and personal word-of-mouth interaction.

While most people are laboring in alienation in front of little phosphorous screens or dangerously talking to others while driving, professional networkers are bonding with others.

And bonding is what atoms and people are driven to do. It's what makes us passionate and vitally alive.

I don't own a cell phone. I can't turn on a computer, and I still prefer my blackberries with cream and sugar. I'm from the old school of baby boomer Midwesterners who still believe in launching business with a handshake and doing one's best to create a win/win in every endeavor. Sideways smiles don't impress me, but I like a good hug.

I'm very passionate about network marketing—more so than ever. As more and more people decide to stop laboring in front of technology, alienating themselves from the one thing that drives both atoms and people, we offer them a wonderful profession based on human interaction and real bonding.

Sure, there's big money in networking, but I'm more passionate about relationships than the monthly income. Take four billion dollars to the moon, live alone in a lead-lined igloo with nothing but a computer and iPod, and see how fulfilling life can really be for the wealthy. I rest my case.

Mark Yarnell is an accomplished author, motivational speaker and international businessperson. Mark is the recipient of the coveted American Dream Award as an outstanding entrepreneur. With eighteen years of applied network marketing experience, he built a successful international distribution organization of more than 300,000 marketing representatives in twenty-one countries.

ACKNOWLEDGEMENTS
BY JOHN MILTON FOGG

This is the part of the book where writers and editors list all the people who help make the book possible, from muses to mentors to mechanics. I run for the dictionary in such cases to make sure I know what I'm doing. It surprised me to learn that the first definition for acknowledge, was "to admit the existence, reality or truth of." I had to scroll down to confirm the meanings "recognition" and "express thanks or gratitude" I expected.

So, I will now express my heart- and mind-felt appreciation for the authors, our designer, editor, printer, and publishers by openly admitting their existence and the reality and truth of how truly remarkable each of them are.

I claimed to bring together more than fifty of the brightest minds in–side–and–out–side network marketing—well–known experts, authors, speakers, trainers, coaches, and especially been-there doing-that now business-building leaders—the best of the best. That has been accomplished. That is who and how the authors are and I appreciate each one of them.

Claudia Volkman is my editor—yes, even and especially editors need an editor. Hardworking, fast, focused, and wise in the ways of words and the people who write and read them, the woman is a joy to work with. Always a pro and always apropos, if you have a book in you, Claudia will bring it out best. You can reach her at: 630.935.3611 and via email at: cvolkman@mac.com.

It's Time... was designed by **Tom Bellucci**. I have known and worked with Tom since the Upline® days. I'm happy to let the look and feel of this book speak for itself. Tom is wonderful to work with and should you choose to do so, you will be beyond pleased and proud. You can contact Tom in Virginia at: 434.466.4666 and via email: tbellucci@comcast.net.

It's Time... was printed by **Action Printing** of Fond du Lac, Wisconsin. Tom "Big Al" Schreiter turned me on to them years ago, and they have been "my printers" ever since. I was told once, "You can have your job 1. Fast. 2. Great price. 3. High quality. Pick TWO!" Gregg Davis, Sarah Birthman, and all the people at Action Printing give you all three—and are absolutely the nicest printing people I've ever worked with. They can be reached at: 800.472.0337 and on the web at: http://ActionPrinting.com.

It's Time... is co-published by two of its authors. They are my friends, associates, and partners. And... one is my upline and the other my coach. You'll learn more about **Leonard Clements** and **Monique Gallagher** on the following pages.

HIGHEST POTENTIAL TRAINING
MONIQUE GALLAGHER

If you wish to achieve bigger goals in network marketing than you've ever achieved before... you'll need a coach- and a good one.

...a proven, results-getting coach who helps you identify and break-through what has stopped you in the past and open up new possibilities that deliver "Authentic Confidence, Sustained Motivation, and Performance."

'I'll say this straight out: I have made more and better self-discoveries, broken through more self-imposed barriers and achieved greater productivity and performance results faster with Monique Gallagher's Highest Potential Training than anything else I've ever experienced.'

- John Milton Fogg

Monique Gallagher is an author, speaker, trainer and business performance coach. Her focus and expertise is on teaching you how to remove the obstacles that prevent people from accomplishing their optimal performance and productivity.

If you are ready to break through your limitations—conscious and unconscious—a great first step is to get her Free Report: 8 Vital Issues a Network Marketer Must Resolve to Succeed at: http:HighestPotentialTraining.com/VitalIssues.

To learn more about Monique Gallagher's coaching and training, contact her at: 888.310.6875 or via email: Monique@Highest-Potential.com.

MARKETWAVE, INC.
LEONARD CLEMENTS

MarketWave is the definitive clearinghouse for accurate, objective information about our industry.

For more than sixteen years, author, speaker, trainer and court certified expert in the field, Leonard Clements has concentrated his full-time efforts on researching and analyzing all aspects of MLM/network marketing.

'When I want the truth... when I've got to separate facts from fiction and learn the real story about any aspect of this business, I call Len. Nobody, and I do mean nobody, has researched and analyzed its history, methods, philosophy, facts & figures and trends, nor exposed the hype, lies, and misconceptions more or better. Len Clements is the expert!'

- John Milton Fogg

Leonard is the author of the controversial book Inside Network Marketing and the best-selling audios Case Closed! The Whole Truth About Network Marketing and The Coming Network Marketing Boom. His website is an extensive resource of research, articles, products, surveys and support. And his free MarketWave ALERT newsletter is a must for any sincere and serious network marketer.

To learn more about Leonard Clements' work, projects, and products, call 800.688.4766, visit the website: http://MarketWaveInc.com, write to MarketWave, Inc., 2406 Canberra Ave., Henderson, NV 89052 or email: MarketWave@cox.net.